Building Feminist Theory

Building

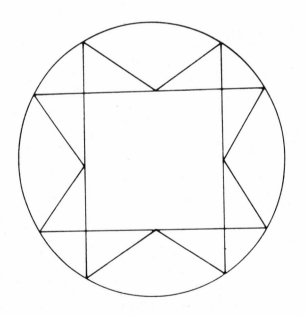

Feminist Theory

ESSAYS FROM QUEST a feminist quarterly

The Quest Staff

Charlotte Bunch
Jane Dolkart
Beverly Fisher-Manick
Alexa Freeman
Nancy Hartsock
Karen Kollias
Mary-Helen Mautner
Emily Medvec
Sidney Oliver
Gerri Traina

The Quest Book Committee

Charlotte Bunch
Jane Flax
Alexa Freeman
Nancy Hartsock
Mary-Helen Mautner

Longman
New York & London

BUILDING FEMINIST THEORY
Essays from *Quest*

Longman Inc., 19 West 44th Street, New York, N.Y. 10036
Associated companies, branches, and representatives
throughout the world.

DEVELOPMENTAL EDITOR   Nicole Benevento
EDITORIAL AND DESIGN SUPERVISOR   Diane Perlmuth
INTERIOR DESIGN   Patricia Smythe
MANUFACTURING AND PRODUCTION SUPERVISOR   Maria Chiarino
COMPOSITION   A&S Graphics
PRINTING AND BINDING   The Hunter Rose Company Ltd.
Cover Printed in U.S.A.

Library of Congress Cataloging in Publication Data
Main entry under title:

Building feminist theory.

   Bibliography: p.
   Includes index.
   1. Feminism—United States—Addresses, essays,
lectures.   I. Quest (Washington, D.C.)
HQ1426.B83   305.4'2'0973   80-28842
ISBN 0-582-28210-1

Printed and Bound in Canada

9 8 7 6 5 4 3 2 1

Acknowledgments

NANCY HARTSOCK "Political Change: Two Perspectives on Power," first appeared in *Quest: a feminist quarterly*, vol. I, no. 1, Summer 1974. Copyright © 1974 by Nancy Hartsock.

LUCIA VALESKA "The Future of Female Separatism," first appeared in *Quest: a feminist quarterly*, vol. II, no. 2, Fall 1975. Copyright © 1975 by Lucia Valeska.

NANCY HARTSOCK "Fundamental Feminism: Process and Perspective," first appeared in *Quest: a feminist quarterly*, vol. II, no. 2, Fall 1975. Copyright © 1975 by Nancy Hartsock.

CHARLOTTE BUNCH "Beyond Either/Or: Feminist Options," first appeared in *Quest: a feminist quarterly*, vol. III, no. 1, Summer, 1976. Copyright © 1976 by Charlotte Bunch.

JANICE RAYMOND "The Illusion of Androgyny," first appeared in *Quest: a feminist quarterly*, vol. II, no. 1, Summer 1975. Copyright © 1975 by Quest: a feminist quarterly, Inc.

CHARLOTTE BUNCH "Not for Lesbians Only," first appeared in *Quest: a feminist quarterly*, vol. II, no. 2, Fall 1975. Copyright © 1975 by Charlotte Bunch.

LUCIA VALESKA "If All Else Fails, I'm Still a Mother," first appeared in *Quest: a feminist quarterly*, vol. I, no. 3, Winter 1975. Copyright © 1975 by Lucia Valeska.

DEIRDRE SILVERMAN "Sexual Harassment, Working Woman's Dilemma," first appeared in *Quest: a feminist quarterly*, vol. III, no. 3, Winter 1976–77. Copyright © 1976, 1977 by Quest: a feminist quarterly, Inc.

MARILYN FRYE "Who Wants a Piece of the Pie?" first appeared in *Quest: a feminist quarterly*, vol. III, no, 3, Winter 1976–77. Copyright © 1976–77 by Quest: a feminist quarterly, Inc.

MICHELLE RUSSELL "An Open Letter to the Academy," first appeared in *Quest: a feminist quarterly*, vol. III, no. 4, Spring 1977. Copyright © 1977 by Michelle Russell.

NANCY HARTSOCK "Staying Alive," first appeared in *Quest: a feminist quarterly*, vol. III, no. 3, Winter, 1976–77. Copyright © 1976–77 by Nancy Hartsock.

KAREN KILLIAS "Class Realities: Create a New Power Base," first appeared in *Quest: a feminist quarterly*, vol. I, no. 3, Winter 1975. Copyright © 1975 by Quest: a feminist quarterly, Inc.

MARY MCKENNEY   "Class Attitudes & Professionalism," first appeared in *Quest: a feminist quarterly*, vol. III, no. 4, Spring 1977. Copyright © 1977 by Quest: a feminist quarterly, Inc.

BEVERLY FISHER-MANICK   "Race and Class: Beyond Personal Politics," first appeared in *Quest: a feminist quarterly*, vol. III, no. 4, Spring 1977. Copyright © 1977 by Quest: a feminist quarterly, Inc.

LINDA PHELPS   "Patriarchy and Capitalism," first appeared in *Quest: a feminist quarterly*, vol. II, no. 2, Fall 1975. Copyright © 1975 by Linda Phelps.

JANE FLAX   "Do Feminists Need Marxism?" first appeared in *Quest: a feminist quarterly*, vol. III, no. 1, Summer 1976. Copyright © 1976 by Quest: a feminist quarterly, Inc.

CHARLOTTE BUNCH   "The Reform Tool-Kit," first appeared in *Quest: a feminist quarterly*, vol. I, no. 1, Summer 1974. Copyright © 1974 by Charlotte Bunch.

BEVERLY FISHER-MANICK   "Put Your Money Where Your Movement Is," first appeared in *Quest: a feminist quarterly*, vol. I, no. 2, Fall 1974. Copyright © 1974 by Quest: a feminist quarterly, Inc.

GINNY APUZZO AND BETTY POWELL   "Confrontation: Black/White," first appeared in *Quest: a feminist quarterly*, vol. III, no. 4, Spring 1977. Copyright © 1977 by Quest: a feminist quarterly, Inc.

JACKIE ST. JOAN   "Who Was Rembrant's Mother?" first appeared in *Quest: a feminist quarterly*, vol. II, no. 4, Spring 1976. Copyright © 1976 by Jackie St. Joan.

GRACIA CLARK   "The Beguines: A Medieval Women's Community," first appeared in *Quest: a feminist quarterly*, vol. I, no. 4, Spring 1975. Copyright © 1975 by Quest: a feminist quarterly, Inc.

JOANNA RUSS   "Reflections on Science Fiction: An Interview with Joanna Russ," first appeared in *Quest: a feminist quarterly*, vol. II, no. 1, Summer 1975. Copyright © 1975 by Quest: a feminist quarterly, Inc.

NANCY MCDONALD   "The Feminist Workplace," first appeared in *Quest: a feminist quarterly*, vol. III, no. 3, Winter 1976. Copyright © 1976 by Quest: a feminist quarterly, Inc.

ALEXA FREEMAN AND JACKIE MACMILLAN   "Building Feminist Organizations," first appeared in *Quest: a feminist quarterly*, vol. III, no. 3, Winter 1976. Copyright © 1976 by Quest: a feminist quarterly, Inc.

Many women, while not on the *Quest* staff during the period this book represents, have given generously of their time, skills, and resources over the years to sustain *Quest*. Dorothy Allison, Denise Burch-Davis, Jackie MacMillan, Arleen Rogan, and Cynthia Washington deserve special recognition for their long hours of consistent commitment to *Quest*. Others we wish to thank for their general support of *Quest* in an ongoing way are June Arnold, Peg Averill,

Dolores Bargowski, Joanne Brooks, Scarlet Cheng, Carol Clement, Casey Czarnik, Judy Davis, Jo Delaplaine, Marge DuMond, Elizabeth Frazer, Cynthia Gair, Bertha Harris, Judith Jones, Valle Jones, Sue Kahan, Ginger Legato, Sue Lenaerts, Catherine Leonardo, Jacqui Linard, Linda McGonigal, Prudence McKinney, Liz Milbrandt, Leslie Montgomery, Andrea Morrell, Nancy Myron, Coletta Reid, Lee Schwing, Shirl Smith, Beth Stone, Margaret Streitenberger, Juanita Weaver, and Helen Young. Further, in its formative period, *Quest* received crucial assistance from Dolores Alexander, Rita Mae Brown, Jean O'Leary, the Institute for Policy Studies, and the women in the Women's Center/IPS Feminist Theory class. We wanted to list the names of all the women who worked on development committees, provided manuscripts and graphics, and donated labor and money over the years. But the list included over two hundred people, so instead, let us simply say thank you, for without all of you and our readers, *Quest* would have never been possible.

Finally, we would like to thank our editors at Longman Inc., who have been both unfailingly patient and sources of encouragement and good advice.

Contents

Acknowledgments   v

Gloria Steinem   Foreword   xi

Charlotte Bunch   Introduction   xv

PART ONE   Power and Practice   1

Nancy Hartsock   Political Change: Two Perspectives on Power   3
Lucia Valeska   The Future of Female Separatism   20
Nancy Hartsock   Fundamental Feminism:
   Process and Perspective   32
Charlotte Bunch   Beyond Either/Or: Feminist Options   44

PART TWO   The Politics of Everyday Life   57

Janice Raymond   The Illusion of Androgyny   59
Charlotte Bunch   Not for Lesbians Only   67
Lucia Valeska   If All Else Fails, I'm Still a Mother   74
Deirdre Silverman   Sexual Harassment, Working Women's
   Dilemma   84
Marilyn Frye   Who Wants a Piece of the Pie?   94
Michelle Russell   An Open Letter to the Academy   101
Nancy Hartsock   Staying Alive   111

PART THREE   Feminist Perspectives on Class   123

Karen Kollias   Class Realities: Create a New Power Base   125
Mary McKenney   Class Attitudes and Professionalism   139

Beverly Fisher-Manick   Race and Class:
   Beyond Personal Politics   149
Linda Phelps   Patriarchy and Capitalism   161
Jane Flax   Do Feminists Need Marxism?   174

PART FOUR   Organizations and Strategies   187

Charlotte Bunch   The Reform Tool Kit   189
Beverly Fisher-Manick   Put Your Money Where
   Your Movement Is   202
Ginny Apuzzo and Betty Powell   Confrontation: Black/White   212
Jackie St. Joan   Female Leaders: Who Was Rembrant's Mother? 223
Gracia Clark   The Beguines: A Medieval Women's Community   236
Joanna Russ   Reflections on Science Fiction   243
Nancy MacDonald   The Feminist Workplace   251
Alexa Freeman and Jackie MacMillan   Building Feminist
   Organizations   260
Suggestions for Further Reading   268
Resources   273
Index   275
About the Authors   279

Foreword

One morning last week, I listened to a radio commentary in which a famous woman educator praised a particular conference held at a local college. At last, she said, the women's movement was beginning to come of age. For the very first time, feminists had talked about the difficult issue of class difference among women.

I felt a rush of frustration. Where had she been all these years? Misunderstanding seemed to settle like a cloud around this hapless woman, and on the conference she described. *What kind* of class differences could there be on New York's most expensive campus, I thought? Why not take the students to a factory in Queens?

When my frustration subsided, I realized that this educator had not meant to be patronizing (or matronizing): she was just reacting honestly to an incomplete view of what women had been doing in the 1970s, the first full decade of American feminism's Second Wave. As for the conference itself, any meeting that looked at the true class differences among women, and not just at the class differences among the men they were attached to, was valuable. But that rush of frustration—the feeling of a sitting dog being told to sit—is very familiar to many women who have been active feminists for more than a year or two. Society in general and the media in particular tend to deal with women's political messages the same way they deal with women individually: they treat them as either invisible or not serious. No wonder that after a while even the most forceful woman begins to wonder if she's really alive.

This ignorance of feminism's message also leaves the woman who is just beginning to question the gender-based power structure around her—perhaps the participants at that college conference as well—with the lonely and time-consuming necessity of reinventing many wheels. It becomes less a question of building on feminist knowledge than of recapitulating it over and over again.

This book pulls together in permanent, portable form the works of a group of feminists who have spent most of the past decade thinking about subjects that may still be considered "new": class divisions experienced by women as both workers (unpaid in the home or paid in the work force) and as the most basic means of production (the means of reproduction); the varying realities of race and culture; redefining power and the polarized options allowed by patriarchy; the politics of sexuality and spirituality; new forms of organizations, leadership, strategy, and communication; and perhaps most of all, the integrity of the process of change as part of the change itself. If there is any mark of feminist theory, it is this shared belief that no accidental result or conscious goal can be ultimately helpful to women unless women ourselves have taken part in making the change—and thus been changed by the process. In other words, the end cannot fully justify the means. To a surprising extent, the end *is* the means.

These essays were themselves created by a process that included this integrity of involvement. You won't find in them the pyrotechnics of masculine-style confrontation or polarizing. They strive to be inclusive, not exclusive—and one of their rewards is a timelessness not spoiled by easy putdowns or modish references. They also are altruistic and purposeful enough to be part of a larger process that includes the reader; if you feel moved to figure out extensions or alternates after reading them, I think their authors would be very pleased. As feminists, the authors include the reader's thought process as an indispensable part of this book—as well as of this longest and most profound revolution.

For the "old" feminist, this anthology is a relief and a blessing. Much of our early transformational thinking and discovery took place in small groups like this one and resulted in writing that was very influential but not popularly available. The ulcer-producing frustration of being kindly advised to consider some subjects—a subject that years of life's energy may have gone into exploring—can now be relieved by saying, "Here. Read this book."

Futhermore, almost every feminist, no matter how "old," will learn from and be surprised by the depth and breadth of insight and analysis that has been collected in these pages.

For the "new" feminist, there will be the great pleasure of recognition, learning, and discovery of support and time saved by reading about a few wheels already invented.

For the reader disinterested in feminism, this anthology will provide many bridges to more traditional areas of interest, as well as many revelations of incompleteness of any social theory that just assumes the existing substructure of sexual caste to be "natural." Since that structure rumbles with earthquakes of change, any theories built on it are likely to crack or slowly erode. Students and teachers of political philosophy, sociology, economics, theories of revolution, and other related subjects might think of incorporating this and other feminist books in their curricula. It's hard to imagine such courses being considered complete or credible much longer; not without breaking the patriarchal habit of labeling everything that happens to the male half of the world "political" (and therefore changeable) and everything that happens to the female half "cultural" (and therefore changeless).

As for the adversaries who consider feminism too revolutionary, too upsetting of applecarts based on birth and unearned privilege, they will discover here that they are absolutely right. This book offers the considerable pleasure of confirming all their worst suspicions.

I am only one of many readers who have followed *Quest* from its beginnings. Though its distribution has been small until now, I have met women as far away as India and Australia who have been sustained by its words and its courage to exist. I also know some of the problems that go into making an alternate structure, trying to work in a new way, and surviving in the expensive and complicated world of publishing. Even more important, there are both the frustrations and rewards of learning the feminist lesson that a revolution, like a house, cannot be built from the top.

I'm glad to be able to say thank you in public to the women of *Quest*. They have enriched and included me, as well as many more readers, both past and to come.

The making of this book is also a gift; it will allow me to stop circulating my battered issues of the original. I can now buy copies for friends.

Beginning with the woman on the radio.

Gloria Steinem
New York City
April 1980

Introduction

Quest: a feminist quarterly was born amid the enthusiasm of the women's liberation movement in the early 1970s. The story of *Quest's* development revolves around a dozen women in Washington, D.C., who struggled, with the help of many others, to bring to life a national journal of feminist political thought. But to talk about *Quest's* early years involves several stories. It is a story of feminist theory and its evolution in the women's movement, of tensions between theory and action and between intellectual and activist demands. It is the story of a feminist group determined to create a nonauthoritarian work process based on feminist principles of cooperation and sharing of skills that would also meet the rigorous demands of publishing. It is a story about the effort to build a feminist institution with an independent economic base controlled by women. *Quest's* stories reflect the 1970's spirit and struggles, successes and failures that took place in the decentralized radical wing of the women's movement in the United States. While *Quest* continues to publish in the 1980s, this introduction looks back on the journal's initial five years in order to provide a context for the essays reprinted in this book.

In its early stages, the women's liberation movement was fueled by our sense of discovery, our sense of sisterhood and unity among women. Consciousness-raising groups had provided a structure for exploring shared oppression and the camaraderie of the early zap actions had given us a powerful sense of our potential. But that unity was short-lived as we soon discovered our very real differences of class, race, sexuality, and politics. In 1972, just when the movement's political activity was expanding through marches and greater public visibility, internal schisms had divided women into small isolated units grouped around special interests and political priorities.

In 1972, Washington, D.C., had spawned two national radical publications, *Off Our Backs*, a feminist news journal, and *The Furies*, a lesbian feminist analytical paper. As the nation's capital, Washington is a place where the line between local and national politics frequently blurs; the local women's movement was therefore very involved in national projects and debates. At this time, the movement was strong but fragmented, reflecting the tensions developing around the country between socialists and antileftists, straight feminists and lesbians, black women and white women. This fragmentation was at its worst when two activists from The Furies (then recently disbanded) convened a city-wide meeting in November to discuss what could be done to lessen the schisms in the movement and strengthen cooperation and power. That meeting led to the formation of a discussion group composed of diverse activists from various feminist projects—the Rape Crisis Center, Women's Legal Defense Fund, and the Women's Center. Six months later, the group decided to start a national journal to explore issues of movement strategy and theory from an activist perspective.

As founders of *Quest*, we saw the journal as one part of developing viable strategies for political change, not as the ultimate goal of the group. Thus, we wrote in our statement of purpose: "*Quest* is not an end in itself but a process leading to new directions for the women's movement possibly including such concrete forms as regional or national conferences, a national organization or a political party." Karen Kollias elaborated on how we saw the magazine in the Introduction to the first issue:

> Our goal is to promote a continuing, active search for ideologies and strategies that will bring about the most comprehensive change by the most effective and humane methods. . . . We are about open political forums. *Quest* wishes to explore differences and similarities in ideologies and strategies among the various segments of the women's movement. . . . We are about strategies. *Quest* wishes to contribute to the evolution of better strategy and tactics, to be a process for evaluating previous theory and practice. . . . We are about change. We assume that the women's movement, and those involved in it, consider complete and fundamental change as a primary goal. . . . We are about ideology. The time has come to expand feminist ideology. Differences in geographical location, race, class, sex preference, religion, age and other factors must be included for a broader, more realistic ideology that moves toward a workable base for unity.

The activists who began *Quest* felt that political strength and clarity would come from exploring feminist analysis from a fairly wide range of viewpoints within the movement.* *Quest* was envisioned as a tool for the already committed, not as a mass-audience magazine. Its aim was to stimulate more political dialogue among organizers, researchers, writers, and activists in the women's liberation movement, in women's studies, in women's rights organizations, and in other social movements.

*The initial *Quest* organizing group was Dolores Bargowski, Rita Mae Brown, Charlotte Bunch, Jane Dolkart, Beverly Fisher-Manick, Alexa Freeman, Nancy Hartsock, Karen Kollias, Mary-Helen Mautner, Emily Medvec, Gerri Traina, and Juanita Weaver.

QUEST as Political Theory

The *Quest* staff was activist in temperament but viewed theory as important to the success of activism. We wanted to articulate a feminist theory out of the daily lives of women and the work of the movement, and we wanted to direct that theory toward a workable strategy for the future.

We saw that a written analysis of concrete movement experiences, both successes and failures, was crucial to advancing feminist theory and developing strategies for change that built on previous work rather than on repeating previous mistakes. We invited activists to write about their initial ideas in political work, about their feminist principles, and about what happened when their strategies for change were put into practice. We felt that critical assessments of movement experiences were necessary to link theory and activism in the effort to meet intellectuals' demands for research, the substantiation of theoretical assertions, and organizers' needs for immediate solutions. *Quest*'s uniqueness lies in this struggle to be politically relevant to current issues *and* intellectually rigorous in developing the long-term implications of theory.

The staff of *Quest* considered certain questions of class, race, and sexual oppression, as well as strategic and organizational matters such as leadership, to be of paramount importance to this evolving theory. Our focus on these questions grew out of our own backgrounds, our experiences in the women's movement, and our knowledge of other struggles for change. For example, partly because many of us had worked in the civil rights movement in the 1960s, and partly because we lived in a predominantly black city, we saw issues of race as fundamental. Most of us were familiar with the literature on the black liberation movements, and several staff members maintained close contact with local politics and community organizations in Washington, D.C.

Our focus on the issue of class also grew out of our experiences. Over half of the original *Quest* group came from lower- or working-class backgrounds, and most of us had experienced the strains that class differences produced in the movement. We saw examining class not as a "male Left" imposition but as essential to the vitality and authenticity of feminism.

Lesbian feminism was another central theoretical and political commitment for the original *Quest* staff, regardless of individual sex preference. Our understanding of the significance of lesbian oppression and our experiences in the very bitter gay/straight split in Washington, D.C., convinced us that it was important to incorporate this political perspective into all aspects of feminist analysis, developed by lesbians and nonlesbians alike.

In addition, our various movement experiences led us to explore strategic issues such as conflict in the movement centered around questions of power, leadership, and organizational structure. For example, we felt that individual leadership should be encouraged and that problems and experiments with leadership should be openly discussed in the movement. This set us apart from many feminists who were antileadership at the time. We also insisted that we were not a "collective." We maintained that some responsibilities could not be shared and that addressing problems of power and responsibility went far beyond simple questions of collectivity. We wanted activists to tackle the tough problems underlying movement controversies over things like money, reformism, separatism, and socialism. Although we were generally anticapitalist, we thought that women should develop an analysis of socialism independent of the debates of the male Left in the United States, for the male Left had not only oppressed many women, but still treated "women's issues" as secondary.

In seeking to ensure that these and other issues would be covered in *Quest*, we decided to have a broad theme for each issue of the journal.* We developed an overall conception of each volume; then the four theme issues within it built on one another. For example, in the second volume, the four themes focused on aspects of change: the envisioning of a future society, the kind of revolution it requires, the organizations and strategies involved, and the role of leadership. The use of themes helped link theoretical and practical questions and highlight the connections between different issues.

Developing articles for *Quest* was a political education and a lively process for the staff. Manuscripts that sparked our interest were often discussed extensively and aggressively rewritten; movement organizers were interviewed, seduced, and cajoled to get their insights and operating theories onto paper. Many articles were written by women on the staff, often growing out of our discussions of the issues involved in the theme. Since these essays represented the process and energy generated by the group's struggles around what we considered important, they constitute a high percentage of the articles we have chosen for this collection.

QUEST Process as Group

Each issue of *Quest* began with the staff's identifying a theme area and forming a development committee, usually about eighteen

*The themes in volume 1 were Processes of Change; Money, Fame, and Power; The Selfhood of Women; and Women and Spirituality. The themes in volume 2 were Future Visions and Fantasies; Theories of Revolution; Organizations and Strategies; and Leadership. The themes in volume 3 were Kaleidoscope One (our first nontheme issue); Communication and Control; Work, Work, Work; and Race, Class, and Culture.

months prior to publication. The development committee for each theme consisted of at least one *Quest* staff person and several other individuals, many desiring to work on one particular theme and some interested in working closely with *Quest* to "try it out." The development committee structure evolved over the first year as a way to meet several needs simultaneously. It brought new people and ideas into *Quest*, adding fresh experiences, perspectives, and enthusiasm. This approach also helped maintain a stable core of staff members while providing a gradual process for introducing to our group other women who might later join the staff.

The first responsibility of each development committee was to imagine all the questions that its chosen theme could and should address. It advertised the theme in advance, solicited articles, and reviewed all the copy received in order to make recommendations for consideration to the full staff. The full staff was then responsible for reading the recommended articles, for making final selections along with the development committee, and for assigning editors to work closely with each author. The staff might also direct the development of more manuscripts to fill gaps.

While copy development consumed much time, it was only one aspect of the production of the journal. Like many feminist projects, we saw our group's methods of dividing work and responsibility and sharing power and leadership as an important aspect of developing and testing feminist political theories. The mechanics of our process evolved to meet our unique needs. The following details are presented not as a blueprint for structure but to illustrate our belief that with trust and creativity, feminist projects can build effective structures based on participatory processes.

In the last two issues of our second volume (1976), we published a Report to the Readers describing the *Quest* process. In one issue, Jane Dolkart, as spokesperson for the staff, wrote:

> In essence we have a system of shifting horizontal leadership based on our individual skills and time commitments. . . . We see ourselves as equals in that we all perform essential tasks for *Quest*, but we do not see ourselves as identical. Each individual staff member must take responsibility for the work within some given area. In that work, she is delegated authority to make certain kinds of decisions and handles both the creative and mundane parts of the task. Thus, while we do not all do the same things, our division of labor is horizontal and no one does only the "best" or the "worst" parts of a job. . . .
>
> Although we do not have a hierarchy, those who work full-time on *Quest* have more responsibility for and knowledge of the intricacies and problems of day-to-day operations, and therefore, have more decision-making authority. . . .
>
> As the need and desire for additional staff developed, we had to set out more specific criteria for staff. We developed written criteria aimed both at evaluating persons interested in joining *Quest* (for example,

extent of previous political experience, prior work with *Quest*, etc.) and at giving those interested an accurate picture of the commitment we would expect.

Clear work processes and explicit guidelines on which we built our structure combined with our common political goals were crucial to the success of our endeavor. Although in many cases friendships did develop, they were not all-important nor seen as mandatory in order to keep us working well together. Finally, our process also had to allow for our political needs as activists. Dolkart notes:

> Since every minute of meeting time and of our lives could be taken up in the details and decisions related to producing a journal, we found that we had to insure that we kept in touch with politics generally, and with movement activity in particular. We decided to begin each of our weekly meetings with a one-hour political discussion, our subjects ranging from internal politics to more general political questions. Second, in an attempt to reach out more to the feminist community in D.C., we have conducted a political seminar following each *Quest* issue and are initiating a feminist political theory course. We are still struggling to develop more ways to keep ourselves actively involved with politics while maintaining *Quest* as a journal.

QUEST as a Feminist Institution

The Report concluded by recognizing that *Quest*'s political goals sometimes conflicted with the daily demands of producing the journal. Maintaining the journal took more and more time as we faced the economic realities of small businesses and publications in America. The building of a feminist business therefore became a central issue for us practically and politically. This reality for *Quest* reflected the situation of many feminist projects in the mid-1970s and points to the importance of the story of *Quest* as a feminist institution.

In the first half of the Report to our Readers, Beverly Fisher-Manick outlined the financial and organizational dilemmas *Quest* faced:

> We set goals about quality, and we have largely stuck to those goals. We wanted a woman-produced journal that was readable, graphically pleasing, sturdy and of book quality. . . . We hoped to pay authors and artists adequate fees for their work, and we dreamed, eventually, of paying ourselves salaries for our work. We believe that feminist projects should support women at a decent living standard.
>
> As our financial statement illustrates all too clearly, the income from selling *Quest* does not, by itself, make these goals and dreams possible. Our expenses exceeded income in 1975, even after we had modified some of our goals.
>
> We need urgently to concentrate on promotion and fundraising but we do not have the time. . . . If we cannot raise the funds, then we face tougher decisions.

Fisher-Manick described those tough decisions and the difficulties not only of publishing on a low budget but also of doing the distribution and promotion necessary to make a journal succeed financially. Finally, she called attention to the contradictions in a movement that says it wants autonomy and self-determination yet does not or cannot support the few independent women's institutions that do exist. These kinds of pressures on feminist institutions have driven many projects out of existence. Yet, in spite of these pressures, *Quest* has found ways to adapt and keep publishing a quality journal. It survives in large part because there is a committed feminist community that has sustained *Quest* through hard times. That community needs a place to express its individual and collective experiences in the work of creating political theory and social change. *Quest* has provided one of the few places for that expression. It has also survived because as the original staff began to disperse, other women stepped forward to provide talent and energy to the endeavor. *Quest* produced its fourth volume amid gradual changes in staff and format, and with the fifth volume, a largely new staff emerged. The transition involved dealing again with issues of power, leadership, and responsibility, with the new staff maintaining some of the previous group's process and creating forms of its own. But that is another *Quest* story, one that can be told more appropriately in the next collection of the "Best of Quest," some years hence.

The group of activists who produced the first issue of *Quest* remained together as a core staff with few changes in personnel for almost five years. The first three volumes represent the work and vision of that group with the assistance of dozens of other women. In this collection, we have therefore chosen to publish essays from only those first three volumes. Although each of us who worked on the book had a list of other articles we might have included, this collection constitutes what we have agreed upon as the "Best of Quest" from these volumes.

QUEST in Perspective

Looking back at what we set out to do, *Quest's* evolution shows some real progress and some failures. What is most important, *Quest* has contributed significantly to advancing the idea that there could be, and should be, specifically feminist theory and, especially among activists, that such theory is important to political action. We have challenged the limitations of popular labels and divisions in the movement, such as radical feminism versus socialist feminism, and have sought new feminist definitions of ourselves. In analyzing how class differences and heterosexism affected our assumptions and strategies as women, we have helped demonstrate that issues of class and lesbian feminism are integral to a comprehensive feminist analysis. But while we have affirmed the fundamental importance of issues concerning racism, we have been less successful in significantly exploring just how race and patriarchy are related and what an integrated analysis would look like in this area. Perhaps *Quest*'s greatest success has been in demonstrating the absolute necessity for feminists to examine critically the issues of organizational structure, power, leadership, and money as they affect our movement's growth and strategy. In all areas where we have explored the terrain of feminist theory, we have seen how much more hard work and discovery lie ahead.

Our work on *Quest* in its early years taught us many important lessons. We learned that the full development of the implications of feminism and the creation of a comprehensive feminist world view that combines theory and activism will take time—both the time to think and write about it and the time to engage in more struggles and experiments as women activists. *Quest* played a vital role in advancing that task, although our initial fantasy of having a solid new theoretical foundation on which to build a national organization dedicated to radical change was premature. In the ebb and flow of movement timing, the time did not ever seem right for creating the organizations we envisioned. Further, the constant demands of the magazine's daily survival affected our dreams of other pursuits, such as *Quest* study guides, political classes, *Quest* conferences, books, and *Quest*-inspired organizations. Since we had neither the time nor the resources to pursue these ideas, we learned, as women everywhere have learned, that the demands of economic survival establish the parameters for the pursuit of dreams. Understanding and expanding those parameters must be central to all our theories of liberation.

As we enter another decade of feminist activism, the articles collected here grow in importance. They contribute to analyzing our past and passing on what we have learned so that each individual or group does not have to reinvent the wheel of feminist thought and experience. We chose to reprint these articles because they represent the diverse areas that were of concern to *Quest* and *that are still central to feminism today*: power, reformism, leadership, class, race, sexuality, lesbianism, motherhood, work, and money. Some of the authors fear that their essays are dated because particulars have changed, and each of us has changed in her own thinking. The basic questions raised are fundamental to feminism, however, and *Quest* has found that these particular articles are among those most often discussed, quoted, and used by feminist groups and women's studies courses. Finally, we chose these selections because they are clearly written and present some of *Quest*'s strongest and most provocative statements.

Most of the essays in this book discuss several issues, but we have ordered them according to their primary focus around four central concerns of *Quest*'s first three volumes: Power and Practice, The Politics of Everyday Life, Feminist Perspectives on Class, and Organizations and Strategies. In the section on Power and Practice, we have grouped together articles that offer a general analysis of the overall state of various parts of the women's movement. The Politics of Everyday Life relates what has been conceived of as the "public" world of work to the "private" world of personal relations and therefore combines articles dealing with issues of sexuality and family life with those related to work. In devoting a section to Feminist Perspectives on Class, we demonstrate not only that class has been an important area of feminist concern for some years but also that there are important specifically feminist arguments on the subject. Finally, the section on Organizations and Strategies represents *Quest*'s consistent focus on the need for feminists to learn from what we have done and examine problems and possibilities in our structures and strategies; this section includes several interviews because we sometimes found that the interview format was the only way to get the insights and experiences we wanted from feminist activists onto paper.

We hope that this book will draw you into the experiences and ideas that fueled *Quest* and spur more feminists to engage actively in the development of feminist theory.

Charlotte Bunch

PART ONE

Power
and
Practice

This section on Power and Practice includes theoretical reflections on concepts of power and feminist practice. The articles propose and critique a variety of possible feminist approaches to political action, among them, female separatism, lesbian feminism, socialist feminism, and nonaligned feminism.

Political Change: Two Perspectives on Power

Nancy Hartsock

Feminists agree that the political change we seek means an end to sexism in all its forms, but political change involves more specific and more controversial goals as well. While most of us would agree that free, 24-hour, client-controlled child care and proper health care for women are goals whose achievement would both result from and represent major political change, agreement is not widespread about many other issues, such as the Equal Rights Amendment or campaigns to integrate women into police forces. Does the women's movement see the last two as demands for political change? Some women argue that they are not, while others see them as important and central political changes. In order to work effectively, we must understand what political change means from a feminist perspective and work out criteria for developing and evaluating strategies for change.

Power, Change, and Social Science

Power

Politics is about power—that much is generally agreed upon by practitioners and students of the political—and discussions of politics have included power as a fundamental concern. Most social scientists have based their discussions of power on definitions of power as the ability to compel obedience, or as control and domination. They link this definition with Bertrand Russell's statement that power is the production of intended effects, and add that power must be power over someone—something possessed, a property of an actor such that he* can alter the will or actions of others in a way that produces results in conformity with his own will.[1] Effects on the actions of others are fundamental to this understanding of power.

Social theorists have argued that power, like money, is something possessed by an actor which has value in itself and which is useful as well for obtaining other valued things. In an article on the concept of power, Talcott Parsons, the most influential of these theorists, states that he regards power as "a circulating medium, analogous to money, within what is called the political system," and suggests that we can best understand power by looking at "the relevant properties of money as such a medium in the economy."[2]

Parsons argues that money itself has no value in use but acts as a measure of value. He adds that modern monetary systems require an institutionalized confidence in the system as a whole, and argues that money only works as a medium of exchange within networks of market relationships. By analogy, power "is generalized capacity to secure the performance of binding obligations by units in a system of collective organization."[3] Both kinds of transactions require a system within which they can be managed as symbols.

That Parsons and others compare the uses of power with the uses of money in a capitalistic market society indicates their acceptance of that society's assumptions about the nature of market transactions, and their expansion of these patterns to cover essentially all human interactions. Their analogy of the uses of money and power supports Marx's claim that the development of the importance of money (or, as Marx designated the broader category, exchange value) leads to the transformation of all human activities into patterns modeled on monetary transactions.[4]

Money functions as a universal commodity, since it is defined as the exchange value of other commodities and at the same time has an independent existence. The parallel properties of power are apparent in the distinction between power as a value in itself and the other values one can obtain if one has power.

Marx stressed the historical importance of exchange value in creating a society in which power functions like money when he pointed out that "the influence of exchange over all production relationships can only develop fully and ever more completely in bourgeois society."[5] Only in a society based on the market, in which human interdependence is not personal but based on exchange value, can power come to be sought as a value in itself, and domination of others—or the use of power to "purchase" certain behavior—become the almost exclusive measure of power.

---

*Note on gender: "He" and "men" are not generic terms in this article, but refer specifically to men and not women. Here, "she" is the more generic pronoun.

The idea that power refers to something possessed by individuals (a commodity) and means domination over others can be found in philosophical writing of the seventeenth century where it served as a justification for the ways society was managed and controlled by the marketplace.

Thomas Hobbes, one of the earliest and most influential theorists in this tradition, conceived of society as the structured relations of exchange between proprietors, and of political society as a "device for the protection of this property and for the maintenance of an orderly relation of exchange."[6] In order to form the state, Hobbes argued, each individual gave up "the right of protecting and defending himself by his own power," and turned to the sovereign for protection. "Without that security, there is no reason for a man to deprive himself of his own advantages, and make himself a prey to others."[7] It is not surprising that Marx could say of such a society that we carry both our power over society and our association with it in our pockets.[8] Similar formulations have persisted, all of them based on the assumption that individuals are isolated, in competition, and without community.[9]

These definitions of power aid us in discussing male supremacy. Berenice Carroll notes Bertrand de Jouvenel's statement that "a man feels himself more of a man when imposing himself and making others the instrument of his will," and adds that "it is no accident that the subject of this assertion is 'a man.' The associative links between ideas of manliness and virility on the one hand, and domination, conquest and power on the other hand, are strong and pervasive in Western culture."[10]

Change

Social scientists' discussions of change are based on the same assumptions as their discussions of political power. *Webster's Third International Dictionary* defines the verb *change* as to "to make different," and then distinguishes variation, alteration, and modification from transformation. Social science treatments of change have focused on either societal change or individual change, but have frequently ignored the process or dynamic of change itself.[11]

One major textbook on methodology, *The Language of Social Research*, treats only change in individuals. It presents three methods for measuring individual change.[12] These methods for measuring change assume that change is variance and make little attempt to separate variance from the concepts of modification or transformation. Any difference uncovered in what is measured over time is labeled "change." These methods do not distinguish superficial differences from fundamental social change.

Other social scientists, such as Lasswell and Kaplan in *Power and Society*, understand that political change can involve a transformation. But Lasswell and Kaplan still conceptualize revolution as a change of elites: "the counter-elite cannot attain power without the instrumentality of the mass, but the instrument is a threat to its own position as well as to that of the elite it seeks to supplant." Moreover, "the course of a revolution is sought to be limited by each participant group to the attainment of a favorable power position for itself."[13] Lasswell and Kaplan clearly regard human beings, both individuals and groups, as competitors in a hostile world.

In summary, social scientific discussions of political change give little attention to the process of change itself, and the assumption that the basic units of society are competitive, hostile, and isolated individuals leads to an overemphasis on people taking power for their own advantage, and underemphasis on the importance of change in the institutions and structures of society.

Other Approaches to Political Change

A feminist redefinition of the concept of political change requires an understanding of the women's movement's concern for the relationships of the personal and the political; a perspective on the struggles within the movement over the nature and uses of power, leadership, and organization; sensitivity to the importance of process and interaction in social change; and finally, recognition of the fundamental links between economics and social relationships. Feminists regard change as a process that takes place on several levels: the personal, the group or organizational, and the level of social institutions. Political change, then, involves redefining the self, building different kinds of political organizations, gaining economic power for women, and most importantly, a sense of how each of these arenas for change relates to the interlocking structures of patriarchy, white supremacy, and capitalism. Finally, change at each of these levels must be understood as important not only as a facet of political change in itself but as a precondition for further change, which can take place in several of these structures at once.

The Personal and the Political

> *If what we change does not change us we are playing with blocks.*
> —*Marge Piercy*

Small-group consciousness raising at the beginning of the contemporary women's movement—with its stress on clarifying the links between the personal and the political—led women to conclude that change in consciousness and in the social relations of the individual is one of the most important components of political change. Women talked to each other to understand and share experiences and to set out a firsthand account of women's oppression.

But a great deal of unexpected energy and method came out of these groups. We learned that it was important to build an analysis of sexual politics from the ground up—from our own experiences. The idea that the personal lives of women should be analyzed in political terms both grew out of the experience of women in these groups and served as a focus for continued small-group activity. We drew connections between personal experience and political generalities about the oppression of women: we took up our experience and transformed it through reflection. This transformation of experience by reflection and the subsequent alterations in women's lives laid the groundwork for the idea that liberation must pervade aspects of life not considered politically important in the past. While many of the questions addressed by the small groups were not new, the methodology differed from the practice of most social movements, particularly those in Western capitalist countries.

Stressing the links between the personal and the political led women to conclude that first, a fundamental redefinition of the self was an integral part of action for political change; and second, that the changed consciousness and changed definition of the self could occur only in conjunction with a restructuring of the social relationships in which each person was involved.

In the process of developing a new sense of self, we made many advances. We took good points too far, however, and created new kinds of problems. Charlotte Bunch notes four of them: women have turned oppression into a source of identity but have also made it an excuse for inaction; we have relied on the women's movement to provide a ready-made identity; we have fixed on ideals that we require of all women without attention to what each woman can do well; and we have built identity and respect not on our own strength but on our relationships with other women.[14] Each of these can become a way to avoid creating an independent and responsible self. At the same time, each of these problems represents a successful attempt to create change, and each provides us with one element of a feminist definition of change: change is the process of creating new problems out of our solutions to earlier problems.

Developing an independent sense of self necessarily calls other areas of our lives into question. We must ask how our relationships with other persons can foster self-definition rather than dependence and accommodate our new strengths. What is the role of consciousness in creating change? What kinds of organizational structures contribute to the process of changing our self-concept? How does our sense of self relate to economic issues, to class within capitalism, heterosexuality within patriarchy? Finally, our efforts to develop new selves focus our attention on process and interaction. We constantly confront new situations in which we act out of our changed awareness of the world and experience the changed reactions of others. As Georg Lukacs summarized it, "to posit oneself, to produce and reproduce oneself—that is *reality*."[15] By working out the links between the personal and the political, the women's movement has begun to understand existence as a social process, the product of human activity. The realization that the social world is a human creation and that through our own activity we have already changed important aspects of that world leads to a sense of our own power and provides a source of energy for further changes.

Organization and Leadership

Independent and strong selves at the personal level must be expressed and reinforced by organizations. Discussion has centered on the kinds of organizations that can both express and develop women's strengths, and power within women's organizations has come to be an important issue. While leadership and power are not the only issues important in working out questions of organizational structure, they bear on the central issues of political power, and consideration of those problems is useful.

Reaction against leadership was often a reaction to the earlier experience of some women in male-dominated organizations, but soon it became an issue within the women's movement as well. Women who had been active in male-dominated organizations associated power with "loudmouthed, pushy, ego-centered men,"[16] who advocated a "macho" style of violence and sometimes listed women among the objects to be readily available after the revolution. The predominance in the movement of middle-class women, who lacked the tradition of women's strength and independence more frequent among working-class and rural women, also contributed to the identification of leadership and power as oppressive male characteristics.

"Informal" leaders developed, and some were recognized by the media and transformed into stars, at both national and local levels. Women who had argued for the abolition of leadership and power found that some women were far more influential than others. It is useful to examine this issue as one concerning what kinds of power are legitimate in the women's movement. Women were rightly dissatisfied with the idea of power as money (a value in itself and a possession which enables one to obtain other things) in the male Left.

There are alternative definitions of power that do not require domination of others.

Berenice Carroll points out that in *Webster's International Dictionary* (1933), power is first defined as "ability, whether physical, mental or moral, to act; the faculty of doing or performing something," and is synonymous with "strength, vigor, energy, force, and ability." The words "control" and "domination" do not appear as synonyms.[17] Although this concept of power does appear in contemporary social science, it has not been as important as ideas of power as a form of domination. Christian Bay cites one such definition of power as "any activity where there is accomplishment, satisfaction of needs, mutual attainment of goals not distorted by . . . thwarting . . . experience."[18] Carroll, too, cites arguments about power as the need for activity and achievement, the drive to "interact effectively with" the environment. She also notes that the work of A. Kardiner on the "development of the effective ego" presents a similar view.[19]

Significantly, these understandings of power do not require the domination of others; energy and accomplishment are understood to be satisfying in themselves. This kind of power is much closer to what the women's movement has sought, yet this aspect of power is denied to all but a few women; the common female experience of being treated as though we were invisible can scarcely be characterized as effective interaction with the environment.

One source of the difficulties in the women's movement about leadership, strength, and achievement has been our lack of clarity about the differences between the two concepts of power. A letter of resignation from the women's movement, used by two different women in different cities, expresses some of these problems. They complain of being attacked by their sisters for having achieved something, and of being "labelled a thrill seeking opportunist, a ruthless mercenary, out to make her fame and fortune over the dead bodies of selfless sisters."[20] The letter argues that leadership qualities should not be confused with the desire to be a leader, and, similarly, that achievement or productivity should not be confused with the desire to be a leader (by implication, to dominate others). These statements indicate that women have not recognized that power understood as energy, strength, and effective interaction need not be the same as power that requires the domination of others in the movement.

But we must nevertheless recognize and confront the world of traditional politics in which money and power function in similar ways. Thus, creating political change involves setting up organizations based on power as energy and strength, groups that are structured and not tied to the personality of one individual, groups whose structures do not permit the use of power as a tool for domination of others in the group. At the same time, our organizations must deal with the society in which we live on its own terms—that is, terms of power as control, power as a means of making others do what they do not wish to do.

Recognition of the two faces of power, and of the necessity for working on both levels, means that our organizations must be structured and ongoing. With few exceptions, the radical wing of the women's movement has fragmented into small groups that are difficult to find and join. We cannot create political change until we structure our own organizations to deal with power as domination in the institutions of society. As our sense of self develops, we should be able to experiment more with different forms of organization and to understand how changes in organizational structure increase our ability to control the structures which now control us. Thus, while political change is about changes in power relationships, we are not talking about women simply participating in power relationships as they are at present constituted, but rather using our methods of organization as strategies for the redefinition of political power itself. The organizations we build are an integral part of the process of creating political change, and in the long term can perhaps serve as the groundwork for new societal institutions.

The process is not as easy as it sounds. History provides many confirmations of Lord Acton's famous dictum that power corrupts and absolute power corrupts absolutely. We have seen organizations in the male-dominated Left mirror some of the worst evils of the capitalist structures they said they wanted to replace. We must constantly ask: To what extent must we build organizations that mirror the institutions we are trying to destroy? Can organizations based on power as energy and initiative be effective tools for changing sexist, heterosexist, racist, and classist institutions such as the media, the health industry, and the like? To what extent will both we and our organizations be transformed by the struggle for power (domination)? Can our organizations serve as tools for taking power for women and still lay the groundwork for new nonsexist, nonracist, nonclassist societal institutions? While there are no easy answers to these questions, we must continue to ask them as we work to create political change.

Patriarchy, Capitalism, and White Supremacy

The transformation of our sense of self and the creation of organizations which express our new ideas cannot take place in a vacuum. We change ourselves and our organizations for the purpose of changing the interlocking structures which control our lives. The economic position of women is fundamental to the political change we seek.

Moreover, when we look closely at the economic roles of women we see the ways capitalism, patriarchy,* and white supremacy reinforce one another and how the ideology of individualism provides a philosophical justification for these structures. When we understand that the economic condition of women is maintained and structured by several institutions rather than only one, it becomes clear that the change we are working for cannot succeed in the economic sphere merely by providing paid work for every woman.

Women are exploited as wage laborers just as men are, but our position differs from theirs in three major ways: first, women are heavily concentrated in service and clerical jobs; second, we are paid less than men who do comparable work; and finally, all women, along with minority-group men, are used as a reserve labor force. In sum, we are viewed as supplementary workers to be brought into the money economy when needed and removed when no longer necessary. That more than half the population can be regarded as supplementary workers indicates the strength of the institution of patriarchy and the roles it forces on women.

Western capitalist society presents the middle-class family as the ideal, a unit in which the man has both economic and psychological power over its other members. Family relationships structured in "acceptable" ways act as a stabilizing force for the economic system as a whole. Economic dependence of several people on one wage earner (male or female) and wages so low that both parents must work to support their children are useful resources for capitalism. As one manufacturer pointedly remarked, he prefers married women, "especially those who have families at home dependent on them for support; they are attentive, docile, more so than unmarried females, and are compelled to use their utmost exertions to procure the necessities of life."[21]

The ideology of the family performs other services as well. The proper role of woman is supporter and reconstructor of the male ego after the workplace has damaged it. The male worker's position of domination in the family reverses his own domination by his boss at work and enables him to transfer tensions developed at the workplace to the family, thus lowering the probability that he will focus anger on the workplace.

Patriarchy considers work for wages improper for women and imposes the myth of "woman's place" on working women. Many women believe they are temporary or supplemental wage earners. Patriarchal ideas are also used by the employer to question the motives of

---

*Institutionalized heterosexuality is an important element of patriarchy, and my references to patriarchy in the text include it. The discussion of the importance of the family should be read with this in mind.

women who complain about their jobs. If they are older and single, he dismisses their protests as the neuroses of spinsters; if the women are young, he dismisses their protests as those of temporary workers who will leave when they marry or get pregnant; if they have husbands, they are regarded as both supplementary and temporary; and the problems of women with children to support alone are simply not recognized. That the reality of women's lives often runs counter to these myths does not significantly lessen their impact.

Capitalism makes a place for the economically dependent woman through consumption. According to Friedan, advertising consultants know that finding "bargains" has come to be a housewife's major contribution to the economy of the family, just as the husband's contribution consists of bringing home a paycheck.[22] The upgrading of consumption assumes that every family has at least a middle-class income; contains a woman, a man, and several children; and is supported by the paid labor of one (male) worker. While many women's lives contradict the myth, the ideas it expresses affect us all. Women working for wages can be led to buy things for their families out of guilt for spending time away from home. The woman who must support others is in a double bind: she is blamed for leaving her children and her wages are often so low that she is unable to purchase many of the goods every family "needs."

Women's services in the home are the source of another link between patriarchy and capitalism. The work of housewives increases the real wages of families with two adults[23] and thereby enables them to purchase commodities they could not otherwise afford. At the same time, women employed outside the home still produce a portion of this value in the home. The employment of married women living with their husbands thus provides a measure of expansion in the market for goods and services in boom times. Firing women at other times provides a cushion against the full consequences of recession, since the women's increased home production will partially make up for their lost salaries.

Capitalism and patriarchy in the United States are also linked with white supremacy. The popularization of the myth that black matriarchy is responsible for the problems of the black community is one of the most obvious and vicious links between patriarchy and white supremacy. The efforts by both blacks and whites to make the black family mirror the white middle-class patriarchal family, and efforts to push black women into supportive roles, not only oppress black women but also decrease the energy available for the struggle against white domination. The creation of divisions and hostilities between black women and men is useful to the ruling class to defuse effective attacks on racism.[24]

Second, capitalism requires marginal work forces, and white supremacy as well as patriarchy are convenient instruments for this purpose. Racial and ethnic minorities are used as marginal labor in most advanced industrial countries—Southern Europeans in Germany, North Africans in France. Racial minorities are used by capitalism in other ways as well:

> The extent to which the capitalist class is able to isolate segments of the working class from each other strengthens its position. . . . If one group of workers is able to command higher pay, to exclude others from work, and if the other group or groups of workers are limited in their employment opportunities to the worst jobs and lowest pay, then a marginal working class has been created which benefits the labor aristocracy and to an even greater extent the capitalist class.[25]

Third, minority-group men provide a more varied reserve labor force than women, who are confined to a few types of work. Finally, the idea that the problems of minority-group workers can be traced to "discrimination" alone is an important tool for capitalist control. One writer has argued that ending discrimination as such would make only a small difference in the economic role of minorities.[26] Yet the concept of discrimination, based on an understanding of the individual as a person who carries both her power over society and her association with it in her pocket, helps maintain the belief that employers buy some products (workers) rather than others for reasons as innocuous as preference or taste. They can argue that those of us who object are inconsistent:

> We do not regard it as "discrimination"—or at least not in the same invidious sense—if an individual is willing to pay a higher price to listen to one singer than another, although we do if he is willing to pay a higher price to have services rendered to him by a person of one color rather than by a person of another.[27]

The idea that persons are products whose value is measured by their price, the stress on freedom of "contract" between equals, the assumption that each individual goes to the market with the ability and willingness to pay certain prices to achieve some preferences— all these are implied by the concept of discrimination.

While we have discussed only a few of the links among capitalism, patriarchy, and white supremacy, it is obvious that we cannot end any woman's economic oppression and dependency without at the same time destroying those structures. Power as domination is fundamental to the three; taking power as domination appears to be the only way to take over and transform them.

Ideas and History

It is difficult to refer to the concept of the individual as a structure in the same sense as capitalism, patriarchy, or white supremacy. Nevertheless, these structures could not be maintained without a set of assumptions about what human beings are and what they might become. We cannot work effectively for change without understanding the importance of ideas and recognizing the reciprocal effects of consciousness on actions and organizations.

The content of the intellectual and emotional life of a society is bound up with the way it reproduces its material life. Ideas play the role of justifying, legitimating, and then stabilizing economic changes. As Marx stated, when

> each new class . . . puts itself in the place of one ruling before it, (it) is compelled, merely in order to carry through its aim, to represent its interest as the common interest of all the members of society, that is expressed in ideal form; it has to give its ideas the form of universality and represent them as the only rational, universally valid ones.[28]

Thus, bourgeois philosophers, political economists, and others developed the ideas capitalist society required for its survival and growth, and saw their assumptions as universal and eternal truths about humankind.[29]

Earlier I argued that contemporary definitions of power as domination were based on assumptions of possessive individualism and the requirements of capitalist society. In addition to power, the possessive individual is concerned with the myth of equality and the compartmentalization of life.

The idea of equality as presented by Hobbes begins from a world that in its state of nature is populated by "human calculating machines,"[30] each one basically equal to all the others. Marx argued that the idea of self-interested and fundamentally equal beings was important because capitalism required interchangeable laboring units. Once human equality had become accepted as a universal truth, the argument could be made that since all persons are in fact equal—that is, have "equality of opportunity"—then those who are unable to get as much money as others are solely responsible for their own state.

Nineteenth-century employers consistently objected to labor legislation as interference with freedom of contract. They argued that such legislation encouraged "the workman to look to the law for the protection which he ought to secure for himself by voluntary contract"; the legislation "limits a *man's* power of doing what *he* will with what *he* considers *his* own."[31]

This argument relies on the assumption that the employer and employee are in equal positions of power with respect to each other. This assumption is not accurate, since the laborer cannot survive without selling her labor power; yet it has been widely accepted by those who suffer from it as well as those who benefit. The practice of blaming the victim for her plight is a powerful obstacle to the creation of political change, since it suggests that if those involved were "worth" equality of treatment, they would in fact be accorded equality.

We know from our efforts to break free of them that these are powerful ideas. The idea of the isolated individual who protects and expands his own position allows the ruling classes to justify and expand their positions of dominance as the just reward for having the strength to act on their own interests. Those of us are not so successful are kept from looking beyond ourselves by our shame at failing to expand our power (domination).

The compartmentalization or fragmentation of life is a second corollary of possessive individualism. The system of purchasing labor by the day or hour rather than by lifetimes of loyalty is compatible with the idea that in different spheres one behaves according to different rules. An important separation in industrial society has been between modes of behavior appropriate for the family and behavior appropriate for the workplace or public life.[32] The women's movement has been particularly concerned with the separation of the personal from the political, but this distinction is simply one of many compartmentalizations that divide the world into disparate spheres: the public is separated from the private; professional judgments from human ones; the world of facts (reason) from that of values (emotion).

Anais Nin has commented on this phenomenon from a woman's perspective:

> I have always been tormented by the image of a multiplicity of selves. . . . My first concept of people about me was that all of them were coordinated into a whole, whereas I was made up of a multitude of selves, of fragments. . . . There were always, in me, two women at least, one woman desperate and bewildered, who felt she was drowning, and another who only wanted to bring beauty, grace, and aliveness to people, and who would leap into a scene, as upon a stage, conceal her true emotions because they were weaknesses, helplessness, despair, and present to the world only a smile, an eagerness, curiosity, enthusiasm, interest.[33]

Compartmentalization is a way of separating us from ourselves, but it is also a technique of survival: if we have only the self who is drowning, we die.

W. E. B. DuBois comments on a similar phenomenon among blacks:

> It is a peculiar sensation, this double-consciousness, this sense of always looking at one's self through the eyes of others, of measuring one's soul by the tape of a world that looks on in amused contempt and pity. One ever feels his two-ness—an American and a Negro. . . .[34]

The compartmentalization of the world leads to a fragmentation of the self among working- and lower-class people as well. "Dividing the self defends against the pain a person would otherwise feel, if he had to submit the whole of himself to a society which makes his position a vulnerable and anxiety-laden one."[35]

After passing through the prisms of capitalism, white supremacy, and patriarchy, the compartmentalization of the world takes different forms in middle- and upper-class white women, in minority women and men, and among white working- and lower-class people. But in each, the fragmentation of the self is a mechanism for survival, a way (however damaging to us) of getting by in an oppressive world, a way of coping with the all too frequent failures in one or more areas of our lives. Yet the fragmentation of the self maintains our oppression. By compartmentalizing our lives we implicitly accept individual responsibility for the failures that grow out of our collective oppression and absorb into ourselves the impact of these failures. As long as we fail to challenge the structures controlling our lives, the fragmentation of ourselves is necessary for survival. By contrast, the process of directly challenging patriarchy, white supremacy, and capitalism both creates and requires a sense of ourselves as wholes rather than fragments.

Conclusions

We have returned to the importance of our sense of self, but now can see it as a part of our efforts for political change. Since our sense of self is bound up with the structures of social control, we cannot allow our work for political change to stagnate at the level of personal change. At the same time, we must recognize that change takes place in several areas and both affects and is affected by changes in other areas. We have seen that patriarchy, capitalism, and white supremacy have pervasive effects on all aspects of our lives. Thus, efforts for change in any area should lead us to examine the obstacles to change created by the existence of the other structures as well.

Political change is a process of transforming not only ourselves but also our most basic assumptions about humanity and our sense of human possibility. Political change means restructuring our organizations to reflect our constantly changing understanding of the possible and to meet the new needs and new problems we create. Political change requires strategies that attack the interlocking structures of control at all levels. At bottom, political change is a process of changing power relationships so that the meaning of power itself is transformed.

Our strategies for change must grow out of the tension between using our organizations as instruments for taking and transforming power in a society structured by power understood only as domination, and using our organizations to build models for a new society based on power understood as energy and initiative. Thus, in evaluating a particular strategy we must ask: 1) how it will affect women's sense of self, and sense of our own collective power; 2) how it will make women aware of problems beyond questions of identity—that is, how it will politicize women; 3) how the strategy will work to build organizations that will increase both our strength and competence, and will give women power to use (like money) to weaken the control and domination of capitalism, patriarchy, and white supremacy; and 4) how the strategy will weaken the links between these institutions.

As Juliet Mitchell pointed out, a change in one of several interlocking structures can be offset by changes in the others.[36] This is a particularly difficult question, since weakening the structures that oppress us depends heavily on how the strategy is conceived, followed through, and expanded. How, for example, can support for the Equal Rights Amendment lead to women taking power in such a way that the structures of social relations as they are at present constituted cannot survive?

Finally, we must examine every strategy for change in terms of the understanding of process and interaction it contains: does the strategy contain at least the seeds of its own supersession, or is it a way of forever doing the same things for the same people?

These criteria for evaluating strategies for political change grow out of the four concerns I listed at the beginning of the discussion: the importance of the relationship between the personal and the political; questions of power and leadership in feminist organizations; the importance of process and interaction; and the problems posed by the interlocking nature of capitalism, patriarchy, and white supremacy. Political change can occur only if each of these concerns is an important and continuing element of our thought. They call our attention to the fact that what we mean by political change is structural change.

NOTES

1. See Bertrand Russell, *Power, A New Social Analysis* (n.p., 1936), p. 35, cited by Anthony de Crespigny and Alan Wertheimer, *Contemporary Political Theory* (New York: Atherton Press, 1970), p. 22; Harold Lasswell and Abraham Kaplan, *Power and Society* (New Haven: Yale University Press, 1950), p. 76; and Howard Warrender, *The Political Philosophy of Hobbes* (Oxford: Clarendon Press, 1957), p. 312.
2. Talcott Parsons, "On the Concept of Political Power," in *Political Power*, ed. Roderick Bell, David V. Edwards, and R. Harrison Wagner (New York: Free Press, 1969), p. 256.
3. Ibid., p. 257.

4. Karl Marx, *The Grundrisse*, ed. David McLellan (New York: Harper & Row, 1971), p. 65. The discussion of the development of credit, in which all that one has or is or does can be translated into a measure of one's exchange value, provides an example of how the transformation takes place. See David McLellan, *Marx Before Marxism* (New York: Harper & Row, 1971), p. 176.
5. *Grundrisse*, p. 65.
6. C. B. MacPherson, *The Political Theory of Possessive Individualism* (London: Oxford University Press, 1962), p. 3.
7. Thomas Hobbes, *De Corpore Politico, English Works*, Molesworth ed., 4:128–29, quoted by Warrender, *The Political Philosophy of Hobbes*, pp. 112–13.
8. Marx, *Grundrisse*, p. 66.
9. Christian Bay, *The Structure of Freedom* (New York: Atheneum, 1968), p. 250, and Kate Millett, *Sexual Politics* (Garden City, N.Y.: Doubleday, 1970), p. 23, cite a number of these discussions.
10. Berenice Carroll, "Peace Research: The Cult of Power" (paper presented to the American Sociological Association in Denver, Colorado, September 1971), p. 6. She takes de Jouvenel's statement from Hannah Arendt, "Reflections on Violence," *Journal of International Affairs*, 23, no. 1 (1969): 12.
11. J. A. Ponsioen, in *The Analysis of Social Change Reconsidered* (The Hague: Mouton, 1965), discusses a number of writers.
12. Paul Lazarsfeld and Morris Rosenberg, *The Language of Social Research* (Glencoe, Ill.: Free Press, 1955), pp. 203–81.
13. Lasswell and Kaplan, *Power and Society*, pp. 268–78.
14. Charlotte Bunch, "Perseverance Furthers: Woman's Sense of Self," *The Furies*, February 1973, pp. 3–4.
15. Georg Lukacs, *History and Class Consciousness* (Cambridge, Mass.: MIT Press, 1971), pp. 15–16.
16. Rita Mae Brown, "Leadership vs. Stardom," *The Furies*, February 1972, p. 20.
17. Carroll, "Peace Research," p. 7. The author is indebted to her paper for the scholarly sources discussing power as energy.
18. Bay, *The Structure of Freedom*, p. 248, cited by Carroll, p. 8.
19. Robert White, "Motivation Reconsidered: The Concept of Competence," *Psychological Review* 66 (1959): 297, 310, 318, cited by Carroll, pp. 9–10.
20. Anselma dell'Olio and Joreen, printed in *Chicago Women's Liberation Union Newsletter*, July 1970.
21. Karl Marx, *Capital* (New York: International Publishers, 1967), 1:402.
22. Betty Friedan, *The Feminine Mystique* (New York: Dell, 1963), pp. 214–15.
23. Chong Soo Pyun, "The Monetary Value of a Housewife," in *Woman in a Manmade World*, ed. Non Glazer-Malbin and Helen Youngelson Waehrer (New York: Rand McNally, 1972), p. 192.
24. See Robert Staples, "The Myth of the Black Matriarchy," *Black Scholar*, January–February 1970, p. 15.
25. William K. Tabb, "Capitalism, Colonialism, and Racism," in *Institutions, Policies, and Goals: A Reader in American Politics*, ed. Kenneth M. Dolbeare and Murray J. Edelman, with Patricia Dolbeare (Lexington, Mass: D. C. Heath, 1973), p. 174.

26. Ibid., p. 175.
27. Ibid., p. 167.
28. Karl Marx and Frederick Engels, *The German Ideology*, ed. C. J. Arthur (New York: International Publishers, 1970), pp. 65–66. They also point out that "the ideas of the ruling class are in every epoch the ruling ideas, i.e., the class which is the ruling *material* force of society is at the same time its ruling *intellectual* force."
29. MacPherson, *Possessive Individualism*, has documented the role of these assumptions in political philosophy.
30. Ibid., p. 92.
31. T. H. Green, *The Political Theory of T. H. Green*, ed. John R. Rodman (New York: Appleton-Century-Crofts, 1964), pp. 43–44. Italics mine.
32. On this point see Eli Zaretsky, "Capitalism, the Family, and Personal Life: Part 2," *Socialist Revolution*, 3, no. 3 (May–June 1973).
33. Anais Nin, *Diary, 1931–34* (New York: Harcourt, Brace, and World, 1966), quoted by Meredith Tax, "Woman and Her Mind: The Story of Everyday Life," in *Notes from the Second Year* (1970), p. 15.
34. W. E. B. DuBois, *The Souls of Black Folk* (New York: Fawcett World Library, 1968), p. 16 in Joyce Ladner, *Tomorrow's Tomorrow* (New York: Anchor Books, 1971), pp. 273–74.
35. Richard Sennett and Jonathan Cobb, *The Hidden Injuries of Class* (New York: Random House, 1972), p. 208.
36. Juliet Mitchell, *Woman's Estate* (New York: Pantheon, 1971), p. 120.

The Future of Female Separatism

Lucia Valeska

Every woman on earth can draw strength and courage from the separatist slogan "Power to Women" because every woman has experienced a measure of futility and powerlessness solely due to the fact that she is female. The woman who calls her people "black" will feel it. So too with the woman who is working class, southern white Baptist, Betty Ford, or Elizabeth the Queen. Thus speaks the collective, biologically based history of mothers, sisters, daughters, aunts, grandmothers, nieces, misses, mrs., mses, queens and ladies, milkmaids, whores, and dykes alike. Wherever you are or have been, the power of "Power to Women" gets to you.

Past that, we have some difficulties. So far, biology is destiny, but so are a number of other things. Even though sexism pervades society across class and racial boundaries, still it affects us differentially—especially in our historical, political, and economic development. If the fundamental fabric of society is *paternalistic* (usually associated with a feudal economy) intimacy—emotional, physical, psychological—can be sustained between rulers and ruled. With industrialization, the rise of a *competitive* political economic order gradually numbed the previous paternalistic relationship.

Take black and white America as an example. One of the primary distinguishing characteristics of race relations in a paternalistic system is that it simultaneously places great social distance between the races in combination with a high degree of intimacy. Black "mammies" suckle, toilet train, and tutor white children; and black "uncles" tell stories, teach manual skills, protect and obey the master's entire family. The children, black and white, play and grow together from infancy to adulthood. In each family's daily intercourse, in the quarrels and celebrations, the other maintains a close watchful presence. Sexual contact between the races is never entirely condoned, but it is relatively frequent and practically unavoidable—especially between master and female slave.

The mass migration of poor blacks to industrial centers changes the whole fabric of interdependent and intimate connections between whites and blacks. A new potential for mass black identity and organization emerges, and a different form of racism takes hold.[1]

The effect of industrialization, however, on sex roles is different and varies according to race and class. Black women went through a similar economic transition as did black men in terms of moving out of a paternalistic framework. The fact that many black women remained, or became domestic workers in white households, tempered their transition somewhat, but not enough to keep paternalistic ties with whites intact. The black domestic worker still calls the ghetto home, and she draws her primary political consciousness from that segregated community. Consequently, black women rarely have been severely paternalistically beholden to black men in this country—due to the history of racism here.

The white working-class woman also moved from a thoroughly paternalistic (often rural extended) family into a competitive, industrial work force. The primary difference between her situation and that of the black woman in terms of industrialization is that the white woman temporarily escaped the new competitive order. The transition left her with one foot in the new order and one still heavily ensconced in the traditional family. The traditional family (extended or nuclear) is a paternalistic institution by definition.

Stuck in this particular institution, white middle-class women made a different transition. Until recently they have remained in a paternalistic environment with respect to sex role: having their class identity, economic mobility, and emotional and psychological existence fundamentally submerged in their father's family first and then their husband's. They were not regarded as primary wage earners. Their families did not require their (wage based) economic contribution to survive. Only recently, with the demise of the middle-class nuclear family, are middle-class women being pushed wholesale into a competitive, industrial world. Because they are not ghettoized in the traditional sense, and have no potential for mass mobilization based on geographic consolidation, they therefore have come to view isolated, paternalistic existence in the family and one-to-one ties with men as uniquely insidious.

As we analyze how the distinct realities of class, race, and sexuality influence our lives and the direction of our struggles, it is crucial to note the economic roots of female separatism. Our individual reactions to it will vary according to these diverse origins. Nevertheless, our collective insight must yield a concrete understanding of why ultimately lesbian feminism delivers a unique threat to the complex history of human oppression. Furthermore, while the potential blow to male supremacy is as real today as it was six years ago, the terrible child of the feminist revolution is still emerging.

The first wave of dyke-baiting is over. The word "lesbian" can be uttered in wider circles without causing as many raised eyebrows. The grand convergence of lesbianism and feminism is seen and perceived commonly in plain black and white instead of acid lavender.

Initial militant female separatism, like early women's liberation, has sobered in most quarters. Sisterhood is still powerful, but the "army of lovers" have set aside their spears to make music, poetry, radio networks, bookstores, schools, credit unions, presses, magazines, farms, cooperatives, novels, political theory, health care centers, and record companies. What's more, they are brewing up these projects with a very mixed—some say odd—assortment of women. The virulent strain of strict separatism and even once vehement anti-Leftism appear to be fading into a virtual sea of project-oriented activity.

Consequently some maintain that the issue of separatism is used up—it had its merry, suicidal fling, and died an astonishingly early, if not remarkable, death. From the West Coast a friend writes that the very word elicits deadpan hostility or an active curse. Yet, she adds, "while so many are outwardly against separatism, they continue to live it." Recently, three women from Seattle's *Radical Women* sailed through town on their way home from the Antioch Socialist-Feminist bash. A query on separatism gleaned from them a resounding: "It's dead in Seattle. But," they quickly added, "three-quarters of our membership is lesbian and we're an autonomous female organization."

Meanwhile, on the East Coast, a sporadic rash of charges and countercharges plagues the feminist press. A nonseparatist lesbian is ousted from a separatist workshop.[2] Child care at the West Coast Lesbian History Conference is mucked up in the planning stages over the relative ages of male children. There is a bit of a row at Antioch over whether men should be permitted to watch the children. And a feminist from Canada lashes out against the lesbian imperative, shouting: ". . . what I do with my cunt is my own business!"[3] Omens and rumors abound.

Aside from the fact that it's somewhat bizarre to be pronounced dead on arrival when your eyes are wide open and your blood is running hot, what does it all mean? Where do the contradictions leave us? Can we count up the booty from the first campaign to see what we have got? Undeniably a certain separatist ideology and practice has taken irrevocable, organic hold of the women's movement as a whole. One doesn't argue the merits of all-female projects, only whether or not an occasional intruder should be allowed and under what conditions. Lesbians are no longer greeted with sisterly tolerance but with a sure (if hostile) respect. Although many of the militant, lesbian-only collectives have been short-lived, the cultural revolution they started and sustain thrives. Every spring the latest batch of new-feminist-gays hits the bars on schedule. If their politics seem a bit watered, their numbers alone take up the slack. It is truly a staggering phenomenon. But what has this to do with revolution?

Revolutionary Potential

The feminist movement spans a nearly infinite range of political orientations. Even within individual organizations, large and small, the membership discloses an enormous variety of political development. The reason behind our monstrous diversity is simple: one qualifies for the feminist movement if one is female; it doesn't particularly matter what you think because the overriding impulse of coming together is female oppression alone. But while our strength may be in our diversity, it is also true that our greatest revolutionary weakness can be found there as well.

Revolutionary growth is dependent upon concrete analysis, well-articulated consciousness, specific short- and long-range strategies, and organization to implement stated collective goals. A concomitant effect of well-developed revolutionary growth is progressive polarization, which naturally and logically separates *us* from *them*, compels people to choose up sides and make ready for battle. In a revolutionary situation, one is not given the option of neutrality or even diversity. In this sense of *revolutionary*, the feminist movement clearly falls short. The causes for our shortcomings are complex and numerous. What I would like to focus on here are the revolutionary shortcomings with respect to separatism.

First, what does separatism mean? Speaking academically, separatism is simply another word for segregation. The chief difference between the two is how they are used, by whom, and for what purposes. Segregation is used by the economically dominant group as a means of social control, that is, to maintain and perpetuate a given economic, political, and social stratification system. Whereas separatism is used by the economically disadvantaged in order to radically alter existing political, social, and economic arrangements.

Qualitatively, both separatism and segregation are carried out in degrees with a tremendous variation in emphasis depending on the specific situation. Furthermore, the politics of either can be used by individuals or groups who do not necessarily define themselves as separatist per se.

I compare separatism with segregation because their academic similarities tend to disguise their fundamental practical, historical, and political differences. Separatism arouses liberal wrath because, in the liberal mind, it is instantly equated with segregation and *its* role. An example of this confusion is found in the current national debate over quota versus affirmative action. Legally (and academically) there is no difference between setting aside a number of slots for white males (thus keeping others out) and setting aside a number of slots for ethnic minorities and women (effectively keeping white men out). The difference is in our collective political histories. How the Supreme Court will solve the dilemma remains to be seen. It is differential treatment (legal and illegal) that created the situation and it will, of necessity, be differential treatment that gets us out of it. Differential treatment is illegal, but it is the same everywhere. If you want half your school faculties to be female, there are two options: 1) double the faculty (in the midst of recession and long after the baby boom); or 2) fire half the men. This is why affirmative action is a sham reform in terms of its potential for social change.

There is more than just an academic similarity between segregation and separatism. Both are powerful political devices. While we must continually differentiate between them in terms of who's doing what (the dividing and for what purpose), we must also realize that separation is a weapon we instinctively gravitate toward out of necessity. Keeping men out of women's consciousness-raising groups (mild separatism) can be defined euphemistically; we can say: "It is helpful for us to be together without men, just this one place," or "The women need a space of their own," etc. But the fact remains that keeping men out because they are men is discrimination on the basis of sex. It can be labeled "sexism in reverse" just as accurately as any other form of female separatism. All to belabor the obvious truth that feminism is intrinsically separatist. True, the type and degree of separation practiced varies tremendously within the movement.

Lesbian Feminism

Lesbian feminism is popularly considered the most militant form of separatism. While most women and organizations that label themselves "separatist" are lesbian, the reverse is no longer the case. This is a notable development of the last five years. Ever since the convergence of lesbianism and feminism, lesbianism alone has progressively taken on the dimensions of a national cure for what ails you. Gone are the first lesbian feminists who painstakingly worked their way out of the closet through a step-by-step political analysis of the roots and mainstays of male supremacy. In their place are increasing numbers of women who simply find that relationships with women are better. Many of these women are also feminists—in fact were initially exposed to the "lesbian alternative" through the feminist movement (or through their friend who was active in . . .). But their politics run the same infinite gamut as those in the general women's movement. There are socialists, reformists, women's studies dykes, housekeepers, sorority sisters, and divorced sisters-in-laws. These days any random straight woman can accidentally wander into a lesbian bar, party, classroom, picnic, or ball game, and remain there forever.

On the one hand, the proof is in the pudding. Apparently it wasn't such a bad idea. On the other hand, such riffraff you've never seen. The net effect of our phenomenal population explosion as a people is yet to be tallied, and I shall certainly not attempt it. But one result is that the term lesbian feminist does not communicate what it once did. Some militant lesbian feminists have taken refuge under the label lesbian-separatist. But this too has its difficulties because the lesbian feminist camp itself is divided into what we might roughly call cultural nationalists versus political lesbian feminists. Don't faint if you belong to neither group or both. The labels only represent approximate emerging constellations. No single individual or organization exhibits all the characteristics of one, but rather a general orientation toward one rather than the other.

Both advocate separation of the sexes organizationally, politically, and personally—insofar as separation is possible. The possibility of separating is always exaggerated because, let's face it, men are everywhere. Similarly both constellations advocate collective and individual economic independence for women as a primary strategy for achieving the desired autonomy. Often the differences between the two are in degree rather than substance: there is much exchange between them and some contention; but as they develop, the distinctions become more definite.

Cultural Nationalists

When cultural nationalists speak of revolution, they mean matriarchal revolution; that is, putting women in charge of everything of consequence—from childrearing on down to president. Or rather, they speak of returning women to the power they once held under the grand matriarchies of prehistoric civilization. They tend to see separatism as a strategical end—the only way to reorganize all of society under a truly just, fair, loving, and creative order. It's not clear how we'll get from here to there, just faith that we will. For the time being they emphasize building a powerful female culture with all the necessary accouterments: music, art, poetry, films, religion, science, medicine—all female based. If you press them for a narrow description of their politics, they call themselves anarchists or communalists. They are often outspokenly antiauthoritarian, anti-leadership, and antistructure.

Their general strategy is one of "drop out" rather than the "stir up" orientation of their more politically based sisters. In fact, cultural nationalists look askance at the very word *political* (a male compartmentalization), which to them implies rigidity, authoritarianism, and oppressive forms of control. What is deemed correct or incorrect varies according to individual inclination rather than political analysis or organization.

On the question of separatism, they cover a wide range of militancy. Some are virulently antimale, others may not even call themselves "separatist." They are somewhat content to treat men with a "live and let live" philosophy that is more in line with their general political attitude of noncoercive tolerance toward all living things. But, their general perception of males is that they are irresponsible and not to be trusted with any degree of power.

Political Lesbian Feminists

This constellation is urban based. Those who gravitate toward it are often openly hostile to men and see separatism as essential to the revolutionary growth of women. They view themselves as working toward revolutionary change; but, unlike the cultural nationalists, they see the return of matriarchy as more desirable than feasible. One can distinguish the two constellations with respect to separatism, but *not* in terms of militancy. The political lesbian feminists tend to view separatism as one primary strategy. Other strategies include building class consciousness, developing collective organizational structures (true for nationalists too), fighting capitalism, urging women toward a socialistic base and analysis, and developing institutional economic independence.

It is difficult to differentiate clearly between the politicos and the nationalists. Both hold similar views of women, men, and separatism, and both also suffer from lack of overall theory and organization. Perhaps the fundamental difference is that political lesbian feminists are not so put off by structures, power, leadership, and political analysis. In fact, their emphasis is on how to get from here to there; their intent is to seize power.

Where the specific evolution of these constellations will lead is unknown. It is significant that both evolved from an initial lesbian feminist analysis of the logical direction in which feminism must move in order to become a revolutionary movement. In the following discussion of that analysis, I do not differentiate between them.

Lesbian Feminist Analysis[4]

Knowing that oppression alone is a faulty foundation for revolutionary growth and realizing that sexism, however destructive, comprises a way of survival for all women, the initial lesbian feminist movement started out to build an analysis and platform that would provide the lacking revolutionary direction. When survival itself is dependent on oppression, the first job must be to create an alternative means of survival. The feminist movement provided the initial grist when it politely articulated our right to a separate, viable identity. But the actual political leap from the public arena to the private sphere—where women have lived out an overwhelming percentage of their entire political history—was achieved in lesbian feminist analysis and practice.

It was a natural progression of analysis and events. Once the idea of private politics—fathers, brothers, lovers, husbands, family home, sexuality, and children—fused with the plain old feminist demand for a separate identity, it was only a matter of time. The bedroom just isn't that far from the kitchen. But the analysis goes much further.

The greatest insight that lesbian feminism provided the world is that the institution and ideology of heterosexuality (in its historical development) is a cornerstone of male supremacy. Further, any strategy for liberation that ignores this insight may achieve miraculous social change for millions of people, but it will fail to end male supremacy. By logical (practical, personal, and political) extension, lesbianism comes to play a crucial role in the feminist revolution. It is not my intent to argue the legitimacy of the insight. Such has been done and will continue to be done in greater depth by many others.[5]

The lesbian feminist analysis may strike the standard citizen as virtual madness. But this reaction is not universal. For instance, in 1973 we find one sober, male, Marxist sociologist concluding:

> As long as the vast majority of adult women . . . allow themselves to be linked in a marital or amorous relationship with adult males, it will be difficult for them to join other women in fighting. . . . Until such time as militant feminists will propose a means (satisfying to most women) of dispensing with men, the majority of sisters can be predicted to sell out to the enemy . . . [and] the strategy of female liberation [will be] distinguished from the revolutionary model of class struggle."[6]

The phrase "satisfying to most" catches the eye, because, if nothing else, the lesbian community is apparently providing a healthy number of women with satisfaction. However, van den Berghe is using his point to prove that feminism is inevitably and hopelessly reformist as opposed to revolutionary. The fact that he readily sees heterosexuality as the major stumbling block to feminist revolution is more than interesting.

As a grand conductor of the quality of human life, and the largest worldwide distributor of private, public, psychic, and economic resources, the institution of heterosexuality and the ideology that implements it are never to be taken lightly. It is also true that the only institutional and ideological alternative available is lesbian feminism. Not because the act of women loving women is in and of itself revolutionary (potentially yes, actually no) but because it provides the soil for revolutionary growth. Revolution is never automatic. Initially, lesbian feminism confused possibility with inevitability. When you work hard and long to come up with an astounding first step, you sometimes convince yourself that what follows must surely be easier. This was not, and is not, the case.

Refusing to be men's private property is essential and more than a "personal solution." Heterosexuality is far more than a private matter between a woman and a man; it is, in fact, a mandate that all women be forever divided against each other through a compelling allegiance to one man at home and all men outside the home. While it is possible to refuse to be private property, refusing the public domination of men is virtually impossible. The man is everywhere, at every turn in our existence, holding the reins, creating a constant reinforcement of what we are—economically, politically, and sexually. In order to climb out of the mire of female oppression, one is invariably forced to deal with male authority in a manner that compromises lesbian feminist politics. Consequently a large portion of the lesbian feminist's daily existence—especially on the job—is a living betrayal of what she knows and believes.

Recognizing this reality, the next logical step was the development of strictly lesbian feminist living and working collectives. But with no overall theory to guide their development and no economic base to sustain them, many early efforts in this direction fell prey to instability and political and economic isolation. To remedy the situation, a modified course seemed appropriate. Clearly there has been a shifting of gears—a moving outward into the public sphere. The issue of working with straight women has subsided and has been replaced by this question: with whom can we work to develop economic and political autonomy outside the private sphere?

There has been a simultaneous realization that it isn't heterosexuality per se that must be conquered but the ideological and material base of support it gives to male supremacy. Lesbian feminist analysis is indispensable to the process of destroying male supremacy, but not the end of it. Out of lesbian feminist analysis comes the base opposition to heterosexual hegemony and its role in maintaining male supremacy; but this analysis does not insist that all women become lesbians.

Choosing a modified course is not to admit defeat. In its purest form separatism doesn't work because you cannot cut yourself off from all sources of power and survive. It is something that must be handled by degrees: the more you build on new ground, the farther from the old you get. But it is also dangerous to deny the strength of the initial analysis and move the other way altogether—into an antiseparatist position.

The contradictions that envelop separatism come from a complex of sources not the least of which is that it threatens male supremacy and all those who survive through it. But we should look at some of the problems:

The flurry of exhilarating expectations aroused by lesbian feminism sometimes hits reality with a terrible thud. I don't know why we expect that working and living with women only will pan out so perfectly, but we invariably do. We are an emerging people, in every sense. Centuries of oppression, although they have left their mark, should at least serve to inform the direction in which we move. The work yet to be done is vast enough to dispirit the most stouthearted—especially for the motley crew available to do it.

Come Out! is an eloquent imperative and a grand initial strategy— one that has been taken very seriously by thousands of women. Now many of them are all out there—without child care, jobs, skills, and all those debilitating ties to male privilege. Initial strategy does not create the requisite alternative means of sustenance.

One of the distressing elements of heavy antiseparatism is that it leads many of us to gloss over the extent of our psychological and emotional addiction to male power on an individual level, as well as our survival connections to male power on an individual and mass level. Divisive or not, we must develop and articulate a practice of systematically criticizing our psychological as well as our material dependence on men and heterosexuality.

One of the hardest lessons for lesbian feminists to accept is that there are some straight feminists who are making a more vital contribution to women than some lesbians. But the structural difference between them is still real. Straight women are beholden to male supremacy in a manner that lesbians are not. However, although lesbians have greater potential by virtue of their separation from men, it does not matter where achievement comes from; it is actual contribution that counts the most.

It is inappropriate to say one—straight or lesbian—is better than the other, but it is crucial to analyze and understand the distinctions in revolutionary potential and to submit them to systematic criticism. Ultimately our ability to overcome male supremacy rests upon building an alternative to it. That alternative can come only from developing theory, organizational structures, and economic autonomy.

Divided loyalties will influence the spirit of any struggle, but they cannot be dealt with on an individual basis alone. Only through collective organizational support can we find the courage and strength to accept the changes we must make.

Coalition in the Future

Lesbian feminist separatism as it stands today advances a partial analysis of human oppression. It provides us with the beginnings of an oppositional ideological framework, and posits a number of tactics to give that framework a sturdy material base. It fails, however, to provide us with a revolutionary *theory*, long-range strategy, or the organizational means to implement a revolutionary goal. But neither—in terms of women—have other revolutionary ideologies.

More than having heterosexuality intact, other revolutions have perpetuated it time and again. This is no little problem that can be dealt with by making minor adjustments. For instance, every time a Maoist speaks of the miracle of modern China, I remember that the "incurable" lesbian in that country is summarily executed. This example, and its unbearable implications, compel us to focus on the firm, unchallenged institutional roots of sexism in nonfeminist revolutions.

On the other hand, feminists owe a great deal to those who struggled before us. We have borrowed heavily from their ideas, their analyses, their rhetoric, and their methodology. Certainly that borrowing is not over. But, while lesbian feminists must come to grips with class analysis and socialist revolutionary theory, socialists must deal with our indispensable contribution. Right now we are far apart, thoroughly divided, and held obedient by our mutual oppressors— heterosexuality and capitalism.

The first thing socialists need to do is forget about incorporating us into their theory. The theory must change. And the first thing lesbian feminists have to do is to create a national radical feminist organization. Nobody is going to listen to us—not the socialists, nobody— until they cannot afford to do otherwise. It has little to do with whether or not they like us, hate us, can identify with our principles or not. Rather, it is because male supremacy, wherever you find it, is still a viable system, providing everyone (including socialists) not just with privilege but with survival itself.

To end separatism we must end the causes of it. Unity is essential, but a degree of divisiveness is also essential and inevitable until we have the means to expand our analysis to include the needs of others—practically and ideologically. Collectively, women will use separatism in their struggle for liberation, not because it is right or wrong, realistic or fantastic, difficult or groovy, but because we have no choice. Kings do not sit down with peasants, Americans don't take tea with the Chinese, and whites will not reckon with racism until the collective force of the opposition gives them no choice.

Unfortunately, collective force is rarely the offspring of 100 percent humanistic, democratic procedure. *Might* makes *right* and the weaker opposition must find a way to make itself mightier. The act of building a separate, independent, collective territory (geographic, economic, political, sexual) and a powerful new group identity is indispensable to this process; thus both constellations in the lesbian community are making a vital contribution.

Whatever your opinion of it, female separatism has just as long and viable a future as male supremacy. That's a long haul ahead. In the meantime, regardless of the strategical successes of feminism, individual women will continue to find a perpetual wellspring of freedom, affirmation, strength, and joy in lesbianism. That is, reduced to its smallest conceivable contribution, lesbianism remains a powerful political force.

NOTES

1. See Pierre L. van den Berghe, *Race and Racism—A Comparative Perspective* (New York: Wiley, 1967). van den Berghe expands and details the relationship between economic form and accompanying distinct expression of racism.
2. Carol Edelson and Marlene Schmitz, "Great Southeastern Lesbians," *Off Our Backs* 5, no. 6 (July 1975): 25.
3. "Not A Collaborator," letter to the editor, *Off Our Backs* 5, no. 5 (May–June 1975): 27.
4. For this analysis I am indebted to *Lesbianism and the Women's Movement*, ed. Nancy Myron and Charlotte Bunch (Baltimore: Diana Press, 1975). The collection of articles and essays in this book are indispensable reading for all feminists. Most of the articles were originally published by The Furies Collective during 1971–72; they cover a great variety of issues, with rare depth, poignant analysis, and the tremendous originality that gave birth to and powerfully punctuated the work of The Furies Collective. I must add that the analysis contained in this paper, although greedily borrowed, is too skeletal and bent to my own perceptions, prejudices, and purposes to do any justice to the original. Whatever flaws, exaggerations, or misunderstandings you find, come solely from me.
5. See especially Margaret Small, "Lesbians and the Class Position of Women," in Myron and Bunch, *Lesbianism and the Women's Movement*, p. 49.
6. Pierre van den Berghe, *Age and Sex in Human Societies: A Biosocial Perspective* (Belmont, Calif.: Wadsworth 1973), p. 102.

Fundamental Feminism: Process and Perspective

Nancy Hartsock

Several of the *Quest* staff went to the Socialist Feminist Conference in Yellow Springs, Ohio, in July, 1975. We went because we thought of ourselves as feminists who were socialists, but we discovered that despite the obvious disagreements among the speakers, most of the views expressed from the speakers' platform were in conflict with our politics. This article began, then, from a discussion among the five of us who went, and represents our attempts to respond constructively to the conference. We do not intend the article to be primarily a criticism of the conference, but rather an attempt to set out our own concerns as they emerged through our experience in Yellow Springs.

We found ourselves in opposition not to the stated goals of the conference—the destruction of capitalism, imperialism, and patriarchy* but rather to the framework of analysis in which these concerns were presented. Since the framework was defined by the white, male-dominated Left in the United States (hereafter referred to simply as the male Left), it is clear that, as such, it can only lead a socialist feminist movement to the same paralysis that has immobilized the male Left.

Patriarchal Socialism and Socialist Feminism

The role of the male Left in defining the terms on which socialist feminism is to develop was clear. For example, the speaker who

---

*Although we would not include the destruction of white supremacy under the heading of destroying imperialism, that seemed to be a frequent interpretation at the conference.

opened the conference stated that its concern was with the ways racism, class, and imperialism affect women; she did not say that the conference was concerned with the ways patriarchy affects women. She added that socialist feminism as a movement was concerned with transforming the Left. In response to such positions, the Lesbian Caucus was driven to state that it is legitimate to struggle against sexism "whether or not it is the direct result of capitalism and imperialism."[1]

The conference in general assumed that feminism is a culture, while socialism is a politics. A comparison of the statements of the tasks of two workshops—one relating to the autonomous women's movement and one working with mixed leftist and antiimperialist groups—highlights this assumption. In discussing the relation of socialist feminism to the autonomous women's movement, the session description stresses the need for "politicization (infusing our politics into other groups)."[2] In contrast, sessions on working with mixed leftist groups were to discuss ways to build the Left and "ensure that our analysis is heard in our joint work—the *integration* of sex, class, race, and lesbianism."[3] The difference between infusing politics into an apolitical group and integrating or making one's voice heard in a more powerful political group makes it clear that the conference looked to the male Left to define what is political.

But male Left politics lead to problems in the way we do political work and think about politics—problems resulting from their mode of analysis. And these problems of method lead in turn to difficulties in dealing with substantive areas of concern—how to organize against class society, racism, and imperialism—not to speak of sexism.

The history of the male Left demonstrates that it has no concept of process. As a result, it has been unable to understand the fundamental unity of theory and practice. This separation of theory and practice surfaced in a very traditional form at the conference. "Theory" meant reading and studying a few sacred texts that are frequently recited but seldom connected with reality. "Practice," in contrast, meant organizing other people (never one's self) by applying textbook teachings to their situations. The male Left has forgotten that "it is essential to educate the educator himself. [Their] doctrine must, therefore, divide society into two parts, one of which is superior to society."[4]

The separation of theory from lived reality leads the male Left to adopt the elitist assumptions of capitalist society. Their unexamined and unresisted classism surfaces most clearly in the assumption that the "working class" is incapable of working out its own future; that it needs a vanguard party to lead it to freedom; and that the core of the vanguard party will be made up of a group of people who have memorized the sacred texts and are thus equipped to organize the world. The clear assumption is that the male Left will come to the oppressed masses with Truth, and will make for them a revolution they cannot make for themselves.

The separation of theory and practice and the unconscious classism that accompanies it result in the notion that we work for revolution, not for ourselves and out of necessity, but for others, out of an idealistic commitment. The refusal to recognize that revolution begins in our own lives first and that it concerns our own identities as human beings took many forms at the conference. For example, the subsumption of racism under the more impersonal heading "imperialism" makes it possible to avoid the racism we participate in and practice. The inclusion of a workshop on lesbian organizing among a number of sessions on community organizing lets us avoid the tensions between lesbians and straight women and the problems created by heterosexual privilege. To see questions in this way means that we accept the terms of capitalist society in which politics has to do with "public" life, and in which our personal lives can be kept at a distance from our politics.

The separation of theory from practice leads the male Left mechanically to apply Marx's paradigm of capitalist society as made up of two classes—the bourgeoisie and the proletariat. Many conference speakers gave the impression that once this had been said, the analysis was complete. That the analysis is not complete was obvious in the confusion of so many speakers about the reality of class itself. The reiteration that we are almost all working class (because 90 percent of the United States population has nothing to sell but labor power), and the repeated expression of concern that most of the women at the conference were white and middle class, indicate the difficulties of mechanically applying the two-class formula to concrete reality.[5]

The divisions among those who are not part of the bourgeoisie were not seen as fundamentally important. Problems of sexism,* racism, and other barriers between people were seen only as worth noticing because they prevented united action, not because they represent important social forces in themselves. Thus, the kind of tokenism that has occurred at male Left conferences, where women's concerns are often relegated to a single session, was directed at Third World women and lesbians. Rather than integrate their concerns into all the panels as aspects of the issues taken up by each session, conference organizers asked that Third World women and lesbians share a single morning. The implication of this kind of scheduling is that such con-

---

*And heterosexism is an essential part of sexism.

cerns are special interests and are fundamentally irrelevant to the "real" questions raised by monopoly capitalism.

A final, profoundly disturbing aspect of the Socialist Feminist Conference was its lack of feminism. Very few of the speakers had any concept of patriarchy or saw patriarchy as an important and autonomous social force. Rather, the conference focused almost exclusively on the problems and needs of an ill-defined but unitary "workers' movement." The conference provided little aid in analyzing how the forces of white supremacy, patriarchy, capitalism, and imperialism interact in a specific setting; yet if we do not understand how we are divided from each other in everyday life, how can we work against the forces that divide us?

While we cannot define ourselves as socialist feminists in the terms used at the conference, we feel that the conference itself was very useful in asking what we mean by a feminism that includes a socialist analysis. The exploration of feminism that follows should make it clear that if those who call themselves socialist feminists read and understand Karl Marx, they should develop a better understanding of feminism. As Georg Lukacs has pointed out, orthodox Marxism is not the uncritical acceptance of Marx's results: "On the contrary, orthodoxy refers exclusively to *method*."[6]

Feminism as a Mode of Analysis

Women who call themselves feminists disagree on many things. Many are not socialists at all. One would be hard pressed to find a set of beliefs or principles, or even a list of demands, that could safely be applied to all feminists. Still, when we look at the contemporary feminist movement in all its variety, we find that while many of the questions we addressed were not new, there is a methodology common among feminists that differs from the practice of most social movements, particularly from those in advanced capitalist countries. At bottom, feminism is a mode of analysis, a method of approaching life and politics, rather than a set of political conclusions about the oppression of women.

The practice of small-group consciousness raising, with its stress on examining and understanding experience and on connecting personal experience to the structures that define our lives, is the clearest example of the method basic to feminism. Through this practice, we learned that it is important to build an analysis of patriarchy from the ground up—beginning with our own experience. We examined our lives not only intellectually but with all our senses.[7] We drew connections between our personal experiences and political generalities about the oppression of women; in fact, we used our personal experience to develop political generalities. We came to understand our experience, our past, in a way that transforms both our experiences and ourselves.

The power of a feminist method grows out of the fact that it enables us to connect everyday life with an analysis of the social institutions which shape that life. Application of a feminist method means that the institutions of capitalism (including its imperialist aspect), patriarchy, and white supremacy cease to be abstractions we read about. Through their impact on us they become lived, real aspects of daily experience and activity. In this way, feminism provides us with a way to understand our anger and direct our anger and energy toward change.

Integrating Personal and Political Change

Feminism as a mode of analysis relies on the idea that we come to know the world, to change it and be changed by it, through our everyday activity. The focusing on daily life and experience makes it clear not only that we are active in creating and changing our lives but that reality itself consists of "sensuous human activity, practice."[8] We ourselves produce our existence as a response to specific problems posed for us by reality. As feminists, we cannot avoid the realization that we experience patriarchy on a daily basis and that we must oppose the institutions of male supremacy daily as well, in every area of our lives.

Feminism as a method makes us recognize that human activity is also self-changing.[9] A fundamental redefinition of the self is an integral part of action for political change. But our selves are social phenomena, and take their meaning from the social whole of which we are a part.[10] We do not act in a vacuum to produce and reproduce our lives; changed consciousness and changed definitions of self can occur only in conjunction with restructuring the social (societal and personal) relationships in which each of us is involved. Thus, feminism leads us to oppose the institutions of capitalism, white supremacy, and patriarchy.

A feminist mode of analysis makes it clear that patriarchy, capitalism, white supremacy, certain forms of social interaction, and language all exist for us as historic "givens." While they are not unalterable, the historical structures that mold our lives pose the questions to which we must respond, and define the immediate possibilities for change.[11] Thus, although we recognize that human activity *is* the structure of the social world, this structure is imposed not by individuals but by masses of people, building on the work of those who came before. The shape of social life at any point depends on needs already developed as well as embryonic needs—needs whose production, formation, and satisfaction are historical processes. Developing new selves, then, requires that we recognize the importance of large-scale forces for change and recognize as well that the fully developed individuals we are trying to become can be products only of history and struggle.[12] We can transform ourselves only by simultaneously struggling to transform the social relations that define us: self-changing and changed social institutions are simply two aspects of the same process.

Thus, although we found that many socialists at the conference believe that beginning with personal experience is invalid, a cultural if not bourgeois enterprise, we have come to think that "the coincidence of the changing of circumstances and of human activity or self-changing can be conceived and rationally understood only as *revolutionary practice.*"[13]

Recognizing Process and Interaction

By beginning with everyday life and experience, feminism has developed a politics that incorporates an understanding of process and of the importance of appropriating our past as an essential element of political action. We find that we constantly confront new situations in which we act out of our changed awareness of the world and ourselves and experience the changed reactions of others. What patriarchal socialism sees as static, feminism sees as structures of relations in process—a reality constantly in evolution.

Feminist reasoning "regards every historically developed social form as in fluid movement, and therefore takes into account its transient nature no less than its momentary existence."[14]

Each of the interlocking institutions of capitalism, patriarchy, and white supremacy conditions the others, but each can also be understood as a different expression of the same relationships.[15] This mode of understanding allows us to see the many ways processes are related and provides a way to understand a world in which events take their significance from the set of relationships which come to focus in them.

Since each phenomenon changes form constantly as the social relations of which it is composed take on different meanings and forms, the possibility of understanding processes as they change depends on our grasp of their role in the social whole.[16] For example, in order to understand increased wage work by women in the United States, we need to understand the relation of this work to the needs of capitalism. But we must also look at the conditions of work and the kind of work prescribed for women by patriarchy and white supremacy as *different* aspects of the same social system. In this context, production, consumption, distribution, and exchange are not identical but are different aspects of a unity; a mutual interaction occurs between these various elements.

Feminists cannot separate workplace organizing from community organizing from building a movement. We begin from the perspective that possibilities for change in any area are tied to change in other areas. The precise forms of human activity as it appears in the family, the workplace, or elsewhere are intelligible only in the context of the whole society—including both its past and its future.

When patriarchal socialists separate workplace from community organizing, they demonstrate that they have forgotten that the significance of any form of human activity depends on its relation to the whole.[17] They have forgotten that both capitalism and socialism are more than economic systems, and that capitalism does not just reproduce the physical existence of individuals: "rather it is a definite form of activity of these individuals, a definite form of expressing their life, a definite *mode of life* on their part . . . [and this coincides with] both *what* they produce and *how* they produce."[18] A mode of life is not divisible. It does not consist of a public part and a private part, a part at the workplace and a part in the community—each of which makes up a certain fraction, and all of which total 100 percent. A mode of life, and all the aspects of that mode of life, take meaning from the totality of which they are parts.

Appropriation, Necessity, and Revolution

The feminist method of analyzing experience is a way of appropriating reality. Appropriation (or constructive incorporation) means the incorporation of experience in such a way that our life experience becomes a part of our humanity itself. Clearly, appropriation of things or experiences does not mean simple possession or gratification. Our knowledge of ourselves and our world is an aspect of our appropriation of that world, just as the incorporation of our knowledge into who we are as people changes our world. Appropriation, then, refers to the expansion of human powers and potentialities through the transforming impact of experience.

By appropriating our experience and incorporating it into our selves, we transform what might have been a politics of idealism into a politics of necessity. By appropriating our collective experience, we are creating people who recognize that we cannot be ourselves in a society based on hierarchy, domination, and private property. We are acquiring a consciousness that forces us "by an ineluctable, irremediable and imperious *distress*—by practical *necessity*—to revolt against this inhumanity."[19] Incorporating, making part of ourselves what we learn, is essential to the method of feminism. It is a way of making both our past and our future belong to us.

Feminist Theory and Practice

The feminist mode of analysis has important results for questions of theory and practice. For feminists, theory is the articulation of what our practical activity has already appropriated in reality. In theorizing, we examine what we find within ourselves; we attempt to clarify for ourselves and others what we already, at some level, know.

Theory itself, then, can be seen as an aspect of appropriation, a way of taking up and building on our experience. This is not to say that feminists reject all knowledge that is not firsthand, that we can learn nothing from books or from history. But rather than read a number of sacred texts, we make the practical questions posed for us in life the basis for our study. Feminism recognizes that political philosophy and political action do not take place in separate realms. On the contrary, the concepts with which we understand the social world emerge from and are defined by human activity. We agree with Antonio Gramsci that the philosophy of each person "is contained in its entirety in [her] political action."[20]

For feminists, the unity of theory and practice refers to the use of theory to make coherent the problems and principles expressed in our practical activity. Feminists argue that the role of theory is to take seriously the idea that all of us are theorists since we "engage in practical activity and in [our] guiding lines of conduct there is implicitly contained a conception of the world, a philosophy."[21] The role of theory, then, is to articulate for us what we know from our practical activity, to bring out and make conscious the philosophy embedded in our lives. Feminists are in fact creating social theory through our political action. We need to conceptualize, to take up and specify what we have already done, in order to make the next steps clear.[22]

New Directions

Because feminists begin from our own experience in a specific advanced capitalist society, we recognize that the lived realities of different segments of a society are varied. While it is true that most people have only their labor power to sell (for wages or not), there are real differences in power, privilege, ability to control our lives, and even in our survival chances. We cannot ignore these divisions. Only by recognizing our different situations in their complexity can we use our anger constructively. Feminists have begun to learn about the meaning of class and race by looking at the impact of these divisions on everyday life. We are beginning to understand that our class is not defined by our relationship to the mode of production in the simple sense that if we sell our labor power (for a day or a lifetime), or are part of the family of someone (presumably male) who does, we are working-class. Being working-class is a mode of life, a way of living life based on, but not exclusively defined by, the simple fact that we must sell our labor power to stay alive.

Class distinctions in capitalist society are part of a totality, a mode of life structured as well by sexism and racism. Class distinctions in the United States affect the everyday lives of women and men, whites or black or Third World people, in different ways. Feminism leads us to ask questions about the nature of class distinctions and what they mean in the lives of people every day. It compels questions that recognize that we already know a great deal about class, but need to appropriate what we know—to make it into theory.

The method of feminism means as well that we need to look at the ways patriarchy and white supremacy interlock with capitalism. Our experience provides us with many examples of the ways patriarchy, capitalism, and white supremacy interlock.[23] The myth of black matriarchy, women's role as houseworkers, their functions as part of a reserve labor force, and the participation of women and minorities in a separate and secondary labor market—all these fulfill specific functions for capitalism but would be impossible without the institutions of white supremacy and patriarchy. We need to know more about the nature of these relationships. What are the processes that define them? How are they changing? What are they becoming?

Feminism as a mode of analysis leads us to respect experience and differences, to respect people enough to believe that they are in the best position to make their own revolution. Thus we cannot support the elitism implicit in the concept of a vanguard party. Patriarchal socialists have forgotten that the Leninist model of a vanguard party was developed to "replace a part of the historical process by conscious intervention."[24] That is, it was developed to create a vehicle that could function in the *absence of* the kind of political education that grows from the experience of capitalist society.

Luxemburg argued that even in nineteenth-century Russia, the vanguard party was inappropriate, since there is no "ready made, pre-established, detailed set of tactics which a central committee can teach its membership as if they were army recruits."[25] In general, the tactics of a mass party cannot be invented. They are "the product of a progressive series of great creative acts in the often rudimentary experiments of the class struggle. Here too, the unconscious comes before the conscious. . . ."[26]

Organizations and Strategies

Feminism, while it does not prescribe an organizational form, leads to a set of questions about organizational priorities. First, a feminist mode of analysis suggests that we need organizations that include theory building as the appropriation of experience, as a part of the work of the organization itself. We need systematically to analyze what we learn as we work in organizations. Too often, we have left analysis of our experience to small groups and have limited ourselves to understanding the relationship between personal experience and social institutions. While this is valuable, we need to develop ways to appropriate our organizational experience and to use it to transform our organizations themselves. Some feminist organizations are beginning to raise questions about the process of meetings or about the way work is and should be done. But because so many of us reacted to our experience of the male Left organizations by refusing to build any organizational structures at all, we have only begun to think about the way we should work in organizations with some structure, as opposed to the way we should work in small groups.

We need to build the latitude for change and growth into our organizations rather than rely on small groups for these forces. This means we need systematically to teach and respect different skills, and allow our organizations to change and grow in new directions. We need to use our organizations as places where we begin to redefine the social relations of work, where we begin to live as whole people. We can begin now to create new ways of working that do not follow the patterns of domination and hierarchy set by the mode of production as a whole.

In terms of strategies, we can begin to make coalitions with other groups that share our approach to politics. We will not go into places where we do not work to pass out leaflets, or try to bring people who do not share our experience into our organizations without changing those organizations to take account of and respect their differences. We cannot work in coalitions with people who refuse to face their responsibility for everyday life, with people who will not use their own experience as a fundamental basis for knowledge, with people who refuse to take an active part in their own existence. We cannot work with those who treat theory as a set of conclusions to be pasted onto reality, and who, out of their own moral commitment, make a revolution for the benefit of their "inferiors."

As feminists, we must work on issues that are real for us, which have real impact on daily life. These issues can vary—housing, public transportation, inflation, food prices, and shortages, to name a few. We can work on these issues either with women only, or in coalitions including men. So long as others in the coalition share our method, and so long as those we work with are working for change out of necessity (because they, like us, have no alternative), there is a real basis for coalition.

As we work on particular issues, we must continually ask how we can use these issues to build our collective power. We must ask how our work will help to educate ourselves and others to see the connections and interactions among social institutions. Finally, we must ask how work in a particular area weakens the institutions that structure our lives and how our work uses the processes that define our society to change it.[27]

Conclusion

Feminism makes us recognize that struggle itself must be seen as a process. We must avoid, on the one hand, developing a narrow sectarian outlook, and on the other, abandoning our goal of revolution. We must continue to base our work on the necessity for change in our lives. Our political theorizing can grow only out of appropriating the work we have done. While the answers to our questions can only come slowly and with difficulty, we must remember that we are involved in a continuous process of learning what kind of world we want to create as we work for change.

NOTES

1. "Lesbianism and Socialist Feminism" (paper read at the Socialist Feminist Conference, Yellow Springs, Ohio, July 1975), p. 1. (Mimeographed.)
2. "Building Our Movement and Relating to the Autonomous Women's Movement" (paper read at the Socialist Feminist Conference, Yellow Springs, Ohio, July 1975), p. 2. (Mimeographed.)
3. "Alphabet Soup: Or, Working With Mixed Left and Anti-Imperialist Groups" (paper read at the Socialist Feminist Conference, Yellow Springs, Ohio, July 1975), p. 1. (Mimeographed.) Italics mine.
4. Karl Marx, "Theses on Feuerbach," in Karl Marx and Frederick Engels, *The German Ideology*, ed. C. J. Arthur (New York: International Publishers, 1970), p. 121.
5. On the inaccuracy of this account of Marx's theory, see Georg Lukacs, "What Is Orthodox Marxism," *History and Class Consciousness* (Cambridge, Mass.: MIT Press, 1971), p. 8.
6. Ibid., p. 1.
7. On this point, compare Karl Marx, *Economic and Philosophic Manuscripts of 1844*, ed. Dirk Struik (New York: International Publishers, 1964), p. 140, and Antonio Gramsci, *Selections From the Prison Notebooks*, tr. Quinton Hoare and Geoffrey Nowell Smith (New York: International Publishers, 1971), p. 324.

8. Marx, "Theses on Feuerbach," p. 121.
9. Ibid., passim. See also Gramsci, *Selections*, p. 360.
10. See ibid., p. 352, on this point.
11. Marx and Engels, *German Ideology*, p. 59.
12. Marx, *1844 Manuscripts*, p. 141. See also Karl Marx, *Grundrisse*, tr. Martin Nicholaus (Middlesex, England: Penguin, 1973), p. 162.
13. Marx, "Theses on Feuerbach," p. 121.
14. Karl Marx, *Capital* (Moscow: Foreign Language Publishing House, 1954), 1:20.
15. Marx, *1844 Manuscripts*, p. 119.
16. See Lukacs, "Orthodox Marxism," p. 13.
17. Ibid.
18. Marx and Engels, *German Ideology*, p. 114.
19. Karl Marx, *Selected Writings in Sociology and Social Philosophy*, tr. T. B. Bottomore (New York: McGraw-Hill, 1956), p. 232.
20. Gramsci, *Selections*, p. 326.
21. Ibid., p. 344.
22. On this point, compare Marx, "Theses on Feuerbach," p. 122.
23. I have described this at greater length in Nancy Hartsock, "Political Change: Two Perspectives on Power," *Quest: a feminist quarterly* 1, no. 1 (Summer 1974): 10–25.
24. Rosa Luxemburg, "Organizational Questions of Russian Social Democracy," in *Selected Writings of Rosa Luxemburg*, ed. Dick Howard (New York: Monthly Review Press), p. 285.
25. Ibid., p. 289.
26. Ibid., p. 293.
27. Criteria for choosing strategies are discussed more extensively in Charlotte Bunch, "The Reform Tool Kit," and Hartsock, "Political Change," *Quest: a feminist quarterly* 1, no. 1 (Summer 1974).

Beyond Either/Or: Feminist Options

Charlotte Bunch

The time has come to reassess the experience of the women's movement, particularly with the Left, and to reassert a direction for feminism that is both radical and independent and that integrates the political, cultural, economic, and spiritual dimensions of women's lives. I have chosen to call this direction *nonaligned feminism*. Although the issues discussed here affect all its segments, I am primarily concerned here with the radical portion of the women's movement—by which I mean those feminists who are critical of all patriarchal systems, including U.S. capitalism, who tend to feel alien to those systems, and who are not satisfied only with their reform. Much of my analysis is based on the ideas and experiences of both radical feminists and lesbian feminists, who have most frequently expressed this position in the United States. However, here I have chosen a new term—nonaligned feminism—in order to avoid the limitations of existing labels and suggest new grounds for defining a movement that incorporates the experiences of a wider variety of women.

The need for such a reassessment grows out of the increasing pressure that feminists (as individuals and as a movement) have experienced over the past few years to align ourselves—once and for all—either with or against the Left, either as "socialists" or as "reformists," since this mentality recognizes no other options. And even if we resist that dichotomy, we encounter another one: that between "political/economic" feminists and "cultural" or "spiritual" feminists. Presenting them as mutually exclusive options, this dichotomy distorts the function of each of these spheres and ignores their interrelatedness. As a result, many feminists have begun to feel that they do not quite fit anywhere, that there is little defined space for the pursuit of a feminism that is critical of the United States, very much engaged in politics, and yet independent of the socialist movement.

But I have no intention of succumbing to these choices as defined by others. Although we are not organized around a single goal, I believe that many (if not most) feminists feel limited and confined by pressures to conform to one or the other of those options. And I believe that now, perhaps more than ever, we must resist pressure for a final declaration of allegiance and continue to pursue the fullest implications of a nonaligned but committed and active feminism.

The pressure to choose one side or another of these dichotomies does not come from only one side or any single source but is the result of many factors: our lack of answers in some situations, since a feminist analysis of patriarchy as it affects all aspects of life is still incomplete; women's doubts about our ability to create and effect a new political direction, which often results in either a retreat from politics or an acceptance of the older, better defined traditions of American reformism or socialism; legitimate but often immobilizing concerns about the race and class makeup of the movement, which paralyzes some white feminists with guilt; and finally the difficulties of survival for independent feminists—since white men, whether Left, Right, or Center, generally control most of the resources in our society, if we align with one of them personally, or with their politics, or remain in what they define as women's spheres, we are allowed greater access to those resources.

Under these pressures, the radical portion of the women's movement seems to be fragmenting into three dominant and often mutually exclusive trends: socialist feminism, political reformism, and cultural or spiritual separatism.* While each of these embodies important work, what is disturbing is their general tendency not only to denounce or ridicule the work of the others but also to deny the necessity for an independent feminist framework that would integrate aspects of each and go beyond them to create a synthesized feminist politics revolutionary in its implications for all aspects of our lives.

In this article I begin to explore some of the questions raised by this situation, primarily in terms of pressure to be pro- or anti-Left. In particular, I propose to look at the concept of nonalignment and how it can be useful to feminists; to examine how feminists have dealt with this dichotomy over the past decade and how it is reemerging

---

*Cultural feminism and the women's spirituality movement are certainly different phenomena, but the separatist tendencies in both areas are similar. This is discussed further in "The Feminist Dilemma Today" section of this essay.

today; and to describe how *Quest* functions as a nonaligned vehicle for political debate and analysis aimed at further developing a radical, nonaligned feminism.

The Concept of Nonalignment

The pressure to be for or against the Left is neither new nor unique to the feminist movement. It reflects the polarity dominating our world for at least the past thirty years: capitalism versus communism. In the 1950s, when this polarity was at its height—the cold war between the "Free World" and the "Iron Curtain"—many of the less powerful nations began to act to force open the vise squeezing them into allegiance to one or the other. In particular, leaders of some of the newly independent countries of Asia and Africa called the Bandung Conference in 1955, at which many of the "developing nations" worked together to establish their nonaligned status. As Indian Prime Minister Jawaharlal Nehru proclaimed: "For anyone to tell us that we have to be camp followers of Russia or America or any country in Europe is not very creditable to our new dignity, our new independence, our new freedom, our new spirit." [1]

The nonaligned nations were not always united with each other and did not create one single unifying ideology, but they did establish space outside the control of the two dominant poles (U.S./U.S.S.R.), give legitimacy to the concept of nonalignment, and eventually alter the perception of world forces through the concept of the Third World. These efforts, along with the seismographic crack between Russia and China, made new alliances and new modes of development possible within nonaligned countries, allowing them more political flexibility without making them irrelevant to, powerless against, or totally unaffected by the controls of the major power blocs.*

My purpose here is neither to detail the debates surrounding the nonaligned nations nor to propose that feminists are in an identical position. Rather, I want to establish a historical context for a concept that can be useful to us. "Nonaligned" does not mean neutral; it does *not* mean uninvolved, inactive, separated, or uninterested. Nonalignment is *not* a withdrawal from politics. It simply means that one is *not automatically* attached to one of the dominant lines or factions, and hence it does not preclude taking stands on issues, mak-

---

*While this polarity has diminished some in the past decade, its dominance is still evidenced in many world issues and was certainly a very present conflict at the United Nations International Women's Year Tribunal in Mexico City, Summer 1975. Feminists could gain from further study of the experience of nonaligned nations. A conference in Washington, D.C., on "The Nonaligned Movement in World Politics Today" (Howard University, April 8–10, 1976), revealed that the concept is still evolving and has had varying degrees of political and economic viability in different contexts.

ing coalitions around particular goals, or condemning or commending the actions of other groups or governments. In our context, nonalignment means simply that actions are taken according to an assessment of the particulars involved from an independent decision for or against the Left in general.

Such a concept may sound simple, or to some, simple-minded. It is neither. To be nonaligned is difficult because it requires careful attention and debate to determine what actions are appropriate in each situation. Our positions are based on an emerging feminist analysis of particular issues and how they affect women's interests and long-term feminist goals rather than on preestablished approaches to each issue. For example, in the development of feminist theory, nonalignment requires that we study not only Marxism but many other theories critically, in order to learn where and how they can contribute to the development of a comprehensive feminist analysis. But we neither seek to force feminism into an existing (e.g., Marxist) framework nor reject a given ideology out of hand, as having nothing to offer us.

Nonalignment is not solely a reaction to Left/anti-Left pressures; it is a *positive* stance for feminists. It is an affirmation of our belief in the future, strength, and potential of our own analysis and movement. We do not approach it without a history, without principles, or without politics.

We start from an analysis of patriarchy (in America and elsewhere)—how it manifests itself in capitalism, imperialism, racism, and heterosexism. We start with a commitment to start new processes and to end the oppression of all women, commitments that require us to develop and support efforts that will lead to an end to all forms of oppression. Our greatest potential lies in taking ourselves seriously as a powerful though relatively new nucleus for profound change. Although we may work with and learn from other groups when it is appropriate, our primary purpose must be the expansion of *our* insights and *our* movement as feminists, for in that process, we will create new possibilities, new perspectives on ending all oppression. Our potential rests not in being absorbed into existing ideologies or groups but in actively creating new efforts toward reshaping the political, cultural, economic, and spiritual structures of our world.

Our Recent Past

In the twentieth century, the term "radical" has generally been identified with "leftist" or "socialist." Every political group critical of any or all aspects of the Western capitalist/imperialist/racist/heterosexist patriarchy has been forced to confront its relationship to the most developed opposition: communist nations, socialist movements, and Marxist thought.

In my generation, which came of age in the 1960s, struggle with the question of the Left played a significant role in the civil rights, student, antiwar, and black militant movements. All these movements began with an essentially nonaligned position—critical of America but aloof from the Old Left debates of Marxism. Yet, as they became frustrated with the limitations of reformism in the United States, they discovered that the only available alternative model for change seemed to be Marxism. Over time, they therefore became engaged in those issues; many became intricately involved in the nuances and warfare of the Left; some rejected the Left entirely, either returning to work in the system or dropping out; and a few others, most notably some black leaders, began searching for and are still developing other ideologies not primarily oriented around Marxism, such as Pan-Africanism. While this phenomenon requires more careful study, still it shows feminists clearly that many of our problems are not entirely new and that we should seek to avoid mistakes made by other groups.

My own resistance to the socialist/antisocialist polarity facing feminists at present is not, therefore, simply a question of male versus female politics. Women *can* learn from the experiences of socialist and other movements, and particularly from the black movement's struggles with the questions of race, nationalism, and socialism. For example, we should discuss such questions as the significance of Eldridge Cleaver's seeming rejection of "world communism" embodied in his return to America; why the Black Panthers decided to enter electoral politics, and how Angela Davis views her relationship to the Communist party. And certainly many of the issues raised by socialist critiques—class, the domination of monopoly capital, imperialism—are crucial to any movement for change. But my resistance to this polarity comes from a conviction arising out of my own experience in and analysis of the 1960s, that the terms in which the pro- or anti-Left were argued then did not prove adequate to and were often destructive of those movements.

To be sure, debate with the Left is not new to feminists. In fact, the women's liberation movement and much of feminism's rebirth in the 1960s came out of that debate: women's caucuses in leftist organizations fought first for our right to exist and then joined with the more radical elements from such establishment women's groups as NOW to create an autonomous women's movement, and hence established women's liberation and radical feminism. As important, during this struggle, analysis of patriarchy as the root cause of female oppression developed, and it pointed the way toward both theory and process that go beyond the confines of the capitalist/socialist polarity.

But feminist theory is still young, still evolving toward a total analysis, and thus we are repeatedly subject to pressure that it be subsumed by some preexisting "larger, more complete" perspective. Consequently, in the early 1970s, after several years of experience with women's liberation, many feminists became impatient with our lack of complete answers. This impatience, combined with concern over the Vietnam war and our class and race privileges, led many of us to consider working with the Left again. At the same time, moreover, some leftist groups began a concerted recruitment effort to win back "their women" and tap a now-large women's constituency.

The resulting upsurge of socialist debate in the independent feminist movement took two primary forms: women's antiimperialist study and action groups and attempted takeovers of women's centers and organizations by leftist groups, particularly the Socialist Workers Party. The takeovers, when perceived by independent feminists, led not only to resistance but also to resentment of the Left. The women's antiimperialist movement (of which I was initially a part) included women of many political backgrounds but was dominated then by strife between "socialism" and an emerging female separatism. Those tensions eventually led to splits in groups all over the country, symbolized in dramatic battles over the planning and execution of a North American Indochinese Women's Conference in the spring of 1971.[2]

Thus, out of this resistance to the Left—in both its male and female forms—grew female separatism. In the early 1970s, female separatism was widely discussed and became the prevailing means for maintaining a feminist stance that was neither reformist nor leftist.[3] Simultaneously, lesbians, who were oppressed by radical feminists as well as by reform and socialist feminists, began to articulate lesbian feminist theory and separatism. By 1974, lesbian feminism emerged as the predominant separatist position and led not only to new feminist theory but also to a flourishing of feminist culture, enterprises, and communities. Separatism in both these forms represented the independent and radical posture previously articulated by women's liberation. This period paralleled a similar period in the black liberation movement—a time when establishing one's independence, identity, and ideology, and solidifying a base of power, were the priorities.

Separatism, then, arose out of the instinctive need of feminists to remain nonaligned in order to maintain ourselves as a distinct interest group and create new political theories and strategies. But we learned that separatism has its limits. Perhaps inevitably, separatism seemed to lead to isolation and powerlessness rather than to the politically engaged but independent stance we had envisioned; ultimately, women's interests are not totally separate from the problems being struggled with universally. We are affected by all systems and divisions (e.g., class, race) and by all the practical issues (unemployment, housing, welfare, and police surveillance) and have a stake in how these issues are resolved.

The Feminist Dilemma Today

Emerging out of lesbian feminist separatism over the past couple of years, I and others sought new approaches that would embody an independent radical but nonaligned feminist position. In that search I have become distressed by the movement's fragmentation, its widespread pessimism, introspection, and dogmatism. I want now to examine this phenomenon in terms of the dominant trends mentioned earlier: cultural and spiritual separatism, political reformism, and socialist feminism.

First, while cultural and spiritual feminism are not the same, they have in common a recent flourishing and seem to be the most independent of the Left/anti-Left debates. Yet many, although certainly not all, the activities associated with both trends are increasingly detached from questions of political and economic change and their interaction with cultural and spiritual change. Thus, the energy generated in both these areas, which if combined with a new feminist politics could be a powerful force for change, is instead becoming more "separatist"—that is, more isolated from other struggles. Since culture and spirit are integral parts of all movements for change (culture, for example, reflects the best and the worst of what is happening politically), and since a politics that does not express itself culturally and spiritually is necessarily weakened, then the growing polarization and hostility from *both* sides of the "political" and "cultural" camps is disastrous for feminism. Thus the issue is not whether you work in the cultural, political, economic, or spiritual arena, but what perspective and analysis you bring to your work and how you understand its relationship to the other three areas. The problem I perceive with both present-day popularized "cultural feminism" and "women's spirituality," then, is their tendency to embrace the most negative aspects of separatism and isolate themselves from other areas of struggle; ultimately, this stance contributes to allowing the patriarchal status quo continued domination over most women's lives. Moreover, while my primary focus in this article is not on cultural or spiritual feminism, I believe that their tendency to separate themselves from politics is related to the pressures from many politicos to define pro- or anti-Left as the sole political options for feminists.[4]

Second, for their part, independent feminists who are not primarily involved in cultural or spiritual activities seem increasingly divided among those who are moving toward traditional poltical reformism, those who are moving toward socialist feminism, and those who (like myself) are not aligned with either. Again, the problem in radical feminists' involvement in reform activities is certainly not in the work being done—it is both useful and logical for radicals to engage in a variety of reforms, such as rape crisis centers, legislative changes, credit unions, and the like. The problem is that in building feminist strategies around reform goals dependent on existing political and economic structures, feminists often come not only to accept the limitations of reform but also to *defend* existing institutions instead of continuing to work toward feminist alternatives.

This may occur when feminists' work becomes so dependent on liberal or governmental agencies (e.g., those rape crisis centers, which are funded only through LEAA), that their identities and political futures become tied to maintaining the establishment base for their work, thus precluding their developing a base for radical changes that might eliminate the need for their own feminist institution as well. Another cause for this shift in politics may simply be that working on any feminist reform or institution requires so much energy that longer-range questions get put aside in the struggle to survive. Whatever its causes, many once radical feminists seem to defend the system more and accept the argument that if you are not satisfied with socialism or the U.S. Left, you must necessarily endorse capitalism. The pressure to say that if you aren't pro-Left you must be anti-Left, or vice versa, is coming not only from socialists but also from women engaged in political reformism. While there are exceptions, the general trend is nevertheless so strong that we must examine what is happening to feminists engaged in reform activities and politics and goals during the process. Otherwise, both political reformists and socialist feminists end up denying the revolutionary possibilities in feminism, including its potential to go beyond the old capitalist/socialist polarity.

This brings me to socialist feminism, which (even though generally the New Left in the United States is in decline) is having a resurgence. The problem again is not feminists' desire to discuss socialism or examine issues of class, race, and money from that perspective; they *are* important issues. But socialism does not have a monopoly on their solution. In fact, the women's movement has begun to confront them both theoretically and practically, and in some instances, more successfully than the Left. The problem is that since socialist feminism lacks a radical feminist perspective, what emerges is primarily another effort, frequently guilt-laden, to contort female reality and feminist concepts into some existing socialist framework. Like all contortions, this process is limiting because it precludes the emergence of a powerful feminist analysis that could lead to new approaches to the questions of oppression and change.

As Nancy Hartsock noted in the preceding chapter, several of us from *Quest* went to the Socialist Feminist Conference in Yellow Springs eager to see what new directions in feminist thought/action were being developed. We went because we recognized the importance to feminists of many questions raised by a socialist analysis. But to our dismay, the framework of discussion was rarely feminism and instead was the U.S. white male Left. Hartsock analyzed why this approach does not further our understanding of what socialism can offer feminist development. Let me only add that for me it was also too familiar, too like the earlier feminist/socialist conflicts of 1968 or 1971.

Finally, I am disturbed that many socialist feminists are demanding once more that independent, nonaligned feminists curtail political explorations by choosing to be pro-Left, by declaring that socialism is THE WAY, just as other feminists are demanding that we renounce socialism or embrace spirituality as THE WAY. In public speaking, for instance, I am often asked *what* I am, in such a tone that I know immediately that my answer will condemn or redeem me, no matter what else I say or what *I* mean by the terms in question.

Although the pressure to align with one or another of these mutually exlusive options is not always stated in these terms, it is there, implicitly if not explicitly, in almost all the recent big debates in the women's movement (e.g., in Alpert vs. Swinton; in the Sagaris split, and in the Feminist Economic Network/Feminist Economic Alliance rupture). These debates are characterized by a fanatical insistence that one choose between two opposing forces and that to align with the other side (not to mention, to consider other factors involved) is as much a moral as a political disaster. The Alpert-Swinton controversy embodied this mentality quite clearly.

From the beginning there seemed to be only two very hard moral lines on the Alpert-Swinton issue: 1) you were pro-Swinton (and therefore not a reliable feminist); or, 2) you were pro-Alpert (and therefore anti-Swinton), or you were a dupe of the Left (and therefore hardly a real feminist). The first problem was the absence of facts on which to base action. Thus, while I personally sympathized with Alpert, who seemed to have been condemned without any reliable proof, I felt that an impartial investigation (or at least one made up of advocates on both sides) to establish just what *had* happened should have been the first order of business. (Several individuals did ferret out data, but without the resources or the political legitimacy of an agreed upon national investigation, the success of that effort was seriously hampered.)

In addition to the factual void, the self-righteousness on both sides, and the rigid dichotomy it set up, obscured rather than explored important political issues raised by the situation. What should have been discussed was not whom you trusted—Jane or Pat—but what, if any, genuine common interests exist between the Left Weather Underground and feminism—such questions as whether independent feminists have something to gain by helping leftist groups to survive and grow, and if so, what? Which groups, politics, and people on the Left embody it? What are the specific politics of the Weather Underground (which, by the way, is available in their publications,[5] but which I almost never heard discussed), and how does it coincide or conflict with feminist politics? Is it important for all radical groups to protect the existence of an antigovernment underground regardless of its actions or its politics, and if so, why, and how? Instead of discussing such critical political issues, we were urged to condemn or extol Alpert, most often in the form of demanding whether we were prepared *categorically* to support or oppose the Left.

I do not argue that feminists should never ally with other oppressed groups or with a leftist faction; on the contrary, I favor enlightened coalitions with a variety of groups at different times. But alliance—or withdrawal—should grow out of careful political analysis of feminist goals and an assessment of our common interests, not out of generalized moral mandates. The irony here is that socialist organizations or black political groups do not automatically support *one another* unless they are clear why they want that group to survive and what alliances they want to make with it. (Even the Chinese Communist party, in its thirty years of socialist development prior to taking state power in 1949, sometimes allied with the Chinese Nationalist government—its bitter enemy—against other groups, including other leftists.) Yet the Alpert-Swinton debate, often because it was posed in moral terms, allowed little space for political examination of how different options would affect the future of a radical but nonaligned feminism.

Some individual women, acting from their feminist principles, have expressed dismay over the Left/anti-Left polarity and have asserted their right to make distinctions about which politics and which people on the Left—Saxe, Swinton, Raymond, for example—they would support. Such efforts to respond case by case have often been sneered at as apolitical or as a refusal to take a stand. I believe, however, that they represent the best sort of active but nonaligned feminism. Further, I believe that we must assert ourselves more forcefully in just such a manner, not only in cases involving specific individuals, but also in issues posed in terms of these dichotomies.

A Manifesto for Nonaligned Feminism

Despite the present fragmentation in the women's movement, we believe many feminists are uncomfortable with the growing division between pro- and anti-Left, and between politics and culture or spirituality. We seek a movement that goes beyond those confinements. We are critical of the U.S. political, cultural, economic, and spiritual structures. But as feminists, we are also not satisfied with any existing ideological or strategic model for change. We are prepared to learn from social democratic thought, revolutionary experience, Marxism, and other efforts for change. But our primary task is to develop feminist theory, process, strategy, and direction. Too many issues are not answered by the contemporary Left, Right, or Center stance of the partriarchal world; it is the job of nonaligned feminists to explore those issues.

Our assertion of nonaligned feminism involves keeping the feminist struggle and perspective at the fore as we evaluate all questions, coalitions, and issues. It also recognizes the need to expand what is called "feminist" so that the term responds to the realities of all women, across class, race, sexuality, and national boundaries in order to avoid merely reflecting the interests and needs of only one group.

It requires a willingness to explore every possible source for analysis—not only the works of women but also of men like Fanon, Freud, Galbraith, Mao, Marx, and Proust—regardless of how others have used their insights and without compulsion to declare ourselves a priori for or against any of their theories. It implies an openness to explore coalitions with other forces for change, to evaluate and reassess them constantly, according to how they affect women and our long-range goals. As we engage with others, declare positions on a wide range of issues, and make ourselves available instead of self-segregated, it is also crucial that we keep our own communities, projects, and organizations intact. We must not lose our independent feminist base; it is the source of our political power. It is the inspiration and touchstone for theory and strategy. And it is the source of our personal and communal sustenance.

This is the mandate for nonaligned feminism.

We see *Quest* as one of several vehicles for a nonaligned feminist ongoing debate and analysis. As our first introductory article stated:

> We are about open political forums. *Quest* wishes to explore differences and similarities in ideologies and strategies among the various segments of the women's movement. We are a journal of long-term, in-depth political analysis, a searching-ground for answers to unresolved questions.[6]

Quest's position as a forum can perhaps best be understood in terms of the perspective for nonaligned feminism I have outlined. We do not have a line to push or a final set of conclusions to advocate. But we do have politics, and we have a particular perspective on the crucial theoretical and practical issues facing feminists. In our limited space, we continuously make political choices about what to print. We seek the best elucidation of critical issues from a variety of points of view. In choosing material, we are guided by our nonaligned and radical perspective on feminism. From that perspective, we evaluate what we believe will add most to the development of a strong feminist movement and theory for all women. We are therefore not a liberal forum open to airing all views merely for the sake of equal time. While we do not *all* always agree with each other or with each article that we print, we do agree that each article in some way builds toward an understanding of our past and/or future theories and strategies.

Because we seek articles from different perspectives, within a certain framework, some have been confused about our politics and our printing of "contradictory" views. For example, one woman condemned us for going to the Socialist Feminist Conference, yet when asked if she read what we said about it, she answered "no"; apparently our presence alone was evidence enough for her conclusions. At the same time, others have called us "antisocialist" for our critique of the conference and of other socialist strategies. I could cite many such stories. I mean only to point out that as a result of exploring various facets or polarized questions, we have experienced the extent of the pressures on feminists to choose THE WAY and label others accordingly.

Our search for different perspectives and contributors to *Quest* has led some of us to travel to other cities and attend as many feminist events as our time and money allow.* We have found that the ideas relevant to a strong, nonaligned feminist direction are growing in many different places and under many labels. Out of these experiences and from our first two years of publication, we have concluded that *Quest*, in its search to clarify long-term questions, may have remained too distant from some of the movement's immediate crucial developments and specific controversies. We have begun now to solicit more articles that comment directly on the developments and debates but also attempt to clarify the long-term goals and problems

---

*For example, members of the *Quest* staff have been at Sagaris; the National Congress of Neighborhood Women; regional lesbian feminist conferences; the Feminist Eye-Film and Video conference; the NOW National Convention; the Feminist Economic Network/Feminist Economic Alliance foundings; the Gay Academic Union; the National Radical Feminist, Women and the Law, and Women's Spirituality Conferences.

they involve. We hope that, rather than adding to polarization and recrimination, this process will help directly to link theory and action. We believe that analyzing current events and controversies is important since analysis and debate provide the groundwork for developing new synthesis, new resolution of the old conflicts and problems still plaguing feminism. With this in mind, we welcome you to the third year of *Quest: a feminist quarterly*, and to our ongoing struggle to help build an independent, nonaligned feminism as a way of providing direction and hope for women seeking to change ourselves and the world around us.

NOTES

1. Prime Minister Jawaharlal Nehru, *Economic Review*, May 1955, as quoted in O. Edmund Clubb, *Twentieth Century China* (New York: Columbia University Press, 1964), p. 345.
2. The North American/Indochinese Women's Conference, held in two parts—in Toronto and Vancouver in the spring of 1971—grew out of contact that feminists had with North Vietnamese women in 1970. It was meant to be the first meeting between Indochinese (North and South Vietnamese, Laotian and Cambodian) revolutionary women and explicitly feminist women from Canada and the United States. The battles that ensued in the United States had primarily to do with who should organize and go to the conference and what should be presented there as the content of feminism here. Since this was an international event, it interested many women and quickly embodied all the problems and conflicts among feminists in the radical segment of the movement.
3. Two important statements of female separatism were *The Female State*, a journal printed in Boston in 1970, and "Fourth World Manifesto," a paper written by women in Detroit in response to the organizing of the North American/Indochinese Women's Conferences.
4. Thanks to Bertha Harris and Beverly Fisher in particular for help with the ideas in the section on culture and spirituality. For more discussion of women and spirituality, see Peggy Kornegger, "The Spirituality Ripoff," *Second Wave* 4, no. 3 (1975): 12–18.
5. In addition to the communiqués written from the underground periodically and published in many women's newspapers, see particularly the book, *Prairie Fire: The Politics of Revolutionary Anti-Imperialism*, a political statement of the Weather Underground, printed underground in the United States (May 1974).
6. Karen Kollias, "Spiral of Change: An Introduction to Quest," *Quest: a feminist quarterly* 1, no. 1 (Summer 1974): 7.

PART TWO

The Politics of Everyday Life

In the Politics of Everyday Life we explore questions concerning how we live, work, and see ourselves. Some authors reflect on the contradictions between academic work and a commitment to feminism, the possibilities of achieving gratifying work and creating alternative work structures within capitalism, and sexual harassment at the workplace. Others address the meaning of lesbianism, both as an identity and as a political commitment; the illusion of androgyny; and the dual aspects of motherhood, as a personal relationship and self-definition and as a political-economic institution.

The Illusion
of Androgyny

Janice Raymond

Those of us who have written about androgyny, in an attempt to talk about the depths of the feminist vision or get at what it is that lies beyond the superficial lingo of, for example, "equal pay for equal work," have had very serious second thoughts on the matter. Not that the vision we were and are trying to talk about is any less real but that the use of a word like "androgyny" to describe the process and the end in view adequately describes neither. Etymologically, historically, and philosophically, androgyny presents many problems that were not so evident at first glance.

The etymology of the word, coming from the Greek *aner* and *gyne* (with the masculine classically coming first), gives the impression that if you put the archetypal masculine and feminine together, you will somehow arrive at an adequate whole that just happens to be formed from two inadequate halves. As Mary Daly has phrased it, androgyny connotes "scotch-taping John Wayne and Brigitte Bardot together." Further evidence of this pseudo-organicism can be noted when perusing dictionary definitions of androgyny. Some dictionaries talk about the meaning of androgyny in terms of plant hybrids or in terms of human hybrids.[1] In the latter case, androgyny becomes synonomous with physical hermaphroditism. Nor is the term gynandry adequate. Although the female root comes first here, the primary image is one of the sexual sphinx.

In appearance, the words *androgyne* and *androgen* are quite similar. In fact, androgyny is sometimes spelled as androgeny. Thus to speak of androgynizing humanity comes dangerously close to literally androgenizing humanity. An androgenous humanity is no mere pun in the light of some of the more recent works on sex differences that

have unfortunately enjoyed wide acceptance among feminists. I refer
here specifically to the writings of John Money. In their most recent
work, Man and Woman, Boy and Girl, John Money and Anke Ehrhardt
talk about what they call "fetal androgenization," making connections between fetal androgenization and "tomboyism," the latter
being "a sequel to a masculinizing effect on the fetal brain."[2] Fetally
androgenized females not only develop physical male characteristics
(perhaps an enlarged clitoris or excessive body hair) but also have the
propensity to develop psychosocial conditioned masculine behavior.

> The most likely hypothesis to explain the various features of tom-
> boyism is a sequel to a masculinizing effect on the fetal brain. This
> masculinization may apply specifically to pathways, most probably in
> the limbic system or paleocortex, that mediate dominance assertion
> (possibly in association with assertion of exploratory and territorial
> rights) and, therefore, manifests itself in competitive energy expendi-
> ture.[3]

Androgenization is seen to cause not only biological androgynization
(hermaphroditism) but also psychosocial androgynization (tomboyism, etc.). Money and Ehrhardt are quick to point out that no
corresponding estrogenization is responsible for a normal biological
female differentiation, much less for a so-called feminized male,
biologically or psychosocially speaking: ". . . the antithesis of androgen is not estrogen, but nothing . . . feminine differentiation requires
only the absence of androgen. It does not require the presence of a
feminizing substance."[4] What Money and Ehrhardt are actually
reiterating here, in more sophisticated pseudoscientific terminology,
is Aristotelian/Thomistic biology. Once more, the male comes to be
seen as the active power of generation and the female as the passive
power, or worse, as the totally noneffecting power (read, nonpower).
And once more the female comes to be seen as a "defective male," this
time not due to a moisture in the south wind at the time of conception[5] but to the absence of androgen. Furthermore, it is the presence
or absence of androgen in Money and Ehrhardt that becomes direc-
tive for both physical and psychosocial androgyny. Androgen becomes normative for androgyny.

Similar androgenizing processes have functioned on a mytho-
metaphorical level in the historical and theological/philosophical literature that has dealt with androgynous themes. For example, much
of the Gnostic literature stresses androgyny as a salvation theme. In
the Gospel of Thomas especially, only when the "two become one,"
"when you make the male and the female (not) be female,"[6] will
salvation and the Kingdom of God be attained. In order for androgyny to be attained in the woman, she must first make herself
male. "For every woman who makes herself male will enter the King-

dom of Heaven."[7] No such comparable process is necessary for men to attain androgynous actualization.

Thus the male has a direct route to androgynous being; the female must first of all become male. This hierarchical androgenization of woman is not peculiar to the Gnostic literature alone. It also forms part of the androgynous theme in Plato, the Kabbalah, and the Renaissance mystics.

The split-level hybrid model of androgyny also prevails in current literature on the topic. The prevailing notion of androgyny in Carolyn Heilbrun's *Toward a Recognition of Androgyny* is, as the book jacket acknowledges, that of "the realization of man in woman and woman in man." Heilbrun is in good company here. Unfortunately even the brilliant Virginia Woolf had a similar notion of androgyny in *A Room of One's Own*. She wrote:

> And I went on amateurishly to sketch a plan of the soul so that in each of us two powers preside, one male, one female; and in the man's brain, the man predominates over the woman, and in the woman's brain, the woman predominates over the man. The normal and comfortable state of being is when the two live in harmony together, spiritually co-operating. If one is a man, still the woman part of the brain must have effect; and a woman also must have intercourse with the man in her. Coleridge perhaps meant this when he said that a great mind is androgynous. . . .
>
> It is when this fusion takes place that the mind is fully fertilized and uses all its facilities.[8]

Likewise, Betty Roszak has a hybrid model of androgyny. In an essay entitled "The Human Continuum," which takes great pains to stress that if we even "think of ourselves as 'a woman' or 'a man' we are already participating in a fantasy of language,"[9] Roszak concludes with these words: "Perhaps with the overcoming of women's oppression, the woman in man will be allowed to emerge."[10]

Obviously, Heilbrun, Woolf, and Roszak are each attempting to describe a future vision that will push us beyond stereotyped definitions and requirements of masculinity and femininity. Yet it also ought to be obvious that if this is the desired goal, then we cannot use the language of oppression nor incorporate oppressive definitions of the self into a nonoppressive ideal of the same self. For in reality the language and imagery of androgyny is the language of dominance and servitude combined. One would not put master and slave language or imagery together to define a free person. Therefore, any serious effort to describe an androgynous ideal must take issue with Heilbrun's assertion that ". . . so wedded are we to the conventional definitions of 'masculine' and 'feminine' that it is impossible to write about androgyny without using these terms in their accepted, received sense."[11] Heilbrun fails to perceive here the eminent cooptability of this kind of language.

Androgyny as Cooptation

Cooptation forms another critical theme in the discussion of androgyny. It is not only a word that lends itself to cooptation but the vision it attempts to describe is equally susceptible to cooptation. The grossest example of this kind of cooptation appeared in *Ramparts* in December 1973. Here androgyny was identified with what was called the "third sex." This "new androgyny" was supposedly freed by the technological culture. This freeing, together with "the deep exploration of our psyches by acid and meditation," gave us entrance into exploring "our true and androgynous natures, the anima and animus, both of which we all possess." Men are coming to realize their feminine side and women are "excavating their masculine identities."[12] As models for the "new androgyny," James Nolan gives us the "pansexual rock images" of David Bowie, Janis Joplin, Mick Jagger, and Bette Midler. "David and Mick and Janis and Bette: consider the possibilities."

A fuller notion of the "third sex" emerges, "fertilized" by women's and gay liberation, "both of which began with strains of either man-hating or woman-hating," according to the author.

> It seemed for awhile that Women's Liberation, for all the deep-seated misanthropy it generated, was becoming with a lot of pushy verbalizing and hard-edged power struggling, a caricature of the very masculine traits which the woman despised. Gay Liberation action, with its indigenous misogyny, had taken to playing house in the superficial deco-parlor on narcissism and taste, a realm traditionally ruled over by the very women the gay mentality found so ludicrous. But perhaps these two militant liberation movements were just awkward and adolescent phases we all had to pass through, pimply and self-conscious and blatantly extreme, to arrive at a more whole type of sexual identity: a way of seeing how the other half (of ourselves) lives.[13]

So here we have the ultimate cooptation of the women's movement as an "adolescent stage," which we have already passed through. Androgyny becomes the great leap forward, a synonym for an easily accessible human liberation that turns out to be sexual liberation—a state of being that men can enter as easily as women through the "cheap grace" of the "wider" countercultural revolution. What androgyny comes to mean here, in fact, *is* sexual revolution, phrased in the language of the "third sex." Here women are handed a "mess of porridge for our birthright." Sex (fucking), not power, becomes the basic foundation of liberation.

Given the difficulties with the word, its eminent susceptibility to being coopted, and what we might call the prematurity of it as a vision, is it valid to even try to talk about whatever it is we want to mean when we use the word androgyny? I would answer in the affirmative here, but only if one is fully aware of the aforementioned dangers and corruptions.

A Vision of "Integrity"

It is difficult to know what else to call this vision, if we discard the unsatisfactory term androgyny. However, perhaps we have tried to *name* it prematurely. Therefore, as a transition word, and lacking a better term at the moment, I will hereinafter refer to whatever it is we want to mean when we use the word androgyny by the term *integrity*. My choice of the word "integrity" is a deliberately cautious one and needs some explanation. First, it is an attempt to choose a word which avoids the pitfalls of pseudo-organic connotation. Originally, I thought of using *wholeness* or even *integration*. But both connote putting something together to achieve a desired transformation. There are, however, various and subtle meanings of "integrity" that render it a more adequate term to express a meaningful vision of what many of us previously wanted androgyny to convey.

In comparison to the word *integration*, which is defined as "the making up or composition of a whole by *adding together* or *combining* the *separate parts* or elements," and in comparison to the word *integrate*, which is defined as "to *complete* or *perfect (what is imperfect)* by the addition of the necessary parts" (italics mine), *integrity* is defined primarily in the following way: "The condition of having no part or element taken away or wanting; undivided or unbroken state . . . something undivided; an integral whole. . . . The condition of not being marred or violated; unimpaired or uncorrupted condition; original perfect state; soundness." Integration gives a certain validity to the parts themselves and to an additional process of putting these parts together. In contrast, integrity reverses this connotation and validates an original unity from which no part may be taken. Integrity gives us a warrant for laying claim to a wholeness that is rightfully ours to begin with and from which centuries of patriarchal socialization to sexual roles and stereotyping has detracted. An intuition of integrity in this sense is characteristic of the texture of be-ing (becoming) and prior to cultural definitions of masculinity and femininity. It is an "original" state of be-ing before the "fall" of patriarchy, an original state that does not reside in a static historical past as original or primal conditions are prone to do, but which resides rather in the intuitive wanderings of a mytho-historical past which has the potentiality of generating for all of us a future vision of becoming, beyond a gender-defined society.

A Process Toward the Future

Finally, I think it is only valid to talk about a vision of integrity if one talks about how one gets there, given our present point in history. Here I take Cynthia Secor's point very seriously when she states: ". . . my objection to the term androgyny is a goal without any blueprint for getting there; a kind of moral imperative without any strategic direction."[14] What follows is certainly not a blueprint, but it is at least an intimation of a process which is presently ongoing; for "the future is now."

First, we cannot talk about integrity without talking about what Emily Culpepper has termed "gynergy." Gynergy is the woman power/spirit/strength that is building up in "women identified women." There is no shortcut to integrity without what I would want to call a prior intuition of gynergy. In a previous article, I wrote about an intuition of androgyny.[15] I see more clearly now that what I was more adequately describing was an intuition of gynergy. Various philosophers, most notably Jacques Maritain, have written about the intuition of being, and what I am now calling an intuition of gynergy takes its starting point in this ontological process. Gynergy, at its depth, is a question of the power of being.

When discussing the intuition of being, Maritain emphasized that modern existentialism had cut off the more primary concept of being (*ens*, or that which exists or whose act is to exist) from the concept of existence. That is, it had isolated the concept of being from that of existence. When this intuition occurs, one suddenly realizes that a given entity exists and exercises its highest activity of being in its own way, which is total and totally self-assertive.

In a critical sense, Maritain's conception of the intuition of being is too individualized and thus loses its social impact and minimizes the issue of power. In contrast I would say that the intuition of gynergy being described here takes *power* very seriously and has a definite social emphasis. In origin, it proceeds not only from an individual woman's realization of her own power of being but from a collective consciousness (i.e., a feminist collective consciousness of nonbeing and being). It therefore has a fundamental social, as well as individual, direction. Being is partly known from nonbeing, and women are now beginning to realize and act on the nonbeing we have been conditioned to. At its most destructive level (which paradoxically is the beginning point of liberation), oppression is an inundative intuition of nonbeing. As Tillich has stated, "The question of being is produced by the shock of our stunted personhood and lack of power."

Women have been first to recognize this basic stunting and sexual alienation because we have felt most heavily the weight of its oppression. Sexual alienation has also been destructive to men, but there are profound differences in our respective degrees and manifestations of oppression. Few, if any, men have had the shock of nonbeing that women have experienced in coming to realize a consciousness of sexual oppression. And, until men perceive the basic nonbeing that an oppressor is immersed in, they will continue to enjoy the benefits of sexual oppression and alienation. If and when this realization for men ever occurs, it will "complete" the intuition of gynergy, *not* in the sense of "balancing" gynergy of the "andergy" (Goddess knows we have enough male negative energy dominating the planet), but in the sense of men becoming woman-identitied. Thus an authentic andergy would be *rooted* in *gynergy* or have its source in gynergy. If and when this identification occurs, we might well begin to talk about an intuition of integrity. Obviously this means very different things for men than for women. It would probably mean relinquishing male-privileged power, prestige, status, and goods. It would mean a lot of other things also, but it is up to men who think they have a glimpse of gynergy to figure out what this can mean for their own lives.

One thing it would definitely mean would be the acceptance of some form of separatism. Thus, we cannot talk about integrity without talking about separation. There is no way to move toward integrity without political polarization between women and men, a polarization that may separate us in every sphere of human activity from the conference room to the bedroom. To deny this would be to say you can have meaningful integrity and transformation without conflict and vindication. As stated before, integrity without polarization would be just another form of "cheap grace." Integrity is not simply a matter of men and women together (no pun intended). It is not simply a matter of powerless women and powerful men "dialoguing" about the possibilities of the intuition of integrity. This kind of answer trivializes the whole issue of power and short-circuits the necessity for gynergy to manifest itself among women. It is this notion of integrity that enables people like James Nolan to brand feminism as an "awkward and adolescent phase we all had to pass through, pimply and self-conscious and blatantly extreme, to arrive at a more whole type of sexual identity." It is this notion of integrity that sees pseudo-organicism as the essence of liberation, and polarized struggle as its aberration. It is this notion of integrity that directs women once again to others instead of to ourselves. And it is this notion of integrity that makes men the ultimate beneficiaries of feminist struggle without really having to struggle themselves. Women need this integrity discovered separately. We have little sense of ourselves as selves, much less as a people who have named who we are and who we want to be. Gynergy resulting from separatism is calling us into existence.

In the final analysis, gynergy is a process opening us to an as yet unknown future. It is an open teleology. Goal-talk seems to have an inability to grasp the notion of infinity and at some point insists upon closing the circle. Integrity is an unfolding process of becoming. It contains within itself an insatiable generativeness, that is, a compulsion to reproduce itself in ever diverse fashion. Its generativeness is that of insufficiency striving consciously for richer and more varied being, the fullness of which is always the quest. Ultimately, integrity is perhaps best described as a quest for transcendence.

NOTES

1. See for example, the listings "Androgynous" and "Androgyny" in *The Compact Edition of the Oxford English Dictionary*.
2. John Money and Anke Ehrhardt, *Man and Woman, Boy and Girl* (Baltimore: Johns Hopkins University Press, 1972), p. 103.
3. Idem.
4. Ibid., pp. 60, 63–64.
5. *Summa Theologiae* I,92,I, ad I.
6. *Logion* 22:pl. 85, vs. 20–31.
7. *Logion* 114:pl. 99, vs. 18–26.
8. Virginia Woolf, *A Room of One's Own* (New York: Harcourt, Brace and World, 1929), p. 102.
9. Betty Roszak, "The Human Continuum," in Betty Roszak and Theodore Roszak, *Masculine/Feminine* (New York: Harper & Row, 1969), p. 304.
10. Ibid., p. 306.
11. Carolyn Heilburn, *Toward a Recognition of Androgyny* (New York: Knopf, 1973), p. xv.
12. James Nolan, "The Third Sex," *Ramparts*, December 1973, p. 24.
13. Ibid., p. 25.
14. Cynthia Secor, address to the Modern Language Association Forum, December 1973.
15. Cf. Janice Raymond, "Beyond Male Morality," in *Women and Religion*, ed. Judith Plaskow and Joan Arnold Romero (rev. ed.; Missoula, Mont.: Scholars' Press, 1974), pp. 115–25.

Not for Lesbians Only

Charlotte Bunch

The following is an expanded and revised version of a speech given at the Socialist Feminist Conference, Antioch College, Yellow Springs, Ohio, July 5, 1975. Many of the ideas expressed here about lesbian feminist politics were first developed several years ago in The Furies. Nevertheless, I am continually discovering that most feminists, including many lesbians, have little idea what lesbian feminist politics is. This speech takes those basic political ideas and develops them further, particularly as they relate to socialist feminism.

I am listed in your program as Charlotte Bunch-Weeks, a rather ominous slip of the tongue (or slip in historical timing) that reflects a subject so far avoided at this conference that I, for one, want to talk about.

Five years ago, when I *was* Charlotte Bunch-Weeks, and straight, and married to a man, I was also a socialist feminist. When I left the man and the marriage, I also left the newly developing socialist feminist movement—because, for one reason, my politics then, as now, were inextricably joined with the way I lived my personal, my daily life. With men, with male politics, I was a socialist; with women, engaged in the articulation of women's politics, I became a lesbian feminist—and, in the gay-straight split, a lesbian feminist separatist.

It's that gay-straight split that no one here seems to want to remember—and I bring it up now, not because I want to relive a past painful to all concerned, but because it is an essential part of our political history which, if ignored, will eventually force lesbians to withdraw again from other political women. There were important

67

political reasons for that split, reasons explicitly related to the survival of lesbians—and those reasons and the problems causing them are still with us. It is important—especially for political groups who wish to give credence and priority to lesbian issues—to remember why separatism happened, why it is not a historical relic but still vital to the ongoing debate over lesbianism and feminism.

In my own personal experience, I, and the other women of The Furies collective, left the women's movement because it had been made clear to us that there was no space to develop a lesbian feminist politics and life style without constant and nonproductive conflict with heterosexual fear, antagonism, and insensitivity. This was essentially the same experience shared by many other lesbian feminists at about the same time around the country. What the women's movement could not accept then—and still finds it difficult to accept—is that lesbianism is political: this is the essence of lesbian feminist politics. Sounds simple. Yet most feminists still view lesbianism as a personal decision or, at best, as a civil rights concern or a cultural phenomenon. Lesbianism is more than a question of civil rights and culture, although the daily discrimination against lesbians is real and its alleviation through civil libertarian reforms is important. Similarly, although lesbianism is a primary force in the emergence of a dynamic women's culture, it is much more. Lesbian feminist politics is a political critique of the institution and ideology of heterosexuality as a cornerstone of male supremacy. It is an extension of the analysis of sexual politics to an analysis of sexuality itself as an institution. It is a commitment to women as a political group, which is the basis of a political/economic strategy leading to power for women, not just an "alternative community."

There are many lesbians still who feel that there is no place in socialist feminist organizations in particular, or the women's movement in general, for them to develop that politics or live that life. Because of this, I am still, in part, a separatist; but I don't want to be a total separatist again; few who have experienced that kind of isolation believe it is the ultimate goal of liberation. Since unity and coalition seem necessary, the question for me is unity on what terms? with whom? and around what politics? For instance, to unify the lesbian feminist politics developed within the past four years with socialist feminism requires more than token reference to queers. It requires an acknowledgement of lesbian feminist analysis as central to understanding and ending woman's oppression.

The heart of lesbian feminist politics, let me repeat, is a recognition that heterosexuality as an institution and an ideology is a cornerstone of male supremacy. Therefore, women interested in destroying male supremacy, patriarchy, and capitalism must, equally with lesbians, fight heterosexual domination—or we will never end female oppression. This is what I call "the heterosexual question"—it is *not* the lesbian question.

Although lesbians have been the quickest to see the challenge to heterosexuality as a necessity for feminists' survival, straight feminists are not precluded from examining and fighting against heterosexuality. The problem is that few have done so. This perpetuates lesbian fears that women remaining tied to men prevents them from seeing the function of heterosexuality and acting to end it. It is not lesbianism (women's ties to women) but heterosexuality (women's ties to men), and thus men themselves, which divides women politically and personally. This is the "divisiveness" of the lesbian issue to the women's movement. We won't get beyond it by demanding that lesbians retreat, politics in hand, back into the closet. We will only get beyond it by struggling over the institutional and ideological analysis of lesbian feminism. We need to discover what lesbian consciousness means for any woman, just as we struggle to understand what class or race consciousness means for women of any race or class. And we must develop strategies that will destroy the political institutions that oppress us.

It is particularly important for those at this conference to understand that heterosexuality—as an ideology and as an institution—upholds all those aspects of female oppression discussed here. For example, heterosexuality is basic to our oppression in the workplace. When we look at how women are defined and exploited as secondary, marginal workers, we recognize that this definition assumes that all women are tied to men. I mention the workplace because it upset me yesterday at the economics panel that no one made that connection; and further, no one recognized that a high percentage of women workers are lesbians and therefore their relationship to, and attitudes toward, work are fundamentally different from those assumed by straight workers. It is obvious that heterosexuality upholds the home, housework, the family as both a personal and economic unit. It is apparently not so obvious that the whole framework of heterosexuality defines our lives, that it is fundamental to the negative self-image and self-hatred of women in this society. Lesbian feminism is based on a rejection of male definitions of our lives and is therefore crucial to the development of a positive woman-identified identity, of redefining who we are supposed to be in every situation, including the workplace.

What is that definition? Basically, heterosexuality means men first. That's what it's all about. It assumes that every woman is heterosexual; that every woman is defined by and is the property of men. Her body, her services, her children belong to men. If you don't accept that definition, you're a queer—no matter who you sleep with; if you do not accept that definition in this society, you're queer. The original imperialist assumption of the right of men to the bodies and services of women has been translated into a whole variety of forms of domination throughout this society. And as long as people accept that initial assumption—and question everything *but* that assumption—it is impossible to challenge the other forms of domination.

What makes heterosexuality work is heterosexual privilege—and if you don't have a sense of what that privilege is, I suggest that you go home and announce to everybody that you know—a roommate, your family, the people you work with—everywhere you go—that you're a queer. Try being a queer for a week. Do not walk out on the street with men; walk only with women, especially at night, for example. For a whole week, experience life as if you were a lesbian, and I think you will know what heterosexual privilege is very quickly. And, hopefully, you will also learn that heterosexual privilege is the method by which women are given a stake in male supremacy—and that it is therefore the method by which women are given a stake in their own oppression. Simply stated, a woman who stays in line—by staying straight or by refusing to resist straight privileges—receives some of the benefits of male privilege indirectly and is thus given a stake in continuing those privileges and maintaining their source—male supremacy.

Heterosexual women must realize—no matter what their personal connection to men—that the benefits they receive from men will always be in diluted form and will ultimately result in their own self-destruction. When a woman's individual survival is tied to men, she is at some intrinsic place separated from other women and from the survival needs of those other women. The question arises not because of rhetorical necessity—whether a woman is personally loyal to other women—but because we must examine what stake each of us has in the continuation of male supremacy. For example, if you are receiving heterosexual benefits through a man (or through his social, cultural, or political systems), are you clear about what those benefits are doing to you, both personally and in terms of other women? I have known women who are very strong in fighting against female job discrimination, but when the battle closes in on their man's job, they desert that position. In universities, specifically, when a husband's job is threatened by feminist hiring demands, I have seen feminists abandon their political positions in order to keep the privileges they receive from their man's job.

This analysis of the function of heterosexuality in women's oppression is available to any woman, lesbian or straight. Lesbian feminism is not a political analysis "for lesbians only." It is a political perspective and fight against one of the major institutions of our oppression—a fight that heterosexual women can engage in. The problem is that few do. Since lesbians are materially oppressed by heterosexuality daily, it is not surprising that we have seen and understood its impact first—not because we are more moral, but because our reality is different—and it is a *materially* different reality. We are trying to convey this fact of our oppression to you because, whether you feel it directly or not, it also oppresses you; and because if we are going to change society and survive, we must all attack heterosexual domination.

Class and Lesbianism

There is another important aspect of lesbian feminism that should be of interest to a socialist feminist conference: the connection between lesbianism and class. One of the ways that lesbianism has affected the movement is in changing women's individual lives. Those of us who are out of the closet have, in particular, learned that we must create our own world—we haven't any choice in the matter because there is no institution in this society that is created for us. Once we are out, there is no place that wholeheartedly accepts us. Coming out is important, partly because it puts us in a materially different reality in terms of what we have to do. And it is the impact of reality that moves us (or anyone) to understand and change. I don't believe that idealism is the primary force that moves people; necessity moves people. And lesbians who are out are moved by necessity—not by choice—to create our own world. Frequently (and mistakenly), that task has been characterized as cultural. While the culture gives us strength, the impetus is always economic: the expression of necessity is always material. For middle-class women this is especially true—lesbianism means discovering that we have to support ourselves for the rest of our lives, something that lower- and working-class women have always known. This discovery makes us begin to understand what lower- and working-class women have been trying to tell us all along: "What do you know about survival?"

I heard a lot about class analysis when I was in the Left, and some of it was helpful. But it wasn't until I came out as a lesbian and had to face my own survival on that basis—as an outlaw, as a woman alone—that I learned about class in my own life. Then I learned what the Left had never taught me—what my middle-class assumptions were and the way in which my background crippled me as a woman. I began to understand how my own middle-class background was holding me back personally and the ways in which middle-class assumptions were holding back the growth of our movement. Class affects the way we operate every day—as has been obvious in much of what has happened in this conference. And theories of class should help us understand that. The only way to understand the function of class in society, as far as I'm concerned, is to understand how it functions right here, on the spot, day to day, in our lives.

Another way in which class consciousness has occurred in the lesbian community—and I want to acknowledge it because it is frequently one of the things kept locked in the bedroom closet—is the cross-class intimacy that occurs among lesbians. This intimacy usually leads to an on-the-spot analysis of class oppression and conflict based on the experience of being hit over the head with it over and over again. Understand that I am not advising every middle-class woman to go out and get herself a lower-class lesbian to teach her about class-in-the-raw; but also understand that I am saying that there's no faster way to learn how class functions in our world.

Cross-class contact occurs all the time in the lesbian community, frequently without any self-conscious politics attached to it. For example, in lesbian bars, a political process that is often misinterpreted as a purely social process is going on in women's lives. Because there are no men in that environment, the conflicts around class and race—those issues basic to women's survival—become crystal clear, if you understand them not in rhetorical or theoretical terms but in the ways that women's lives are interacting with each other's. This is one reason why a lot of class analysis, particularly the practical kind, has come out of the lesbian feminist movement—analysis based on our experience of class contact and conflict, our recognition of it, and our integration of its meanings in the way we live our lives. This material experience of class realities produces real commitment to struggle and to the class question not out of idealism but as integral to our survival. Idealism can be abandoned at any time. Survival cannot.

I want to be clear about what it is that I am *not* saying. I am not saying that all lesbians are feminists; all lesbians are not politically conscious. I am saying that the particular material reality of lesbian life makes political consciousness more likely; we can build on the fact that it is not in the interests of lesbians to maintain and defend the system as it is.

I am also *not* saying that the only way to have this political analysis is to be a lesbian. But I *am* saying that so far most of the people with lesbian feminist politics who have challenged heterosexuality are lesbians. But ours is not the only way, and we've got to make it not the only way. We, as lesbians, are a minority. We cannot survive alone. We will not survive alone, but if we do not survive, the entire women's movement will be defeated and female oppression will be reenacted in other forms. As we all understand survival more clearly, we see that the politics and analysis of women's oppression coming out of the lesbian's life experience has got to be integrated into the politics of socialist feminism and the rest of the women's movement.

It is not okay to be queer under patriarchy—and the last thing we should be aiming to do is to make it okay. Nothing in capitalist-patriarchal America works to our benefit, and I do not want to see us working in any way to integrate ourselves into that order. I'm not saying that we should neglect work on reforms—we must have our jobs, our housing, and so forth. But in so doing we must not lose sight of our ultimate goal. Our very strength as lesbians lies in the fact that we are outside patriarchy; our existence challenges its life. To work for "acceptance" is to work for our own disintegration and an end to the clarity and energy we bring to the women's movement.

It is not okay, and I do not want it ever to be okay, to be queer in patriarchy. The entire system of capitalism and patriarchy must be changed. And essential to that change is an end to heterosexual domination. Lesbians cannot work in movements that do not recognize that heterosexuality is central to all women's oppression; that would be to work for our own self-destruction. But we can coalesce with groups that share the lesbian feminist analysis and are committed to the changes essential to our survival. This is the basis upon which we can begin to build greater unity and a stronger, more powerful feminist movement.

If All Else Fails, I'm Still a Mother

Lucia Valeska

What I have to say about women and childraising is harsh. I know of no other way to get the message across, so mucked up are we in fear, myth, romance, and historical ignorance of the world's oldest and most significant female vocation—motherhood. The harshness comes from a sense of urgency. Unless we untangle the real features of childraising, the feminist movement will fail to jump its most difficult hurdle.

Three years ago, in the midst of the contemporary lesbian rebellion, as a mother I turned to my lesbian sisters and said: "Mothers will be next and lesbians will look like silly putty in comparison." Mothers outweigh us in numbers, rage, and immobility. When they strike we will come up with them or they will take us down. That is how I felt. Two years later, in an impatient surge toward individual liberation I gave up custody of my three children. As a result, I am a mother and then again I am not. Nonmothers or the childfree measure their words in my presence, and since I've left the fold, most mothers find me fundamentally suspect. But the view from renegade bridge is enlightening.

I see three distinct but occasionally overlapping political camps: 1) the childraisers, 2) the children, and 3) the childless or childfree. These camps share a common oppression, but they are also in direct conflict with one another. Each situation carries a series of contradictions and concomitant ambivalencies, complicated by the separate realities of sex, race, and traditional class divisions. The job of untangling the conflicts, of forging a common struggle, is nearly beyond comprehension, but we must start digging somewhere.

The Childraisers

Mothers are not the only childraisers. Included in this group are lovers; housekeepers; babysitters; nursery, elementary, and secondary school teachers; communal mothers; relatives; friends; feminist aides; and an occasional father. There are what can be broadly defined as primary and secondary childraisers with much variety and several degrees in between. A primary childraiser is the primary source of emotional and economic support for her children. The secondary childraiser is only one of a group of people who is economically and emotionally responsible for the children.

Whether you are a primary or secondary childraiser and what else you do with your time makes a big difference. The myth tells us simply that you are a mother or you are not. But the facts cast the deciding vote, especially regarding the strength or poverty of the self-image you derive from childraising. Ethel Kennedy affords a ready illustration. Tennis, horseback riding, golf, a huge houseful of surrogates, and the Washington cocktail circuit can uniquely influence the self-concept of your basic mother of eleven. The single mother who works a nine-hour shift in order to support her four children will have a different self-image. What we do well tends to create a solid self-concept. What we do poorly results in the opposite. How well we do anything directly depends on the economic and social environment in which we do it. The crunch in childraising comes when you realize that poor mothering and faulty child care are currently built-in givens in the North American social and economic system.

Specific signs of decay are readily apparent. To begin with, we are all familiar with the dreaded question "And what do *you* do?" (*a*) "I'm a mother," (*b*) "I'm a lawyer," or (*c*) "I'm a pig farmer." As a mother I was always tempted to answer with *c* because there are some interesting historical parallels. The primary difference boils down to the fact that pig farming went out a little earlier than motherhood and so you pick up an extra point or two on its antique value. Not even the middle-class American supermom with the greatest resources at her private command can beat the inevitable failure. As the feminist movement legitimizes rebellion, supermom after supermom throws in the towel of her discontent and as often as not returns to school.

If being with children is a joy, why aren't we fighting harder for the privilege? Why is it when you ask for child-care volunteers, everybody in the room contemplates their boot laces? Why is it the mothers and a handful of political stalwarts are inevitably left with the job of consciousness raising (children are human beings too) and organizing child care for meetings, jobs, community, wherever?

The signs are real. The message is clear. If you're looking for a solid self, don't be a mother, or an elementary school teacher, or a child-care center aide at all. Since failure is built into childraising in our society, there is no such thing as a good mother and no such thing as a good self-concept emerging from this work. The situation goes beyond the sole dictates of male supremacy. It has nothing whatever to do with any individual childraiser's advanced skill at maneuvering. There are a number of ingenious, if partial, escape routes that the more privileged work out for themselves. But there you go; it is an *escape*—something to get away from. That *something* transcends good or bad mothering. What is it?

The Changing Economy of Motherhood

Early one morning everybody in the world woke up and decided in unison to hate children. Hence the cure: we all wake up tomorrow morning and decide to love children. Stripped of its rational facade, this is the kind of solution which too often prevails. Many contemporary writers (Jill Johnston, Shulamith Firestone, Germaine Greer, Jane Alpert) talk of returning to the good old days when children were "integrated" into adult society, when they were treated as "small adults" and were a constant presence in the daily life of the community. It's not a bad idea. We could gather up all the children and go marching through the factories, business offices, medical schools, cocktail lounges, libraries, college administrations, board meetings, nuclear laboratories, saying: "Here's three for you and three for you and three for you; keep them safe, happy and intelligent; we'll be back for them in twenty-five years."

The description of an integrated society these writers present resembles an historical truth, which in many parts of the world still prevails. But it is the entire social, technological, and economic fabric of these periods and places that makes the integration of children a viable reality. Many of these integrated children vitally contribute to the economic life of the community: they work from sunup to sundown. But most significantly, their relationship to their mothers is relatively casual.

In any economic setting with an extended family, the mother's relationship to her children is automatically secondary. That is, the children will be raised and *economically supported* by a group of people of which the biological mother is simply one member. This is generally true for all classes, races, and cultures.

The economic settings that maintain a secondary relationship between mothers and children cover an enormous range and variety in life style. They include nomadic communal gathering and hunting peoples, agrarian societies, feudal societies, and early industrial societies. Since these economic forms have prevailed for most of human history, many of the contemporary expressions of motherhood are outgrowths of an economic existence that is now obsolete in most parts of the United States and generally in any advanced industrial setting.

Here's the deal: The nuclear family is the result of an economic system that has come to depend on small, tight, economically autonomous, mobile units. It is essential to capitalism because it not only meets the peculiar production needs of our economy but also fits the requirements of capitalistic consumption. Thus the ideal nuclear family boasts one producer and several (but not too many lest the labor force explode) consumers. It is a middle-class ideal and the norm held out for all classes. Even though the working-class family rarely achieves the ideal, it too believes this is the way life is supposed to be. In the "good" family, the man "works"; the woman is wife, mother, and homemaker.

The nuclear family provided stable family units for the advanced industrial state for a number of years. Now, the very mobility it arose to feed is turning around and killing it. The means of stabilizing and sustaining the old family have progressively disintegrated: neighborhoods, churches, ministers, relatives, etc. New institutional buffers have taken their place: TV, psychiatrists, psychologists, social workers, family counselors, school counselors, and a huge educational system.

By keeping the nuclear family limping along, these adjustments have eased the new primary relationship between mothers and children. But short of total fascistic control (no divorce, no abortion, no child care), the attempt is economically doomed. The U.S. government has failed to salvage an institution that served it well. The stopgap adjustments have not been sufficient. Psychiatrists no longer even attempt to "save" marriages: they help people through "transitions." The divorce rate soars, giving the nation a new choice and women and children a new deal. Either the old nuclear provider supports two, three, or four families, which most men can't or won't afford, or middle-class women join the labor force with unmatched vengeance. All this at a time when the number of jobs is rapidly shrinking.

Meanwhile, back at the homestead, the children are waiting to go to school to make this new deal possible. For a mother of three, that's a minimal wait of nine years on diaper duty before she is free to look for "work." Upon finding that job, she also finds she must be away from home for at least eight hours a day not including travel time. Most children's school days run two to four hours short of this requirement. Talk about credibility gaps, here we have a possibility gap. Welcome, ladies, to the working class.

But long ago, they moved middle-class women out of the extended family, Mexican, Irish, Italian, Jewish neighborhood. Mother still lives in Pocatello, Aunt Jean is in an institution up in Rhode Island; so who now will watch the kids? Arise the new child-care center: haphazard, unfunded, disorganized, and expensive. A college-educated woman earns less than a male with two years of high school training. If you even find a job, do you grasp the size of the paycheck coming in, minus babysitting, child care, groceries, moving, housing, and medical costs? This is a framework for built-in failure.

Take a good look at the rhetoric surrounding the issue of motherhood. The term "childless" represents our society's traditional perception of the situation. Since motherhood was the primary and often *only* route to social and economic well-being for women, having children was a material asset, and to be "childless" was historically negative. Indeed the term was often directly equated with "barrenness." Few women were autonomous; survival depended on marrying and bearing children. No man wanted a barren woman. So under these circumstances no "sane" woman *chose* not to have children. To be childless still carries a negative stigma, even though the social and economic reality has drastically changed. Consequently the question must we be childless? is loaded.

The term "childfree" represents a new perception of reality in the United States. Not only is motherhood no longer the only route to social and economic well-being, it has become a real detriment—a detriment that is clearly visible when a mother looks for a job, a place to live, babysitters, or child care, whenever she tries to *take* her children any place she goes.

Women must for the first time in herstory leave the nest in order to gain an identity and a living wage. Yet a mother cannot leave the nest because she is the children's sole remaining legal, economic, and emotional representative. When children are barred from any productive role until they are twenty-five years old, it makes the job of representative tenfold what it was in the past. To be a good representative you must be economically solvent, have a solid self-concept (gained elsewhere), and have a great deal of time on your hands.

On another level, the debate between "childless" and "childfree" is purely rhetorical. Clearly, with or without children, women are not free in our society. Even more important, as long as children exist it is a delusion to speak of being free of them. They are still all out there, impatiently clamoring for recognition and support.

Meanwhile, the government takes its own stand. It has already paid farmers not to grow food and workers not to work past a certain magical age. It pays students not to join the labor force and fathers to stay away from home. Now the government is implicitly paying women not to have children. Ford follows Nixon in refusing the necessary funds for child care. Like Nixon, he calls it "economizing and preserving the American family." The new deal for children and mothers amounts to no deal at all. They are being forced into an economic and social transition doomed to failure from the start.

Consequences and Strategies

The situation portrayed presents distinct consequences and strategical possibilities for the three political camps: mothers, children, and the childfree. We must recognize the contemporary condition of women and children as a complex product of economic history. The problem is far more complicated than just the result of bad men in places of power. The grim fact that women in feminist collectives refuse to deal with the dilemma unless mothers literally put them up against the wall is one indication that our situation is not a simple by-product of the ideology of male supremacy.

Think. In general the feminist movement has benefited its members. It has given them a collective identity, which in turn has made them stronger as individuals. Women have given of themselves freely and deeply in order to develop this new strength. Of course we've had our casualties, but in general the prize has been worth the cost. In the case of childraising the prize does not yet equal the cost. We reflect society's perception that mothers, children, and child care are expendable. The "expendability" is often expressed in statements such as "Child care is a reformist issue." But this expendability of mothers and children is built into the economic system that controls all of us.

Mothers

Mothers must make it militantly clear that they are not expendable. The economic changes that have made motherhood a national disaster area can be changed. National and local budget priorities and consciousness can be rearranged to suit job, educational, and child-care needs. Of course the privileged, be they men in power or your so-called childfree sisters, will *never* give up their advantages out of the goodness of their hearts. They need to know that the price of not dealing with your situation is greater than the cost of dealing with it—that whatever endeavor they are involved in simply cannot proceed without meeting your needs. You are raising their children; they must provide the resources to do the job adequately. Mothers everywhere must caucus, organize unions, and put an end to their isolation through collective action. There is a lesbian mothers union, based in California, and mothers should use this as a beginning model for collective effort.

In the meantime, if an individual mother's situation is unbearable, and if the option of custody transfer is remotely feasible, she should give this option serious consideration. It is the surest, quickest, most effective strategy available for personal survival. It is also a political statement. It says in no uncertain terms: "If my community will not provide me with the freedom I need to rebuild my life, then I will take it for myself." For a growing number of women, custody transfer is more than an option. It is a necessity.

The potential tragedy is not that children and mothers are lost to each other but that the decision is made in a social vacuum. There is virtually no community support. The so-called experts—psychologists, counselors—paint an invariably gloomy future for you. Even the most liberal, nonjudgmental shrink tends to lose her cool at the mention of custody transfer. The one I consulted rose up out of his chair and shouted: "You can't do that." Fortunately, I disregarded this "advice" and proceeded. What women need is some one or group to share positively both the decision and the transition with them.

No mother makes this choice easily. Both the social taboo and the mother's entire conditioning conspire to keep it out of the realm of serious possibility. Another obstacle is the false assumption that the decision will be complete and irrevocable—a "here today, gone to-morrow" finality. Such is not usually the case. The details, including psychological consequences for both mothers and children, will vary with the individual situation.

Whether a child is raised by her uncle, her grandmother, two people, or a group of people, and what kind of people they are, makes all the difference in the world. My own three children have two sets of parents (one lesbian, one heterosexual), and four functioning grand-mothers. They spend summers with my lover and me, and the school year with their father and another mother. The transition was gradual. My oldest child moved in with his father three years ago. A year later the two younger ones joined him.

In our case the change was a necessity, economically and emotion-ally. Perhaps we could have scraped by economically, although I had no vocational skills and was still working on a college degree. But emotionally the situation for me as a single mother was disastrous. My two-year stint in the women's movement had allowed a vast res-ervoir of rage to surface. The open resentment at being trapped began to far outstrip the pleasures of mothering, and the daily burden was too great for me or my kids to bear. That a healthier situation was available was a stroke of luck and privilege for which I shall be forever grateful.

Children

A key feature of industrialization is that the "workplace" is far re-moved from the home, which gradually leads to the segregation of children from the "business" of the world. As industrialization and technological development proceed, the discrepancy between adult and child spheres grows. Children must be set aside for longer and longer periods of their lives before they can play an integral, responsible role in the life of the community. At the same time, increased mobility combines with supermedia to expose children to a constant flow of new situations and a complex environment that demands they grow up more quickly than ever.

In essence, we have mass-produced a nation of young people who are extremely sophisticated, while we have simultaneously denied that sophistication any serious expression. Because children are segregated and constantly held down, they have developed their own culture, with values, codes of honor, and means of social control that clash with the adult ones. Even though children are packed neatly away in their ghetto—the American public school system—we cannot avoid bumping into them, because there is trouble brewing in the ghetto.

Like other oppressed people, children have begun to organize, to demand basic rights and responsibilities commensurate with their abilities. As with other oppressed groups who begin to rebel, society has reacted negatively to these initial efforts. Just as rape has become a national sport, razor blades and arsenic in Halloween treats and armed guards in the corridors of our best middle-class junior highs have become standard. These reinforce the children's own conclusion that they live in a state of siege.

Segregation of children has had one potentially liberating consequence: it significantly dilutes the impact of where they lay their heads at night. It is no longer possible for adults to stamp out pint-sized replicas of themselves through the nuclear or traditional family. The individual child's destiny is increasingly determined by her own community. In this respect, children are in part seeing to their own liberation. But their situation is still unique for two reasons. First, their condition is temporary by definition. Second, they are by nature to some extent dependent on the adult community. That's where we come in.

A well-developed industrial system changes children from an advantage to a deficit. Under other economic systems, children materially contribute to a family's wealth and well-being, and eventually the young take care of the old. Not so today. This change has tremendously influenced both our perception and treatment of children. No amount of sweetness and light, innocence or charm, can outweigh the fact that they are a pain in the ass and cost a lot of money. Since our perception of children comes from a specific social and economic environment, it can be changed only by altering that environment. The cost of childraising can no longer be shouldered by private individuals. Childraising must move from the private to the public sphere, from the individual to the local and national community. *My* children must become *our* children.

We have begun this transition—witness the education industry. But we are dragging our heels all the way. If we compare need with designated resources, the educational establishment today is a mere welfare program. By and large the treatment of children in it is comparable to the treatment of welfare recipients. Imagine how different funding for education and child care would be, if the grandchildren of our national Congress people were in public child care from three months of age up!

In making the transition from *my* children to *our* children, we can and must change the consciousness of our sisters first. And then, we change the nation. But society's perception of children will not change until we create a viable role for children and give them the resources to fulfill that new role.

In the meantime, child hating must go. It should not be replaced with old platitudes on the natural virtues of children or life with them. Rather, it should be replaced with a firm understanding of why children are "unacceptable" in our society, and a concrete strategy to include children in our thoughts and actions.

Any organization or gathering is practicing child hating if it does not arrange for quality, feminist child care by the "childfree." Furthermore, any person who says: "But I don't particularly like children," is practicing child hating. She is letting society's negative stereotype of children take over her mind. There is as much variety among children as there is among individual women. How can you dislike all of them? The statement comes from one who perceives children as an *inferior* group that is not worthy of her personal recognition or time. Struggles against racism and sexism have set our minds bolt upright on these issues. The casualness with which child-hating statements are made and received is a measure of our lack of consciousness of this issue.

The Childfree

All women who are able to plot their destinies with the relative mobility of the childfree should be encouraged to take on at least one existing child, part time or full time. Love that child, teach her something she might otherwise never learn, show her respect she might not find elsewhere. Oh yes, and be consistent. Let one child in your community grow to expect and rely on your coming just as she relies on the air she breathes. You should not do so because the experience will be joyful but because it is politically necessary for the growth of all women and children. Then if joy comes, halleluja!

To have our own biological children today is personally and politically irresponsible. If you have health, strength, energy, and financial assets to give to children, then do so. Who, then, will have children? If the childfree raise existing children, more people than ever will "have" children. The line between biological and nonbiological mothers will begin to disappear. Are we in danger of depleting the population? Are you kidding?

Right now in your community there are hundreds of thousands of children and mothers who desperately need individual and community support. It is not enough for feminists to add to this population and then help out in their spare time. A growing number of young women are indeed beginning to resist having their own biological children—mostly from a sense of self-preservation. But the new childfree must not only take conscious control of their reproductive organs, they must also see that true self-preservation depends upon the survival of their entire community—one that includes living children.

We must develop feminist vision and practice that includes children. We must allow mothers and children a way out of the required primary relationships of the nuclear family. This can be done only by forging new relationships, with economic and emotional underpinnings, between children and the childfree. At this historical moment the goal is a moral imperative only. Moral imperatives have a habit of hanging out there in thin air until hell freezes. It is the responsibility of nonmothers to end the twin tyrannies of motherhood and childhood as they are lived today, but the childfree will not do so until mothers and children light a big fire of their own.

Sexual Harassment: Working Women's Dilemma

Dierdre Silverman

In May of 1975 Working Women United, an organization in Ithaca, New York, held a Speak-Out on Sexual Harassment. We defined sexual harassment as the treatment of women workers as sexual objects. This problem permeates all aspects of women's work.

Sexual harassment begins with hiring procedures in which women applicants are judged not only for their work skills but also for their physical attractiveness (and, in some instances, sexual receptivity). It continues when job retention, raises, or promotions depend on tolerating, or submitting to, unwanted sexual advances from co-workers, customers, or supervisors. The form of these advances varies from clearly suggestive looks and/or remarks to mild physical encounters (pinching, kissing, etc.) to outright sexual assault. In all instances, the message is clear: a woman's existence as a sexual being is more important than her work.

The speak-out attracted a great deal of support in the Ithaca area, with the realization that this was a collective and not an individual problem. Sexual harassment has received considerable coverage in the establishment media as a result of the speak-out. An article in the *New York Times* was picked up by papers around the country, and *Redbook* made sexual harassment the subject of its January 1976 reader survey.

In examining coverage of the issue in the liberal media, two trends emerge clearly. The first is that media focus is on upper-middle-class, mostly professional, and businesswomen, although it is clear that sexual harassment affects women workers at all occupational levels.[1] Second is the lack of analysis; an unwillingness or inability to understand the meaning of sexual harassment in our (capitalist, patriarchal) society, and to see why it has only recently emerged as a feminist issue. Such analysis is the task of feminist theory, and a beginning is attempted below.

The Prostitute as Paradigm

It is my contention that the paradigm for interactions between men and women in our society is that of the prostitute and her customer. In this exchange, the man provides money (in various forms: cash, commodities, lifetime economic support, employment), and the women provides sexual services (literal or symbolic).[2]

In the same way that conventional prostitution is an economic answer for the hooker, other prostitution exchanges provide economic solutions for most women. Women's economic position demonstrates the need for such solutions. Overall women's income is 57 percent of that of men.[3] This percentage has *declined* steadily since 1955.[4] In addition the unemployment rate for women is consistently higher than that for men,[5] even though many women retreat to housewife status and are less likely to be counted among the unemployed.

The picture is even worse for women who try to make it on their own. In 1969, 47 percent of families living in poverty were headed by women. Only 38 percent of female-headed families had incomes over $5,000.[6] The economic security women do establish depends on men. For it is men, as husbands, employers, supervisors and customers who provide women with the opportunity to work and advance as paid workers, or to live and work in economic security as housewives.

This trade of money for sex is fairly clear in some forms of interaction. Our patterns of dating, courtship, and marriage are examples of this. On dates, men pay, and women are expected to repay with sexual favors.[7] In marriage, men are legally required to provide economic support, while women are required to provide sexual services. Currently, only in Michigan is rape within marriage recognized as a crime.[8] The wife is legally seen as the husband's sexual property. He does not break the law by demanding or taking what is his. (The wife who refuses her husband's sexual approaches may be seen, in legal terms, as violating her marriage contract.)

Even those women who are the most traditional in values and behavior recognize this relationship. For women who follow the Total Woman and Fascinating Womanhood guidelines, the payoff is not only in greater marital (and thereby economic) security, but in presents. Students come to Total Woman classes with glowing reports of the refrigerators, mink coats, or other rewards their husbands have given them in return for their sexually submissive games.[9]

Teaching girls how to hustle is one of the functions of the nuclear family. James Bryan, in a 1965 study, "Apprenticeships in Prostitution," describes the work of the pimp and the older prostitute in teaching the novice girl how to perform.[10] This apprencticeship system differs only in label from the more conventional socialization within the family, in which the daughter learns, by watching her parents' interactions, how to hustle men. In *Working*, Studs Terkel's hooker respondent describes the ease with which she turned her first trick: "I wonder why I was so willing. . . . It wasn't traumatic because my training had been in how to be a hustler anyway. I learned it from the society around me, just as a woman. We're taught how to hustle, to attract, to hold a man and give sexual favors in return. . . . It's a marketplace transaction."[11]

In our society, women have little choice about hustling, whether they do it as professionals or as amateurs, for one lifetime trick or for a series of customers.

Women at Work

Women can try to opt out of the hustling role by working outside the home. In spite of low wages and poor promotion possibilities, outside employment offers women a chance at independence. However, sexual stratification in our society assures that most working women will be trading one form of independence on men for another. Sexual harassment at work is one manifestation of this dependence.

In a recent survey conducted by Working Women United, 70 percent of the respondents had experienced at least one instance of sexual harassment on the job. Ninety-one percent of the respondents saw such harassment as a "serious problem for working women." Those who had personally experienced sexual harassment were asked how many times it had happened. The median figure was three instances, with over half the respondents reporting "a lot," "often," or "more than ten times." The respondents' median age was twenty-six and they had been working, on the average, only seven years.

Respondents were asked to describe the most recent instance of sexual harassment they had experienced. The statistics presented refer to the description each woman gave of that one instance. In more than half the incidents described, the man or men doing the harassing were in work positions superior to the respondent. Another 18 percent were customers or clients. Thus, about two-thirds of the men were in a position to exert some economic pressure on the respondent. In addition, 41 percent of the respondents described harassment involving more than one man.

Sexual harassment happens to women of all ages and all occupational groups. One respondent mentioned an incident that occurred when she was ten and working as a child model; another's experience occurred at age fifty-five. In this survey, clerical employees and waitresses were most frequently harassed; our respondents' occupations covered a wide range. Working-class women, especially those in service occupations, were more likely to receive physical as well as verbal advances, while for middle-class and/or professional women, harassment was more often verbal. Middle-class women were somewhat more likely to ignore the situation, or attempt to change jobs, in order to avoid confrontation. In spite of these class differences, both in the ways women are approached and in the ways they respond, sexual harassment is a problem that cuts across class lines and affects all women in their capacity as workers.

In popular literature, sexual harassment is treated as a joke of little consequence. The actress who "succeeds" by means of the casting couch, the "Fly Me" airline stewardess, and other stereotypes permeate American/male humor. Are women laughing along?

Respondents were asked to describe how they felt after being harassed. Table 1 shows their responses.

Many respondents indicated multiple reactions, so the percentage total is more than 100 percent. When asked, "Did this experience have any emotional or physical effect on you?" 78 percent answered yes. Consider the following comments:

"As I remember all the sexual abuse and negative work experiences I am left feeling sick and helpless and upset instead of angry."

"Reinforced feelings of no control—sense of doom."

"I have difficulty dropping the emotion barrier I work behind when I come home from work. My husband turns into just another man."

"Kept me in a constant state of emotional agitation and frustration. . . . I drank a lot."

"Soured the essential delight in the work."

"Stomachache, migraines, cried every night, no appetite."

TABLE 1   PERCENTAGE OF RESPONDENTS MENTIONING EACH REACTION

Angry	78
Upset	48
Frightened	23
Guilty	22
Flattered	10
Indifferent	7
Other (alienated, alone, helpless)	27

Many women commented on how the harassment, or their reactions to it, interfered with their job performance. The economic consequences of impaired performance are difficult to measure.

What actions do women take in response to sexual harassment? Respondents' descriptions of their most recent experience are summarized in table 2.

TABLE 2   PERCENTAGE OF RESPONDENTS TAKING EACH ACTION

Complain to the man harassing you	25
Ignore it	23
Pretend not to notice	13
Complain through channels	12
Quit the job	9
Ask for transfer	2
Other (most verbal responses, to the man or co-workers)	16

Ignoring the harassment is an ineffective response. For 76 percent of the respondents who tried this tactic, the behavior continued, and sometimes got worse. In fact, almost one-third of these women were penalized on the job for not responding positively to the harassment. When asked why they didn't "complain through channels," women's responses indicated their weaknesses in the work situation. Forty-two percent felt that nothing would be done; 33 percent feared some negative consequences for themselves, varying from blame and ridicule to concrete penalties at work. For about 20 percent of the respondents, either there were no channels or the harassing man was a part of them.

When respondents did officially complain, no action was taken in one-third of the cases. One-third of the respondents who complained were themselves penalized at work. In a small number of cases, action was taken against the man. The most severe of these was transfer to another workplace or ejection of a customer.

Sexual harassment is a common problem for women workers. It has serious emotional repercussions and interferes with women's work performance. More important, as individuals, women have no effective way to deal with the problem. Whatever their response, women pay.

In our attempt to understand why sexual harassment is so widespread and why women are so unable, emotionally and practically, to handle it, the model of prostitution provides some answers.

Women who earn money may be seen as less dependent on men

then women who are not paid for their work. By extending to the workplace the general pattern of male sexual initiative, and by reinforcing this with the man's superior power to enact job penalties, women's attempt at independence is thwarted. The implicit prostitution-exchange in work situations is that men provide the jobs through hiring and promotion, set salary levels and work conditions, and can terminate employment by firing. Women are employed when, and because, men choose to employ them. In return for these economic favors, women provide sexual services as well as work skills. These sexual services range from providing an attractive female presence to actual sexual encounters. We all know that this arrangement exists, although we may not choose to acknowledge it as a conscious or consistent pattern. Magazines such as *Cosmopolitan* counsel a strategy of passive manipulation and advise women to use this technique for their own advantage.

When women are unwilling to play the game, the presumed understanding is violated and the situation becomes emotionally loaded. A woman who refuses sexual advances at work is breaking her end of the bargain by attempting to establish her independent existence as a worker. It is this act which provokes anger and reprisals from men. And the meaning of this act has created guilt, ambivalence, and uncertainty in the refusing women; they know they are breaking an agreement that they have been raised to honor.

When asked why they did not lodge formal complaints, respondents replied:

"I thought it was *my* problem."

"The importance I have been trained to place on what other people think of me—trying to please other people rather than finding my own rewards, fulfillment, etc."

"HoJo's pride themselves on their friendly, pretty girls—in a sense, they promote my sexual harassment."

"I did not want to get him (the harasser) in trouble."

"No one would believe me."

"I felt I couldn't make a scene by telling anyone in authority over him. I felt powerless and, oddly, honor-bound not to publicly embarrass him."

"I would be seen as cruel and unprofessional."

These women express an inability to deal with the possible repercussions of their complaint. This inability is the result, not just of female socialization, but also of an accurate assessment of the power distribution at work. It is a result, not of individual weakness, but of women's disadvantaged position.

When women enter fields that are traditionally male, or occupy positions of authority over male workers, sexual harassment becomes a tool to thwart their efforts at economic independence. Frequent reminders that, no matter what work a woman is doing, she is still a woman and therefore a sex object, are designed to dampen her identification with her work and limit her success at it. Respondents reported harassment when they were employed as carpenters. filmmakers, auto mechanics, college teachers, social workers, probation officers, or accountants, as well as in other male-dominated fields. Often accompanying these incidents is a shared jocularity among men witnessing them, perhaps in affirmation of their triumph over the "uppity woman."

Sexual Harassment and Feminism

Because sexual harassment is so widespread, and because its consequences for women are substantial, it is necessary for feminists to develop theoretical analysis and practical strategies for dealing with this issue. We must try to understand women's reactions to sexual harassment, as well as how the issue can be used to help develop feminist consciousness.

When the sexual harassment issue surfaced in Ithaca last year, women's reactions were dramatically divided. Many expressed strong support along with relief that what had been seen as a personal problem was in fact a public issue. There was also, even from feminists, a certain amount of resistance. This was expressed in comments like:

"Any woman who has it together can handle something like that."

"That sort of thing only happens to women who are asking for it." (Often accompanied by, "It's never happened to me, because I know how to present myself.")

"Just because one weird guy does something that doesn't mean it's a real problem."

(These comments are all direct quotes from women I spoke with. Any resemblance to discussions of rape five years ago is not at all a coincidence.)

Why were some women denying the relevance of sexual harassment to women's oppression? It was clear that women with class and/or educational privilege were most likely to feel this way. These women, who are the most successful and highly skilled, may be the most threatened by the idea that even they will still be judged as sexual objects. The fact that sexual harassment of these women is more often purely verbal and more subtle than that directed at working-class women may lead to their willingness to deny its relevancy.

It is also important to recognize that middle-class women have far greater job mobility than working-class women. If a problem such as sexual harassment arises, the privileged woman may just find another job, perhaps denying that there ever was such a problem. (I did that myself, at least once.) These women are also more likely to be able to leave the job market entirely. Therefore, for many reasons, sexual harassment is not as harsh an issue for them.

The more male-identified a woman is, the less likely she is to respond to sexual harassment as a serious problem. The fact that experiences with sexual harassment are so common for women suggests that the act of harassing is quite normal for men. When women begin to think of their fathers, husbands, lovers, etc., as the people doing the harassing, resistance stiffens. Defenses that place the blame on women are developed.

To combat this resistance, it is necessary to break through people's tendency to view themselves and those around them personally, outside of structural, political context. This type of consciousness raising, which has been so basic to feminism, can mobilize a great amount of energy around the sexual harassment issue. It should focus on the use of sexual standards and sexual demands on women workers by male superiors as an instrument to divide women and maintain male superiority. When standards of physical attractiveness are used as hiring and promotion criteria, women are set against one another in competitive and self-destructive ways. None of us is ever young enough, or beautiful enough, to work without insecurity about being replaced by someone more attractive. The energy women devote to maintaining or enhancing their physical appearance may very well cause their actual work performance to suffer.

At the Working Women United speak-out, women spoke about the "other side" of sexual harassment: being rejected as a worker because one is "unattractive." They felt resentment of the men in power who made those judgments, but they also felt resentment of the women who were hired because of the way they look. This jealousy and competition keep women fighting among themselves, and not questioning the standards men are using or their right to use them.

Feminists should also regard sexual harassment as a workplace organizing issue. We should push for its recognition as a serious grievance, an intolerable working condition. We should make it clear that sexual exploitation of workers is not a joke.

Recognition and discussion of the issue in workplaces is important, so that women do not feel guilt or fear when they complain about sexual harassment. And it is important to provide organized support for individual cases, to follow up complaints and ensure the development of workplace policies that make sexual harassment unacceptable.

Beyond the workplace, public education campaigns are necessary. If public harassment is continually presented as a joke, or an acceptable part of women's lives, or something for which women are to blame, individual women will remain silent. Those who do object to sexual harassment will not receive necessary social support. Feminists should use available media to publicize and explain the issue, to let women know that they are not alone and that they are not at fault.

It is important that such publicity does not focus on blaming or attacking individuals. The frequency of sexual harassment suggests that virtually all men are actual or potential harassers. What is necessary, instead, is an approach that analyzes the power situation at work, exposes and destroys the stereotypes about women workers, and suggests collective efforts at changing the work situation.

Sexual harassment is an extremely powerful issue; it clarifies men's definition of women, as well as the power relationship between the sexes. Because it deals with women's economic existence, it is an issue that can tie together our experience as workers and as women.

Sexual harassment has been present as a problem, but invisible as an issue. This is because men and women have accepted the idea that men are entitled to take the sexual initiative, especially when they are "paying." Women have not mobilized around the sexual harassment issue because it has been seen as an individual difficulty, and its consequences, even to individuals, have not been acknowledged. By making the consequences clear, and by linking this issue to the basic power relationships between the sexes, feminist analysis and action around the issue can develop.

NOTES

1. Data used in this paper come from two surveys conducted by the Working Women United Institute. The questionnaire was completed by 50 food-service workers at SUNY Binghamton, and by 100 women who attended the Speak-Out on Sexual Harassment.
2. This is hardly a new idea. See writings by Emma Goldman, Charlotte Perkins Gilman, and Simone de Beauvoir, as well as many more recent feminist theorists. In a capitalist society, where relations between people occur in the context of commodity exchanges, the prostitution exchange is only a specific example. It is based on the assumption that women in our society most often have sexuality (including reproduction) as their most "marketable" commodity.
3. Francine Blau, "Women in the Labor Force: An Overview," in Jo Freeman, *Women: A Feminist Perspective* (Palo Alto: Mayfield, 1975), p. 222.
4. Monica Hill, *The Woman Worker* (Radical Women), p. 4.
5. Kathleen Shortridge, "Working Poor Women," in Freeman, *Women*, p. 248.
6. Robert Stein, "The Economic Status of Families Headed by Women," *Monthly Labor Review* 93 (December 1970): 7.

7. Obviously, these customs are related to our conceptions of male and female sexuality. It is naive to think, however, that changing ideas about women's sexual needs and capacities will be sufficient to alter these behavior patterns, without an accompanying change concerning women's economic dependence on men.

8. Changes in rape laws are being considered in Florida, California, and the District of Columbia. Rape in marriage is also a crime in South Australia.

9. Joyce Maynard, "The Liberation of Total Women," *New York Times Magazine*, 28 September 1975, pp. 45–46.

10. James Bryan, "Apprenticeships in Prostitution," *Social Problems*, Winter 1965.

11. "Robert Victor," in Studs Terkel, *Working* (New York: Pantheon, 1972), p. 58.

Who Wants a Piece of the Pie?

Marilyn Frye*

For feminists, the permanent moral problem of how to live becomes the problem of how to live in accord with feminist values; we have to subsist by means that are harmonious with these values, and we have to live well enough to have resources for change and for enduring processes and events precipitated by our own movement. In short, we need more than subsistence; we are committed to getting it in wholesome ways; and we must manage all of this now, within a hostile sexist society. Looking about at people's lives generally, it seems that requiring more than subsistence is a considerable luxury, and so it can seem that a feminist ethic which presupposes that luxury, is necessarily elitist. There is truth in this, but it is not the last word. For one thing, revolution may in fact *be* something of a luxury—its moment is not to be found among the absolutely destitute. And furthermore, if having resources beyond the requirements of material subsistence is deemed a luxury, then a great many of us were born to that luxury as surely as we were born to our oppression as women, and we had better understand what it means and what we should do with it.

For some of us these dilemmas arise concretely in the matters of work and privilege. One apparently rich resource that many feminists have, have access to, or aspire to, is a situation in an establishment institution or profession. Attractions include salaries, fringe benefits, offices and supplies, postage, secretarial services and assis-

*This essay has a long history during which it has incorporated contributions by C. Rene Davis and by Carolyn Shafer who is, among other things, my regular-thinking partner. It got valuable criticism, also from Jane English, Alison Jaggar, Sandra Harding and Adele Laslie.

tants, transportation services, contacts with other persons similarly situated, and respectability. But there are feminists who have been wary of this and have been inclined to reject such situations or aspirations as part of their rejection of class privilege.

Elimination of class privilege, along with race privilege, is certainly a feminist goal; if we ignore it, we will find ourselves outmaneuvered by a strategy of sex integration in middle bureaucracy, which would strengthen white middle-class dominance and divert the force of radical feminism. Part of our defense against this is steady awareness of class and race. Class privilege is offensive; but *privilege* is itself an odd sort of self-regenerative thing which, once you've got it, cannot be simply shucked off like a too-warm jacket.

Privilege in general is maintained by its exercise. It must remain substantially unquestioned by the nonprivileged; and this is achieved through the constant, easy, more-or-less unconscious exercise of it. The constancy and the ease make it seem *natural* and then render it almost imperceptible, like the weight of one's clothes on one's body. As a consequence of this, one cannot *merely* do something that it *happens* to be a privilege to be able to do. The "mere" exercise of the privilege positively contributes to the continuance of privilege. Using it strengthens it. This obviously applies to taking a position in an establishment institution: taking such a job not only uses privilege but builds privilege. And even this is not the worst of it. For, to reject the position is also to exercise privilege. As a matter of fact, it seems more of a privilege to be able to *turn down* a $15,000 a year administrative job than to be in a position to get it in the first place. If the question even arises for a particular woman, then she *has* privilege; and she cannot refrain from having it, whichever decision she then makes. In deciding not to do some lucrative thing one is privileged to do, one is falling back on *other* privileges. The person who does not take the $15,000 job can handle the resulting poverty relatively well because the same skills, training, connections and style that fit her for the job enable her to be a reasonably crafty consumer and manipulator of bureaucratic process, and give her a network of well-connected acquaintances; and she starts out her poverty in good health and forearmed with feminist analysis. For most people, poverty is intolerably destructive; for most people, choosing it would be choosing a form of suicide. Having relative poverty as a genuine and interesting option is itself a privilege.

I see no way to suddenly stop having privilege, or to stop exercising it. I certainly am not saying that privilege is ineradicable absolutely—but one cannot suddenly, by a simple act of will, detach oneself from it (which is perhaps one of the many reasons why "personal" solutions are inadequate). And in the end, if poverty and detachment from establishment institutions would eventually reduce one to having no privilege, it is still far from obvious that feminists should do it. To renounce middle-class privilege is not to extricate oneself from the system but to relocate oneself within it. Joining the lower classes and recruiting members to them may tend more to the support of the system than to its downfall, for it may simply be providing more victims for the more thorough exploitation and oppression that take place at the lower levels of the hierarchy: those more thoroughly oppressed provide more fuel for the machinery.*

Impoverishment and deprivation *reduce* power, vision, and endurance. The idea that Justice and Dignity require Suffering belongs to an ethic of self-denial, a slave morality. All resource is tainted (men have not yet been dispossessed). We recognize this and we aim to change it. Meanwhile, it is not politically incorrect to avail ourselves of the resources available to us.

If the foregoing arguments are sound, then holding a well-paying job is not necessarily in violation of feminist principles. Since virtually all well-paying jobs are establishment jobs, the next rack of problems is generated by *tokenism*. In virtually all middle-income, middle-bureaucracy, middle-civil-service jobs, a woman will be a token woman, since virtually none of these are classified as "women's work." Her existence there as a token woman works for the good of the institution and the ill of women generally. The presence of the token is used to convince both her employers and the rest of the world that the institution is not sexist and need not bother seriously with affirmative action or correcting salary inequities or sexist division of work, while it cheerfully continues to hire and promote men and serve male interests. These goods done the institutions are complemented by various harms done the token woman (one never gets something for nothing). The token woman is generally quite isolated; she will not have the relations with her colleagues that the men have, and thus the whole work situation is not as rich in stimulation, assistance, and comradeship as it is for most men in similar positions. This is likely to affect the quality of her work, or the amount of energy it takes to maintain the quality of her work. And this isolation also aggravates the constant problem of coping with the difficult questions of integrity and compromise that arise for her. She has to decide whether and in what degree she must be a closet feminist; how manly to act in order to be taken seriously; how much, when, where, and with whom to fight over sexist language, sexist jokes, sexist gallantry, sexist assumptions, sexism in hiring and promotion and such consummate evils as sexist dress requirements. If a woman fails to take matters of integrity and compromise seriously, or makes the wrong decisions, she is likely to slip into being one of the boys—a

*Here, in particular, this essay draws on conversations with Carolyn Shafer.

female man. If she takes them seriously and makes the right decisions, she invites the fate of being a *token feminist*, and the whole situation becomes more complicated. My situation as a professor at a university exemplifies this nicely.*

Sometimes I catch a glimpse of myself in a classroom, in a university building, clothed and fed and insured by the university, before an audience brought there by the university; and I am very seriously spelling out and explaining for them as persuasively as I can a radical feminist perception of the world, and coaching them in the arts of right reason and clear vision so they will be able to discover for themselves what is going on in this sexist culture. And the better I am at teaching these things, the more truth I find and communicate, the more good I do the institution. The fact that it allows someone to stand in it and say those things gives it credit in the eyes of the students and the wider public. That I am there saying truths and teaching women makes the whole thing more tolerable for the women. The better I am, the better they feel about being in the university, the more they are inclined to believe that professors know what they are talking about, the more they feel the university really is a place where knowledge will bring them freedom. And the stronger is the institution. But among the truths is the truth that the institution is male-dominated and directed to serve the ends of a male-dominated society, economy, and culture. As such, its existence, not to mention its strength and vigor, is inimical to the welfare of women, and probably to the survival of the species. If the women in the class come to agree with me in belief and perception, they must see me then as an absurd figure. For I am just that. I can try to see myself as someone working as an undercover agent, fomenting restlessness and stirring up radical sentiment and anger, working as a traitor from within, as an agent of the new order. . . . But that gratifying fantasy is absurdly counterbalanced by the fact that I am doing all this fomenting quite openly, *in the pay* of the institution, with the blessing of the patriarchy, in the context of a grading system, and with the students learning through all of this that the university is a good place, a place where freedom reigns. The university is in the business of authority; by bestowing its authority on selected token representatives of nonstandard views, it enhances its own authority, which is used and designed to be used in the maintenance and justification of male hegemony over knowledge.

Tokenism is painful, and either resolution of the problems of integrity and compromise—joining the boys or becoming a token feminist—immerses the woman in the absurdity. For the token feminist, the thing must eventually come down to the question of

---

*The subsequent paragraph draws on conversations with Rene Davis.

when, over what issues, and with what provocation to fight the battle that will lose her her job; or when to reject the absurdity and resign. It is inevitable that it comes to this question. If she is a feminist, her tolerance for sexist abuse must have a limit; if she is unable or unwilling to risk her job, she has no limit; if she can risk it, she eventually will.

The conclusion here is, of course, that a feminist should not be too dependent upon her establishment job. And this is not peculiar to establishment jobs; anyone living and acting in a manner calculated to bring about changes in her situation must keep her options open. Economic flexibility is needed by anyone who is sticking to some principles. But there are factors contributing to dependence that are of particular significance to a feminist working an establishment job—especially in the kind of emotive or psychological relationship one has to the institution in which one works.

I began to see these questions of relationship through a discussion with another woman professor about the role and life of a feminist in such a position. There was much agreement, until we got to the question of reforming the university. She claimed the university's ideals were fine and could be made to live up to them; that one should work for reform in the institution, and this would help reform society. I claimed that these "ideals" were not really the university's ideals at all but a public relations hype, and it was never meant to live up to them and never would. What emerged was a crucial and profound difference of *affect*, not of opinion. She was *loyal* to the university and its professed ideology, she had *faith* in the institution; I had neither faith nor loyalty. As she talked, it became clear that her loyalty was rather like filial love or patriotism. I have seen such loyalty also among those who have worked for a long time for one of the large paternalistic corporations.

The pathology of institutional loyalty seems to come from at least three sources. First, the institution keeps the person on the payroll, increasing salary and benefits a little faster than the cost of living goes up. Second, there is the matter of exclusivity, of fraternal bonding, especially in loyalty to a profession. This has a nice additional twist when the subject, a sister, is being taken in as a brother. A third source of loyalty lies in the fact that one gains status and identity from one's position in an established institution, profession, or the like. One *is* a professor; one *is* a physician; one *is* the director of the women's studies program. The bestower of such meaning and identity is the bestower of self-respect, of personhood (or it seems to the love-struck employee). One is grateful, and indebted, almost as to one's heavenly creator.

An institution, profession, corporation, or such, to which one feels loyal, which one loves, has a great deal more than mere economic power over one. The threat of being fired, in one form or another, is laced with overtones of the threat of rejection by a loved one, ostracism by the brotherhood, and annihilation through loss of identity. I believe that for mere mortals these are irresistible forces.

The various sorts of dependence upon institutions which can undermine the feminist's ability to make proper use of an establishment employment as a resource for herself and the movement bear a rather obvious similarity to the sorts of dependence the stereotypic wife has on the stereotypic husband. She is tied to him by economic neccessity and by feelings of owing him loyalty because he supports her, and she loves him because she derives her sense of meaning, her identity and status, from his gracious association with her. The first salvation of woman from her fallen state, through her love and marriage to Prince Charming, was a disaster; remarrying Prince Charming now, deceptively clothed as a title and a good salary, would be a disaster of the same magnitude and type.

It is, I find, a fundamental difference between me and many other feminists I know as colleagues that I judge the opposition of interests between women and sexist (misogynist) institutions to be such that we can be united with them in matrimony or brotherhood or alienated from them in sisterhood. The duality is so sharp because these antiwoman institutions offer (or pretend, to offer) livelihood and identity; and women, the dispossessed and invisible, are dying for these. As a consequence of this the integrity of a feminist working within such an institution must depend on her alienation from it and the constancy of her adversarial relation with it. This orientation is maintained, not negatively through resistance of temptation or a system of coercive pressures and checks from other feminists, but positively, through woman-loving.

This woman-loving that supports one's spiritual independence of the establishment institutions supports best if it is not closeted. The publicity of a primary and loving identification with women places one in a position both with respect to the agents of the institution and with respect to other women, of having to live up to it or be a fool or a fake. And the openness of one's woman-loving feminism is necessary also to be realizing one of the most important benefits one's own establishment employment can have for other women. This is the benefit of space in which they can be women and feminists without fatal opposition and depreciation. One's status, authority, recognition, and power, however modest, are conveyed to those with whom one is identified. Respectability, like guilt, travels by association, without specific effort and without specific control; and respectability purchases space. Every time one woman moves or acts, she makes room for other women to move, to act, to be—*if* her womanness is overtly present as a salient factor in the situation, and *not* if she is masquerading as a man or a neuter.

The material benefits of establishment jobs include the income, the insurance, the access to duplicating machines and space for meetings, the material support of one's feminist work through use of paid "company time" for work, organizing, prosletyzing, etc. One can and should share the wealth and resource within the community of feminists through income sharing, use and support of membership in feminist operations such as credit unions, health clinics, women's centers, bookstores, and so on. And one's position and whatever accumulation of savings it makes possible can serve a community and not just one person or one household, as sort of cushion for emergencies—medical, spiritual, monetary, cop-and-court, welfare.*

There are material and political benefits to be derived from having some of us working establishment jobs. But integration into the establishment bureaucracies is not woman's final answer. I do not think we can change the existing government, health, military, business, or educational establishments significantly enough from within to bother it. The internal structures of these institutions are designed to maintain a privileged elite and to organize even that elite in dominance-subordinance patterns. The health and welfare of women ultimately require entirely different ways of organizing things. If we were to try to transform the existing structures, our success would depend partly on enlightenment but largely on numbers. We would have to transcend tokenism. As long as a substantial majority of men are benefiting from the male-dominance within the institutions and in the world served by the institutions, and as long as men are in the substantial majority in these institutions, there is simply no reason why they should want, tolerate, or encourage enlightenment. The structures maintain the tokenism, which in turn protects the structures.

My conclusion, for now, is that a feminist can conscientiously hold and use an establishment position *if* she is simultaneously cultivating skills, attitudes, identity and an alternative community, with and in which she can function without that position, and which will keep her honest while she has it. One day, when some who have been working straight jobs, and some have not, and all have been inventing new ways to survive and thrive, and when the evolving negotiations between my conscience and my patience set a new shit-limit, which is found unacceptable by my employers; one day the time will be right for me to leave my post on the boundary and move into the new space.

*So far, in my community, the handiest way to handle this seems to be through share-securing loans through the local feminist credit union. This is far from perfect, but it is much better than strictly personal control of allocation, and it spreads the benefits beyond one social circle.

An Open Letter to the Academy

Michelle Russell

It's not as simple as talkin jive: the daily struggle just to stay alive.
—Nina Simone, Revolution I

The starting points for my remarks on women in the academy are historical and situational, personal and political: categories that the women's movement has encouraged us to connect but not to debase. I speak as someone who was born into a revolutionary socialist tradition, who has had the benefit of what Westerners call a "classical humanist education," who has defined teaching as her life work and who, for a variety of reasons, pursues that work outside of the institutional framework of a university.

Much has been written and said of late concerning the knowledge explosion, the interdisciplinary possibilities of women's studies, and the institutional restructuring that form the immediate context for a consideration of women in the academy. I would like to widen the discussion to address the responsibility of women's studies to those outside the academy's walls: the mass of women whose lives will be fundamentally affected by the version of reality developed there, but who, as yet, have no way of directly influencing your direction.

To begin with, some reflections on the academy as it now exists are now in order. For me, the academy has become a mental ward, an ivory tower that harbors and encourages the slow madness induced by social isolation. Its predisposition, intellectually, is to regard anything dead as good, and the living as suspect and intrusive. Like any suburb, it is clean—pruned, well-manicured, sanitary—but psychotic. Its social isolation is technologically masked by the availability of WATS lines, xerography, and archives. But these act only as surrogates and substitutes for direct contact with the world. They constitute the major aspect of the "privilege" you experience. Beyond this, you *pay* in order to reduce your contact with people. You *pay* for sanctuary. The sanctuary lies in suspension.

The suspension is somewhere between the fifteenth and nineteenth centuries. Bound by feudalism, the age of Enlightenment, and the bourgeois revolution, it hardly provides a viable standpoint from which to approach present-day reality. It is only useful insofar as we define ourselves in a critical relationship to that past which the academy deifies as "the march of civilization."

When I do that, the one constant, historically, culturally, politically, and economically, which winds like a black snake—coil, rope, whip—through those centuries is colonialism; not civilization, but the triumph of barbarism in the guise of progress. From the Inquisition and the Crusades to the current incarnation of J. C. as President, I see the institutionalization of the vigilante tradition in the uniform of the state, with all the robes and trappings of high office. *And the primary political and cultural role of Western women and the academy in that process has been to rationalize it.* European and Anglo-American women have acted as the domesticators of subject peoples, indoctrinating them into the manners of servitude and providing the illusion of protection once in captivity; while the academy has acted as the ideological apologist for conquest in the name of civilization. This is your missionary tradition: smallpox carried in blankets to natives by nurses backed by bibles and swords.

The examples of this process can be documented ad nauseum. The point is, for black people, the oppressive pendulum of imperialism's timeclock has swung precisely between assimilation and annihilation, between the velvet glove and the iron fist. And we have become adept at recognizing the continuity of its swing.

Even in the context of the so-called liberal atmosphere of American universities in the 1960s, it was clear, as I wrote then, almost ten years ago:

> Black studies programs, although an apparent departure from the "equal rights" mode of struggle, is only the latest phase in America's domination over us. To understand how serious the situation is, all we need do is to compare the major characteristics of African slavery and colonialization in the U.S. with the process by which blacks are brought into established institutions of higher education. The parallels are striking and instructive.
>
> In the initial stages of African colonialization four things occurred which we can identify as "Before Arrival" (B.A.) prerequisites. First, "recruitment" channels had to be established between European slavers and Africans in positions of trust and power who would act as mercenaries against their people. Second, African mercenaries and European colonizers had to cooperate in collecting and selecting large populations "suitable" for transport to the New World. Third, those who were "lucky" enough to be chosen had to undergo the shock of passage, usually with other blacks of different tribes whose local customs had previously set them apart rather than binding them together.

And fourth, upon landing in America, the blacks who survived had to submit to a plantation diaspora which was the final complement to the systematic separation and disruption of families and tribes that had begun with recruitment.

Once ensconced in the plantations of the New World, there were still more tests to pass. After a trial period during which Africans were consistently excluded from the language and customs of the plantation social system, it was decided that the slaves could be used most effectively if certain "liberalizing" procedures were followed. To facilitate our ability to take orders (and be satisfied exclusively with that) we were taught only the vocabulary of our specific jobs. To undermine our sense of nationhood and inculcate identification with our masters, there was widespread rape and mongrelization of our people. Once this was accomplished, our colonizers felt it was safe to let us congregate, but only for activities (like religious worship) considered peripheral and non-antagonistic to doing the master's work. And finally, with emancipation (the end of our enforced stay as non-paid workers on the plantation) we were granted the "privilege" of becoming either rural tenant farmers or joining an underemployed urban class and incurring a monetary indebtedness to the system which had been built through our oppression.

With a very slight transposition of vocabulary (for Before Arrival, read the Bachelor of Arts; for Africa, read the South and for the New World, the North; for diaspora, read brain drain; for plantation, read college system; for mongrelization, read integration and cultural diversity programs; for religious worship, substitute Black Studies; and for tenant farming, substitute the monetary aid system by which black students are consistently given loans over scholarships), the whole process becomes a perfect metaphor of the dynamics of black educational colonization in America.[1]

While for us, the lessons of this experience have been driven home with unmediated force, white women have often been caught in the middle. As a victimized, accomplice population in this process, you have been confused. Your oppression and exploitation have been more cleverly masked than ours, more delicately elaborated. The techniques, refined. You were rewarded in minor ways for docile and active complicity in our dehumanization. At base, the risk of your complete alienation from the system of white male rule that also exploited you was too great to run. The perpetuation of the race depended upon your reproductive capacity: your willingness to bear and rear succeeding generations of oppressors. If you think this is far-fetched, you have only to look at the struggle for abortion being waged now by women in Italy who must contend with Fascist legislation passed in 1930 and still in force which explicitly declares "abortion is a crime against the sanctity of the race." While your reproductive function has been the only reason for your relative protection in the colonizing process, ours, on the contrary, has sharpened the knife colonialism applies to our throats and wombs. Witness government-sanctioned mass sterilization in Puerto Rico, New York, and Brazil.

I draw on these discrepancies in our condition not to assign blame or to suggest that you are blind to the implications of this process. We also know that history is full of examples of white women rejecting the cultural and economic blackmail that kept you in service. You walked out on your jobs: in the home, in mills and mines, in heavy manufacturing, in bureaucracies. Occasionally, small minorities succeeded in creating artistic and intellectual communities that sustained elements of a culture independent of the dominant commodity relations of bourgeois society. But, on balance, that history—the one of your resistance—is still to be discovered and amplified by this generation. All of you. That is why you are important.

What Stories Will You Tell?

At this point in the history of the American academy, a substantial section of the white female population is being selected and is choosing to take on the civilizing function as well as the domesticating one. Many of you even come from social origins that the academy deems suspect, backgrounds that you are supposed to grow out of, or, at least, leave at the gate. Be that as it may, you are there, defining the legitimate areas of your study and concern. And you must decide if you are going to lend your minds as well as your bodies to reproducing the hierarchies and inherited privilege that shore up colonialism's power.

The central question, of course, is "What version of civilization will you construct?" What stories will you tell each other and leave for future generations? What truths will consistently inform your plot? How will you define yourselves in relation to the central patterns of domination in the world, and how will you align on the side of freedom? How rigorously will you face your own past with all its warts?

If your field is literature, for example, and you are interested in the pastorale as a form in Western civilization, how central will Georgia be to your vision? Not Walden woods, or the Bois du Bologne, or Arcady, but your President's home state? In 1941, it produced the following statement by Billie Holiday:

> Southern trees bear a strange fruit
> Blood on the leaves and blood at the root
> Black bodies swinging in the Southern breeze
> Strange fruit, hanging from the poplar trees.
> Pastoral scene of the gallant South
> The bulging eyes, the twisted mouth

Smell of magnolias, sweet and fresh
Then the sudden smell of burning flesh
Here is a fruit for the crows to pluck
For the rain to gather, for the wind to suck
For the sun to rot, for the tree to drop
Here is a strange and bitter crop.[2]

What will you do with that? Will you let the academy dismiss it as literature because it is a song? Degrade it as history because of its creator's social origins? Or ignore it politically because it contains no explicitly "feminist" statement? Will you teach it in its own terms—which is to say, educate yourselves to what its terms are?

Are you willing to go further, to "Portrait in Georgia," and deal with the historical and cultural implications of what the face and form of white women evoke to Jean Toomer, who writes in 1923:

Hair-braided chestnut, coiled like a lyncher's rope,
Eyes—fagots,
Lips—old scars, or the first red blisters,
Breath—the last sweet scent of cane,
And her slim body, white as the ash of black flesh after flame.[3]

Will you treat that as the exception, or the rule? And after making that decision, in what context will you accept the new "first lady of the land" as a sister? If you are redefining the canon, in what pantheon will you place Nina Simone?

If your field is history, and you are interested in the persistence of the social division of labor inherited from plantation economy, what status will you accord Bessie Smith's *Washwoman's Blues* as a historical document? What importance will you assign to the cultural expression: "Lord I do more work than 40-11 Gold Dust twins." And the washwoman's aspiration: "Rather be a scullion, cookin' in some white folk's yard; I could eat up plenty, wouldn't have to work so hard." And will you feel confident quoting her and Bessie Jackson against Herb Guttman in assessing the consciousness of black women as they made the transition from rural to urban circumstances?

What weight will you give Emma Shield's account of the structure of the tobacco industry, and how will you unearth the consciousness that flowed between black and white women under the following conditions:

Negro women are employed exclusively in the rehandling of tobacco, preparatory to its actual manufacture. Operations in the manufacture of cigars and cigarettes are performed exclusively by white women workers. Negro women workers are absolutely barred from any opportunity for employment on the manufacturing operations. The striking differences in working conditions which these occupational divisions provoke are further facilitated by the absolute isolation of Negro workers from white in separate buildings. . . . It is not unusual to find the white women workers occupying the new modern sanitary parts of the factory and the Negro women workers in the old sections which the management has decided to be beyond the hope of any improvement.[4]

The principles of exclusion, isolation, and marginalization are consciously built into that part of the production process black women are allowed to do. The persistence of a colonial division in the heart of a capitalist setting here is the fundamental structural reality conditioning the relations between black and white women.

As a labor historian, you may go on to discover that, as more privileged victims in the industrial process, white women's economic role vis-à-vis black women consistently has been the work force breaking into production at the point when its organization is in transition from a semifeudal, patriarchal mode to an industrialized one. White women are then in the position of paving the way for black women's entry into those jobs just at the point when necessary skill levels decline, speed-up becomes routine, and the interchangeability and easy replacement of workers becomes rationalized. Food processing and office work are two labor-intensive examples. And, conversely, when specifically arduous or culturally onerous conditions of labor, considered "off-limits" to white women, come under improved regulation, the black women traditionally employed there get displaced. The whole area of domestic labor, which under capitalism has developed its own hierarchal organization, is the clearest expression of this pattern.

Domestic labor means cooking, cleaning, washing, ironing, and the care of those who consume the products of that work. As socialized processes under capitalism, that labor market translation of those activities is personal service, restaurant and hotel work, and laundry work. In the post–World War I period, when black and white women both lived through the experiences of filling the vacancies in production left by departing soldiers, the "return to normalcy" in domestic labor looked as follows:

> With the fixing of the minimum wage in the hotels, restaurants, etc., at $16.50 for a forty-eight hour week, and the increasing number of white women, Negro women were to a very large extent displaced. Wages for domestic service for the rank and file have fallen in the past twelve months (of 1921) from $10 a week without any laundry to $7 and $8 with laundry work.
>
> Only two of the Washington, D.C. laundries are today paying the minimum wage. The average wage in the other laundries is $9 per week and a few workers get as little as $6. Ninety percent of these laundry

workers are Negro women. As soon as some of the laundries began to fear that they would be forced to pay the minimum wage they began to ask the employment bureau about the possibility of obtaining white girls. Now that they are not paying the minimum wage they are perfectly satisfied with Negro women.[5]

We could continue in this vein. The question is, will you?

If your field is anthropology, how will you extend the work of Zora Neale Hurston? If your field is law, what will you say about Scottsboro and Emmett Till, Inez Garcia and Joanne Little? If you are a social scientist, or a "communications specialist," what status will you give to "gossip" and "commiseration"? If you are a home economist, will you produce studies on the functions of the kitchen in immigrant, slave, and Latin communities in the United States? And what new categories of meaning will you develop to help people distinguish between cooking and eating? If your field is biology, how will you effectively combat the genetics of Schokley, Jensen, and Hernstein? Or in medicine, what relationship will you establish with the following account of midwifery:

> The wives and daughters of workers and farmers rely on folk remedies, some of them extremely dangerous—parsley, anise and other vegetable extracts, phosphorous potions made out of the ground-up head of matches. And then there is a kind of midwife. ... Always available through the female grapevine, she charges little and she will never betray your secret. Often she is sympathetic, a poor woman helping other poor women. Her operating room is often her kitchen. Her usual method is to insert into the uterus a probe a little larger than a needle. The probe is left in the uterus, after which miscarriage follows—sometimes accompanied by infection, sometimes attended by death.[6]

How will your work help alter these conditions?

Beyond the search for heroines and transcendent moments of victory, what will you do with everyday life? And, once you decide all these things, will you put your findings in a form to be of use to a woman with five children who works the night shift in a bakery?

The question is this: how will you refuse to let the academy separate the dead from the living, and then, yourselves, declare allegiance to life? As teachers, scholars, and students, how available will you make your knowledge to others as tools of their own liberation?

This is not a call for mindless activism, but rather, for engaged scholarship. These are not new questions. But they must be answered anew by every generation whose minds and energies are bent in the direction of the future. It is a pathway that has its perils.

In pursuing the imperatives suggested by this orientation, many of us have been forced outside the university's walls. But we continue to work. For many of us who have gotten pushed out of the traditional academic settings in the past ten years, and for many who did not succeed in pushing their way in, pedagogy has become peripatetic. We go where invited, under auspices where we usually must critique, in hopes of making contacts that will be useful at some future date. At best, this activity feels like swimming in the sea of the people; at worst, it's treading water. And while, through years of practice, many of us have arrived at principles of effectively sharing knowledge, the present circumstances call for fresh thinking and quick study.

Our teaching opportunities mut be created—in conference, private homes, buses, offices, churches, the streets. Sometimes they involve three or four days of intensive, round-the-clock interaction with hundreds gathered together. More often, they are meetings of two, three, five people who may or may not have previous knowledge of each other but who share a common situation. Our intervention is meant to break through the anonymous character, the isolation in the midst of thousands, that most people regard as "normal." It requires meeting masses of people on their turf, and on their terms. Interaction. Not "lectures to" or "reading about" or "observations of"—but *working with*. It requires participating in the rhythms of their daily lives with the object of giving greater coherence and articulation to that experience, as it is lived. It is a process that does not fit neatly into a 50-minute hour or a disciplinary definition of "field of study" or a classroom on a campus.

For those who define this as our life work, the present exclusionary trend in the academy is a spur to activity. Rescinded open admissions policies, budgetary cutbacks, curtailed veterans' benefits, and faculty layoffs have demanded that new contexts for meeting be developed. Those who want to learn and those who want to teach are finding each other through media other than the classroom.

While you have the temporary luxury of libraries and archives to sustain you in a conversation with one another, and the leisure to consult a common set of references, we carry our texts in our heads and on our backs. Those we hope to influence must be struck with the truth, applicability, orginality, and familiarity of our formulations in passing. *Our wit must stick and have the veracity of experience digested, not just books well-remembered. We teach in the world.*

The roadwork demanded is gruelling. We sleep while sitting and stand while eating. And we must answer for the consequences of our theories in action.

Let's say we want to interact with women. Our critical appreciation of their home life must embrace iridescent icons, clear plastic sofa covers, curling irons, prizefighting, the fine print in a UAW contract, and a work schedule that may allow Thursday and every other Sunday off. Abstract declarations of sisterly solidarity in these situations won't do. We must have a perspective on automatic cookie-cutters, modular auto assembly, and silicone surgery and, at some point, relate all of them to commodity fetishism under capitalism. We must be able to explain the consciousness of Jane Fonda in *Klute*, of Elizabeth Ray and Margo St. James (and even throw in a comment about white slavery in the Victorian era)—not in a semester, but in a half an hour and on a moment's notice. When hard questions are put to us, we cannot say, with smugness, "That is not my field"; we can only say, "I don't know."

We must have a stock of stories to tell—the funnier, the better—in an idiom that draws us and our subjects closer together. Over coffee. Over kitchen tables. In employment offices where women stand and wait for hours only to be told they didn't bring the right papers to qualify for relief.

We must demonstrate the capacity to organize the information we get from people in ways which help all of us move toward wholeness. That is what our education should enable us to do.

Our academic training is of little help. Everything that the bourgeois university has succeeded in disassembling (by department, division, period, class, race, and status), we must bring together again. That is the imperative of consciousness raising that I and those like me, in Detroit, and elsewhere, experience as we go about our work. It is what's waiting for you if you have anything beyond self-satisfaction in mind. It cannot be accomplished in four years, or deemed successful by a committee after oral and written exams. Some of its dimensions are suggested in remarks made by Fidel during a visit to Chile before the coup:

> This is a tiring, arduous trip not because of the lack of oxygen in the pampas where the saltpeter mines are located, or the lack of humidity in the North, or too much rain or cold in the South but because it entails an endless pilgrimage, without any physical or mental rest. At times it is a lonely trip. One would like to arrive in a place and have three professors who would brief one, in a matter of minutes, on the history of where one is and thus have a certain degree of reference to back up one's statements when faced with these problems. But as life would have it, we have to tackle our task as travelers all by ourselves in these circumstances.[7]

If women's studies does anything, it should act as a bridge to make that journey easier and less lonely. We need the resource that your situation can provide. That is why I say, "Rapunzel, let down your hair." Make it a rope for your own descent from the tower to the earth; from the house to the world; from isolation to community; from bondage to freedom. Struggle where you are in ways we can use. By whatever means necessary. And for the empowerment of us all.

NOTES

1. Michele Russell, "Erased, Debased and Encased," *College English*, 1969.
2. Billie Holiday, "Strange Fruit," a recording.
3. Jean Toomer, *Cane* (New York: Liveright, 1951).
4. Emma L. Shields, "The Tobacco Workers," *Black Women in White America* (New York: Vintage,1973), p. 253.
5. Elizabeth Ross Haynes, "Two Million Women at Work," *Black Women in White America*, p. 256.
6. Ellen Cantaro, "Abortion in Italy."
7. *Fidel in Chile* (New York: Monthly Review Press, 1971).

Staying Alive

Nancy Hartsock

*Gray is the color of work without purpose or end, and the cancer of
hopelessness creeping through the gut.*

—Marge Piercy, To Be of Use

*You're there just to filter people and filter telephone calls. . . . You're
treated like a piece of equipment, like the telephone. You come in at nine,
you open the door, you look at the piece of machinery, you plug in the
headpiece. That's how my day begins. You tremble when you hear the
first ring. After that, it's sort of downhill. . . .*

*I don't have much contact with people. You can't see them. You don't
know if they're laughing, if they're being satirical or being kind. So your
conversations become very abrupt. I notice that in talking to people. My
conversations would be very short and clipped, in short sentences, the
way I talk to people all day on the telephone. . . . When I'm talking to
someone at work, the telephone rings and the conversation is inter-
rupted. So I never bother finishing sentences or finishing thoughts. I
always have this feeling of interruption. . . . There isn't a ten minute
break in the whole day that's quiet. . . . You can't think, you can't even
finish a letter. So you do quickie things, like read a chapter in a short
story. It has to be short term stuff. . . . I always dream I'm alone and
things are quiet. I call it the land of no-phone, where there isn't any
machine telling me where I have to be every minute. The machine dictates. This crummy little machine with buttons on it–you've got to be
there to hear it, but it pulls you. You know you're not doing anything, not
doing a hell of a lot for anyone. Your job doesn't mean anything. Because
you're just a little machine. A monkey could do what I do. It's really
unfair to ask someone to do that.*

I don't know what I'd like to do. That's what hurts the most. That's

111

why I can't quit the job. I really don't know what talents I may have. And I don't know where to go to find out. I've been fostered so long at school and I didn't have time to think about it.

—*Studs Terkel,* Working

Whether we work for wages or not, most of us have come to accept that we work because we must. We know that the time we spend on things important to us must somehow be found outside the time we work to stay alive. We have forgotten that work is in fact fundamental to our development as human beings, that it is a source of our sense of accomplishment, and an important aspect of our sense of self.

Work is an especially important question for feminists since in our capitalist and patriarchal society the work that women do goes unrecognized, whether it is done for wages or not. Housework is not defined as work at all, but rather as a "natural" activity, or an expression of love. Only in the last few years have women as a group demanded that housework be recognized as important work. Women who work for wages simply have two jobs—the one, though unimportant and temporary, recognized as work, and the other, completely unrecognized.

The liberation of women—and all human beings—depends on understanding that work is essential to our development as individuals and on creating new places in our lives for our work. We must develop a new conception of work itself. To begin this process, we must clarify what is wrong with the capitalist and patriarchal organization of work and define the requirements of *human* work. We must critically evaluate the ways we are structuring work in feminist organizations, where we can experiment, and invent ways to use our work for our development as human beings.

Estranged Labor

The receptionist has described the way most of us feel about our work—that it is not important and that the pace is often set by machines or by people who are not involved in the work itself. Work is something we must do, however painful. In our society, work is, almost by definition, something we cannot enjoy. Time at work is time we do not have for ourselves—time when creativity is cut off, time when our activity is structured by rules set down by others. The increasing use of unskilled labor (or more precisely, the skills everyone is taught in public schools), and the increasing application of scientific management techniques in manufacturing, the office, and even the home (as home economics) all contribute to the feeling that many jobs could be done by machines and that people should not have to do them. In these respects, housework does not differ fundamentally from women's wage work. Housewives too experience the isolation described by the receptionist, while the phrase "just a housewife" expresses the cultural devaluation of housework.

The work most of us do has been described by Marx as estranged labor—time and activity taken from us and used against us. Work that should be used for our growth as well-rounded human beings is used instead to diminish us, to make us feel like machines. Estranged labor distorts our lives in a number of ways, most of them illustrated by the receptionist's description of her work.* She expresses what Marx described as our separation from our own activity at work when she says, "the machine dictates. This crummy little machine with buttons on it," so that "you can't think."[1] We are not in control of our actions during the time we work; our time belongs to those who have the money to buy our time. Women's time in particular is not our own but is almost always controlled by men. Our time is not our own even away from work. The rhythms of estranged labor infect our leisure time as well; our work exhausts us, and we need time to recover from it. As a result we spend much of our leisure time in passive activities—watching television, listening to the radio, or sleeping.

In addition, Marx pointed out that our work separates us from others, preventing real communication with our fellow workers. Often our work separates us physically from others. Some manufacturers deliberately put working stations too far apart for conversation among employees. But just as often, we are kept from real contact with others not by actual physical barriers but by roles, status differences, and hierarchies. The receptionist points out that although she is surrounded by people, she has little contact with them. Competition on the job also separates us from others. We are forced into situations in which our own promotion or raise means that someone else cannot advance, situations where we can benefit only by another's loss.

Patriarchy, too, in giving men more power over women, separates us from real contact with other human beings. And here, too, the patterns of our lives at work invade our leisure as well. The receptionist says, "I never answer the phone at home. It carries over. The way I talk to people has changed. Even when my mother calls, I don't talk to her very long. I want to see people to talk to them. But now, when I see them, I talk to them like I was talking on the telephone. . . . I don't know what's happened."[2]

---

*All this is more true for working- and lower-class women than for middle-class professional women. Women who are lawyers, for example, have much more control over their work, but the patterns that are so clear for most women (whether we work for wages or not) also structure and limit the ability of any woman to control her own work.

Finally, estranged labor prevents us from developing as well-rounded people and keeps us from participating in the life of the community as a whole. Marx argued that rather than participating in community work for joint purposes, our survival as individuals becomes primary for us, and prevents us from recognizing our common interests.[3] Our own activity, especially our actions in our work, separates us from other people and from the people we ourselves could become. We work only because we must earn enough money to satisfy our physical needs. Yet by working only to survive, we are participating in our own destruction as real, social individuals. Worst of all, even though we recognize the dehumanization our work forces on us, we are powerless as individuals to do anything about it. Patriarchy and capitalism work together to define "women's work" as suited only to creatures of limited talent and ambition; the sex segregation of the labor market ensures that women's work will be especially dehumanizing. The receptionist speaks for most of us when she says she doesn't know what she wants to do. We all have talents we are not developing but we don't really know what they are. As she says, we haven't really had the chance to find out.

Work: The Central Human Activity

Because of the perverted shape of work in a patriarchal, capitalist society, we have forgotten that work is a central human activity, the activity through which the self-creation of human beings is accomplished.[4] Work is a definition of what it is to be human—a striving first to meet physical needs and later to realize all our human potentialities. Marx argues that our practical activity, or work in the largest sense, is so fundamental that social reality itself is made up of human activity (work).[5]

Our work produces both our material existence and our consciousness. Both consciousness and material life grow out of our efforts to satisfy physical needs, a process that leads to the production of new needs. These efforts, however, are more than the simple production of physical existence. They make up a "definite mode of life." "As individuals express their life, so they are. What they are, therefore, coincides with their production, both with *what* they produce and *with how* they produce. The nature of individuals thus depends on the material conditions determining their production."[6] Here individuality must be understood as a social phenomenon, that human existence in all its forms must be seen as the product of human activity—that is, activity and consciousness "both in their content and in their *mode of existence,* are *social: social* activity and *social* mind."[7]

Finally, Marx argued that the realization of all human potential is possible only as and when human beings as a group develop their powers and that these powers can be realized only through the cooperative action of all people over time.[8] Thus, although it is human work that structures the social world, the structure is imposed not by individuals but by generations, each building on the work of those who came before. Fully developed individuals, then, are products of human work over the course of history.[9]

As we saw, however, capitalism perverted human work, has distorted the self-creation of real individuals. The fact that a few use the time of a majority for their own profit or their own pleasure makes work into a means to life rather than life itself. The work we do has become estranged labor; and as a result, our humanity itself is diminished. Our work has become a barrier to our self-creation, to the expansion and realization of our potential as human beings. Work in a capitalist and patriarchal society means that in our work and in our leisure we do not affirm but deny ourselves; we are not content but unhappy; we do not develop our own capacities, but destroy our bodies and ruin our minds.[10]

By contrast, creative work could be understood as play, and as an expression of ourselves. "In creative work as well as genuine play, exhaustion is not deadening. . . . When one selects the object of work, determines its method, and creates its configuration, the consciousness of time tends to disappear. While clock-watching is a characteristic disease of those burdened with alienated labor, [when we work creatively], we lose ourselves, and cease to measure our activities in so many units of minutes and hours. . . ."[11]

Alternatives to Estranged Labor

The perversion of our work, then, is the perversion of our lives as a whole. Thus our liberation requires that we recapture our work. Ultimately we can do this only by reordering society as a whole and directing it away from domination, competition, and the isolation of women from each other. What would work be like in such a society? What models can we look to for guidance about ways to reorganize work?

We know that a feminist restructuring of work must avoid the monotonous jobs with little possibility of becoming more creative and the fragmentation of people through the organization of work into repetitive and unskilled tasks. Although we have some ideas about what such a reorganization of work would look like, the real redefinition of work can occur only in practice. While our alternative institutions cannot fully succeed so long as we live in a society based on private profit rather than public good—a society in which work and human development are polar opposites—feminist organizations provide a framework within which to experiment. The organizations we build are an integral part of the process of creating political change and, in the long run, can perhaps serve as proving grounds for new institutions.

Some examples of alternatives to estranged labor occur in science fiction. There are worlds, for example, in which high status relieves one from the necessity to consume and provides a chance to work. To move up in that world means to move from a life of high consumption to a life of low consumption and work. In *The Female Man*, Joanna Russ describes a world where no one works more than three hours at a time on any one job except in emergencies, and the workweek is only sixteen hours. Yet, she says, Whilewayans work all the time. Marge Piercy, in *Woman on the Edge of Time*, shows us a future in which all the work is done by machines, and women no longer bear children. The high level of technology makes it possible for people to work at things that satisfy them, and spend only a small part of their time on supervising and overseeing the production.[12]

There are, however, contemporary alternatives. The Chinese restructuring of work does not depend on changes in technology but rather operates on two assumptions: first, creativity is an aspect of all kinds of labor, and ordinary women and men on ordinary jobs can make innovations and contributions to society that deserve honor and reward; second, all work that helps build a new society should be treated with the new significance previously accorded only to mental labor. The Chinese, too, have been concerned with avoiding the star mentality, and have argued instead that those who are capable of helping others should make that, rather than their own advancement, a priority. Thus, in China, to lead means to be at the *center* of a group rather than in front of others.[13]

These examples of alternatives to estranged labor draw our attention to the organization of the labor process itself. Feminists, in developing new organizational forms, have been concerned with two related factors that structure the estranged labor process in our society—the use of power as domination, both in the workplace and elsewhere, and the separation of mental from manual work. By understanding the ways these two aspects of estranged labor mold the labor process as a whole, we can correct some of the mistakes we have made as a movement and avoid making others in the future.

Power and Political Change

In an article on power, I argued that social theorists have generally conceptualized power as "the ability to compel obedience, or as control and domination."[14] Power must be power over someone—

something possessed, a property of an actor such that he* can alter the will or actions of others in a way which produces results in conformity with his own will.[15] Social theorists have argued that power, like money, is something possessed by an actor that has value in itself as well as being useful for obtaining other valued things.

That power can be compared with money in capitalist society supports Marx's claim that the importance of the market leads to the transformation of all human activity into patterns modeled on monetary transactions.[16] In this society, where human interdependence is fundamentally structured by markets and the exchange of money, power as domination of others (or the use of power to "purchase" certain behavior, which diminishes rather than develops us), is what most of us confront in our work.

There are other definitions of power. Berenice Carroll points out that in *Webster's International Dictionary* (1933), power is first defined as "ability, whether physical, mental, or moral, to act; the faculty of doing or performing something," and is synonymous with "strength, vigor, energy, force, and ability." The words "control" and "domination" do not appear as synonyms.[17] In this definition of power, energy and accomplishment are understood to be satisfying in themselves. This understanding of power is much closer to what the women's movement has sought, and this aspect of power is denied to all but a few women; the experience described by the receptionist can scarcely be characterized as effective interaction with the environment.

Feminists have rightly rejected the use of power as domination and as a property analogous to money, but in practice our lack of clarity about the differences between the two concepts of power has led to difficulties about leadership, strength, and achievement. In general, feminists have not recognized that power understood as energy, strength, and effectiveness need not be the same as power that requires the domination of others.

We must, however, recognize and confront the world of traditional politics in which money and power function in similar ways. For those of us who work in "straight" jobs (whether paid or not) and work part-time in feminist organizations, the confrontation occurs daily. Those of us who work full-time for feminist organizations confront power as domination most often when our organizations try to make changes in the world. Creating political change requires that we set up organizations based on power defined as energy and strength, groups that are structured, not tied to the personality of a single individual, and whose structures do not permit the use of power to dominate others in the group. At the same time, our organi-

---

*"He" and "men" here refer specifically to men and not women.

zations must be effective in a society in which power is a means of making others do what they do not wish to do.

Mental and Manual Labor

One of the characteristics of advanced capitalist society is the separation of the conception of work from its execution.[18] This division between mental and manual labor—which also shapes the process of estranged labor—is an expression of the power relations between the rulers and the ruled, and is closely related to the concept of power as domination. Having power and dominating others is commonly associated with conceptual or mental work; subordination, with execution, or with manual (routine) work. Women form a disproportionate number of those who do routine work and rarely are insiders in capitalist rituals and symbols of know-how.

As the Chinese have recognized, subordination and lack of creativity are not features of routine work itself but rather are aspects of the socialist relations within which the work takes place. A feminist restructuring of work requires creating a situation in which thinking and doing, planning and routine work, are parts of the work each of us does; it requires creating a work situation in which we can both develop ourselves and transform the external world. Our work itself would provide us with satisfaction and with the knowledge that we were learning and growing. It would be an expression of our own individuality and power in the world.

The Development of a Feminist Workplace

Specific questions about how to restructure the labor process can be grouped under the two general headings of problems of power and problems about the division between mental and manual labor. Attention to these two factors can provide several specific guidelines. First, overcoming the domination of a few over the majority of workers in an organization requires that we have control over our own time and activity. Second, we need to develop possibilities for cooperative rather than competitive and isolated work; we need to develop ways for people to work together on problems rather than for one (perhaps more experienced) person to give orders to another.

We need to recognize the importance of enabling people to become fully developed rather than one-sided. We need to make sure that women can learn new skills well enough to innovate and improve on what they have been taught. We need to make space for changes in interests and skills over time. We need to include elements of both mental and manual work, both planning and routine execution, in every job we create. Finally, we must recognize the importance of responsibility as a source of power (energy) for individual members of feminist organizations. To have responsibility for a project means to have the respect of others in the group, and usually means as well that we must develop our capacities to fulfill that responsibility. The lines of responsibility must be clear, and unless the organization is large, they will often end with a single individual. Having responsibility for some parts of the work done by a group allows us not only to see our own accomplishments but also to expand ourselves by sharing in the accomplishments of others.[19] We are not superwomen, able to do everything. Only by sharing in the different accomplishments of others can we participate in the activities of all women.

Collectives and Cooperatives Work

Given these general guidelines, how should we evaluate one of the most common forms of the organization of work—the collective? Here I am concerned about one type of collective—a group that insists that the work done by each member should be fundamentally the same. This kind of organization is widespread in the women's movement, although not all groups that call themselves collectives function in this way. For example, the Olivia Records collective maintains all lines of individual responsibility for different areas of work.[20]

Just as the women's movement erred in its almost universal condemnation of leaders—and its mistaken identification of women who achieved with those who wanted to dominate—we have, through working in collectives, many times simply reacted against the separation of conception from execution. Collective work is our answer to the isolation, competitiveness, and the monotony of the routine work forced on us in capitalist workplaces. But collectives can at the same time reproduce some of the worst features of estranged labor— the separation of the worker from her own activity, the loss of control over her work, and the separation from real cooperative work—that is, work *with* rather than simply beside others. It can cut us off from real growth as individuals. This happens when collectives reproduce power as domination of others and at the same time reintroduce the division between conception and execution.

Informal rather than formal domination of some members of the collective by others often results from the attempt to avoid hierarchal domination by avoiding formal structure altogether. What is in theory the control of the entire group over its work becomes in fact the domination of some members of the group by others. Some members of the group lose control over their work to those who are more aggressive, although perhaps not more skilled. Also, informal decision making, which assumes that every collective member has the same amount to contribute in every area, can result in reducing opportunities for cooperative work, work that recognizes, combines and uses the differing skills and interests of members of the group to create something none could do alone.

In the attempt to make sure that every task is done by every member of the group, those who were less involved in setting up particular tasks are deprived of a sense of accomplishment—a sense that their activity is an individual and unique expression of who they are, a contribution to the group from which the group as a whole can benefit. By rotating all members through the various tasks of the group, and by insisting that every member of a collective do every activity that the group as a whole is engaged in, the collective, in practice, treats its members as interchangeable and equivalent parts. It reproduces the assembly line of the modern factory, but instead of running the work past the people, people are run past the work.

We are not all equally capable of planning and doing every task of the groups in which we are involved, although we may have some special skills in a particular area. For example, while I am incapable of doing layout or paste-up for *Quest*, I am a competent editor. If much of the work done by one member of the collective has been designed and planned by someone else, the accomplishment and creativity involved in designing a system for doing routine work is not possible. Instead, the tasks are already planned and one learns new operations, planned by someone else. The separation between conception and execution has not been overcome.

One reply to this criticism is that learning skills is important and that collectives provide a place to learn new skills. While we can agree that women very much need to learn new skills, it takes time to reach the point where we can be creative with a new skill. We need to *learn* skills rather than simply try out new things. One of the best ways to learn a skill completely is to be entrusted with full responsibility for one or more aspects of the operation.

In sum, my criticism of this form of collective work is that it is simply a reaction against being forced by the capitalist, patriarchal organization of work to do a single task over and over again. Requiring each of us to do everything is not a creative response and cannot provide a real alternative to estranged labor. A creative response allowing us to move toward unalienated labor requires that we examine the root causes rather than the surface appearances of estranged labor in our society. We should recognize, for example, that learning skills by working for long periods of time on one aspect of the activities of a group does not necessarily produce the estranged labor of capitalist society. If we recognize that the problem is not simply doing one kind of work for a long period of time but rather results from the social relations that surround the work process—power as domination of others, and the separation of conception from execution in our work—we can respond to the real problems of work in feminist organizations. Thus, learning skills means not only learning the physical operations involved in a particular kind of work but learning how to organize and set up that work in the best way—from the perspectives both of efficiency and of self-development.

Conclusions: The Fragility of Alternatives

Even if we correctly identify the factors that structure the labor process in our society, the alternatives we construct can be only very tenuous. Work in feminist organizations will exist in the tension between reformism and conformity on the one hand and simple reaction to work in our society on the other. Our strategies for change and the internal organization of work must grow out of the tension between using our organizations as instruments for both taking and transforming power in a society structured by power understood only as domination and using our organizations to build models for a society based on power understood as energy and initiative. Work in feminist organizations must be a way of expressing and sharing with others who we are and what we can do, a means of developing ourselves, as well as a place to contribute to the struggle for liberation. There are real pressures to reproduce the patterns of estranged labor in the interests of efficiency and taking power. At the same time, there are pressures to oppose estranged labor by insisting that each of us do every job. We can develop correct strategies only by critically examining the practical work we have done as we attempt to maintain organizations in which power is recognized as energy and in which we work to overcome the divisions between mental and manual labor.

NOTES

1. Studs Terkel, *Working* (New York: Pantheon, 1972), p. 30.
2. Ibid.
3. Karl Marx, *Economic and Philosophic Manuscripts of 1844*, ed. Dirk Struik (New York: International Publishers, 1964), pp. 112–13. The account of alienation is taken from pp. 106–19.
4. Herbert Marcuse, *Studies in Critical Philosophy*, tr. Joris De Bres (Boston: Beacon Press, 1973), p. 14; Karl Marx, *1844 Manuscripts*, pp. 113, 188.
5. Karl Marx, *Capital* (New York: International Publishers, 1967), 1:183–84.
6. Karl Marx and Frederick Engels, *The German Ideology*, ed. C. J. Arthur, (New York: International Publishers, 1970), pp. 42, 59.

7. Karl Marx, *1844 Manuscripts*, p. 137.
8. Ibid., p. 17.
9. Karl Marx, *The Grundrisse*, tr. Martin Nicolaus (Middlesex, England: Penguin, 1973), p. 162.
10. Marx, *1844 Manuscripts*, p. 110.
11. Stanley Aronowitz, *False Promises* (New York: McGraw-Hill, 1973), p. 62.
12. Respectively, Frederick Pohl, "The Midas Plague," in *The Science Fiction Hall of Fame*, ed. Ben Bova (New York: Avon, 1973); Joanna Russ, *The Female Man* (New York: Bantam, 1975), pp. 53–56; and Marge Piercy, *Woman on the Edge of Time*. (New York: Knopf, 1976).
13. See Marilyn Young, "Introduction," *Signs* 2, no. 1 (Autumn 1976): 2, and Mary Sheridan, "Young Women Leaders," *Signs* 2, no. 1 (Autumn 1976): 66.
14. "Political Change: Two Perspectives on Power," *Quest* 1, no. 1 (Summer 1974): 10–25.
15. See Bertrand Russell, *Power, A New Social Analysis* (N.P., 1936), p. 35, cited by Anthony de Crespigny and Alan Wertheimer, *Contemporary Political Theory* (New York: Atherton Press, 1970), p. 22; Harold Lasswell and Abrahan Kaplan, *Power and Society* (New Haven: Yale University Press, 1950), p. 76; Talcott Parsons, "On The Concept of Political Power," in *Political Power*, ed. Roderick Bell, David V. Edwards, and R. Harrison Wagner (New York: Free Press, 1969), p. 256.
16. Marx, *Grundrisse*, p. 65.
17. Berenice Carroll, "Peace Research: The Cult of Power" (paper presented to the American Sociological Association, Denver, Colorado, (September 1971), pp. 6–7.
18. Harry Braverman, *Labor and Monopoly Capital* (New York: Monthly Review Press), especially pp. 70–121.
19. As Marx put it, "I would have been for you the mediator between you and the species and thus been acknowledged and felt by you as a completion of your own essence and a necessary part of yourself and have thus realized that I am confirmed both in your thought and in your love. In my expression of my life I would have fashioned your expression of your life, and thus in my own activity have realized my own essence, my human, communal essence." In David McLellan, *The Thought of Karl Marx* (New York: Viking, 1969), p. 32.
20. Ginny Berson, "Olivia: We Don't Just Process Records," *Sister* 7, no. 2 (December–January 1976): 8–9.

PART THREE

Feminist Perspectives on Class

In this part, on Feminist Perspectives on Class, we analyze the relations among class, race, and gender as part of the continuing development of a multiclass and race feminist theory and practice. Some articles explore the effects of class on the way women live, work, and think in connection with the problems class poses for feminist practice. Others investigate the relationship between patriarchy and capitalism, and the adequacy of orthodox Marxism as a base for feminist theory and practice.

Class Realities: Create a New Power Base

Karen Kollias

The women's movement has been defined as an educated, white middle-class one, and for most of its participants, this definition holds true. The most obvious reason for this is that its middle-class originators organized around needs and experiences that reflected their background. Nevertheless, there are feminist organizers from lower- and working-class backgrounds, and some of us have tried to integrate class consciousness and class-oriented issues into the women's movement—but not with much success.

If a truly representative feminist organization is to be created, then we must find concrete ways to incorporate class and race issues in a clear ideology. But so far, these topics have been misunderstood, forgotten, ignored, or misused. As a result, action around these issues has been minimal and in many cases has caused further splits within the movement.

To be an effective tool for social, political, and economic change, the women's movement must know how to utilize money, power, and organization. While these skills often are lacking among middle- and upper-class women, they are part of the lives of lower- and working-class women. Economic conditions have forced many of us to develop strong self-concepts, roots for group identity, and the responsibility of accountable leadership.

The movement has a lot to learn from lower- and working-class women, whether or not they are feminists. But, until the movement can project an analysis of feminism that exposes the ways capitalism and racism further divide and oppress women, it cannot expect our further participation.

I work from three assumptions: both white and nonwhite lower-

125

and working-class women need the women's movement to further their struggles for change; the movement has to act on class and race issues to create a powerful base for change for all women; and these struggles must create a society that doesn't depend on anyone's oppression.

This article defines three commonly lumped together groups—the lower class, the working class, and the working poor; it shows how strong self-concepts, a group identity, and leadership qualities develop from class experiences and create a certain perception of the power structure; it points out how the movement has been classist and racist in its theories and strategies; and finally, it provides some suggestions for ways feminists can deal with class and race in developing an effective political organization.

What We Need to Understand

Theoreticians, from the Old Left to present-day liberals, as well as many "class-conscious" people, see all who are neither upper nor middle class as the masses or the working class. My purpose is to distinguish among these classes in order to show the necessary and consistently overlooked *positive* qualities such women often possess. I cannot account for *all* lower- and working-class women, or provide "the definition" of these three groups. Nor do I examine the weaknesses supposedly inherent in these class experiences—too much has been said about them already. Instead, I congratulate our strengths.

One critical distinction among the working class, the working poor, and the primarily urban lower class is that for the working class, upward mobility is possible; for the working poor and the lower class, the chances for upward mobility are slim. Family and economic experiences are most important in shaping women's lives. I therefore focus on them while examining class differences among women, showing how varying experiences mold their perceptions of society.

The Working-Class Family

Most working-class families are supported primarily by men. The jobs available to these men are fairly secure, often unionized, and require some level of marketable skill. At the same time, they offer little or no room for intellectual challenge and advancement—and, hardly ever, for power. The family income can vary widely, depending on unions and skills, but often it is sufficient to meet immediate needs as well as modest desires.

Higher education is usually reserved for men. Community colleges and state universities may be possible for some women, but the reality for women is most often a high school degree and possibly a secretarial or vocational school. Most working-class women are married and mothers long before a middle-class woman receives her B.A.

A reasonable economic level often leads to the means for upward mobility. Parents consciously push their children to "be more" and will put out more than they can afford for higher education if the opportunity arises. They identify with middle-class families in consumption patterns and by living outside industrial areas. In their struggle for social acceptance they are likely to emphasize the differences between themselves and the lower classes.

For the women, running the home is the clearly defined role regardless of other activities. Economically, she may not have to work, but she often does so to help in the struggle for upward mobility. Her attentions and efforts are spent primarily in the home as wife and mother. From a limited study of southwest Chicago's working-class women, Kathleen McCourt notes that they were quick to state not only that their husbands and children weren't overlooked in favor of community activities, but in fact, that she

> still has dinner on the table every night at the right time. She still keeps her house neat and clean. She still supervises her children. No matter how important the women may perceive their working in the community to be, it is defined within the household as secondary. It is not sufficiently important that the traditional distribution of household chores be re-aligned to make more room for it.[1]

The mother is the controlling force within the family. She mediates between the institutions (church, school, city government) and her family; she provides moral support to a husband who feels powerless, alienated, and unimportant in his job; she assesses the larger society and provides both some of the money (if she works) and most of the direction in the family's move to identify with the middle classes; she keeps the family out of the danger of economic hardship by close management and distribution of its income; plus she coordinates all the domestic chores.

The Working-Poor Family

Working-poor families are usually supported by the unskilled, male or female, who are relatively insecure because they are not unionized. Since fewer males are heads of households, many women must support their families alone, on low wages from exhausting service jobs, such as waitresses, sales clerks, or domestic workers. Many hold down two jobs, one of which (like sewing or ironing) can be done at home. All the income is needed for day-to-day necessities, so there is little left over for upward mobility.

A high school education is common, but working-poor children may be forced to drop out of school to get a job to help support the family. It is usually the women who are expected to quit school. Sometimes dropouts finish high school at night, but because of economic need, marriage, or both, night school often is not possible or considered vital. Higher education is seldom available and given less stress than in the working class.

Working-poor families lack the money to relocate and often stay in the same urban communities for generations unless forced out. Even though their housing is usually poor, the common conditions of the neighborhood, as well as family roots, have the potential to create strong bonds.

The options for women are few, virtually ensuring early marriage—in an effort to start over, or more simply, because there are no other choices. Since finances require her to work, the working-poor mother has little time or energy to devote to her children's "proper" socialization. Children are raised more independently than those of the working class and grow up quickly, soon finding themselves with most of the responsibilities of running the home, particularly if they are female.

Working-poor women, starting at an early age, are used to making decisions that affect others and have had to develop confidence in their ability to confront day-to-day responsibilities. They have to provide needed income, often alone, as well as provide family security and physical welfare. They tend to be strong because they have survived hard economic realities; this is particularly true for those who cannot depend on men as an additional means of security or support.

The Lower-Class Family

Lower-class family existence is characterized by a continuous daily struggle; employment is usually temporary, unstable, and undesirable. While most lower-class families are headed by women, these women do not have any real control over their situation. They are responsible for raising their families by themselves, and many are dependent on welfare for their income. Johnnie Tillmon, National Welfare Rights Organization spokeswoman, describes the welfare system:

> A.F.D.C. (Aid to Families with Dependent Children) is like a super-sexist marriage. You trade in a man for the man. But you can't divorce him if he treats you bad. He can divorce you, of course, cut you off anytime he wants. But in that case, he keeps the kids, not you.[2]

Lower-class women must take whatever work they can find to try to meet expenses—usually unskilled, unorganizable jobs that lack stability or possibilities for advancement. Many such jobs mean long night shifts. Since capitalism, racism, and sexism are interrelated, an extremely large percentage of lower-class families are nonwhite. While female-headed lower-class families have the least financial resources for handling crises (medical disabilities, break-ins, rapes, drugs, etc.), they are most vulnerable to them.

The very young are left alone with other children or with older relatives. Children are responsible for themselves and for others very early; educational opportunities are inadequate and uninspiring. Those in school are often forced to drop out to find work, or feel the uselessness of any education that cannot provide immediate cash security. There is little emphasis on dating and romance, but many younger women see pregnancy or marriage as a way out. Daily struggle is their education more often than not.

So noticeably absent are male heads that lower-class urban areas often look like female communities. Female children see their mothers as the root of the family—a model of strength—unlike their middle-class counterparts.

In addition to economic hardships, lower-class women face constant bourgeois criticism: they are "unfit mothers" for leaving the children unattended if they find a job, or "lazy bitches sucking off the system" when they stay home to care for the children. Struggle means fighting to survive, standing up against these "moral" attacks, and not taking anything for granted. The lower-class woman has to surface all her strengths to survive and, in the process, develop other positive qualities as well.

The further the family is from general social benefits—a good income, a secure and meaningful job—the more dominant are the women. These conditions create the experience necessary for confronting and potentially changing the system. This also illustrates a relationship between class, sex, and race in relation to the power structure.

What We Need to Learn

The objective economic conditions in all three of these classes are neither pleasant nor desirable. However, they have generated some strengths and attitudes that are essential for understanding and confronting the power structure: a strong self-concept, group identity, and accountable leadership, all of which are closely related and therefore provide continuous, cyclical support to one other. Strong self-concepts help build a trusted group identity, which, in turn, provides accountable leaders. Similarly, strong leadership can project strong self-concepts and instill the roots for group identity.

Self-Concept

A political movement will project the strength and confidence of its representatives through their self-concepts. And clearly, self-concept is determined by one's life experiences and how one handles objective life conditions. But while the movement states that women must be strong, many feminists fear strong women and label those with assertive, confident personalities as "too aggressive."

Lower- and working-class women have been forced to surface their strengths in order to survive, and often have had to assume responsibility for others as well. While most women have some element of strength within them, many simply haven't had to develop it, because of their comfort and economic security.

One of the major issues of the women's movement has been to eliminate women's weakness and replace it with confident independence. This is partly because middle-class women who have some kind of protector (a successful husband or father) feel a lack of control over their own lives and have felt the need to organize around that. This is valid within its own class context.

Middle-class models of strength have primarily been men, and strength is usually equated with power. Lower- and working-class women, especially nonwhite women, on the other hand, have seldom been able to depend on someone else for their decisions or maintenance. The process of taking active control over their lives, and of influencing those close to them, has given them a lifetime of experience with decision making of the most basic nature—survival. This decision making becomes part of what makes for a strong self-concept.

In a system run by men, for men, decisive power is naturally equated with men. This, perhaps, explains some middle-class women's fear of a decisive, strong female. But in a system or subsystem in which women make decisions, decisive power doesn't assume undesirable connotations. For the only "masculine" attribute of power comes from the perception that now certain men control how things are run; power *per se* isn't inherently negative. This can be translated into a political goal: *women want not only to achieve certain rights within a system, but also to get a part of the decision-making power governing that system.*

It follows, then, that women with strong self-concepts should be models for women seeking that confidence. This doesn't mean that poor women should be idolized. It does mean that a woman might find both a motive and a model for expanding her self-concept through the influence of these women. However, this strength should not be mistaken for economic control, which is much harder to achieve while capitalism still exists.

Group Identity

Group identity allows for commitment, risk taking, accountability, and the establishment of mutual trust. These attributes are vital for groups seeking to be a unified political force. Group identity doesn't just happen; certain objective economic and social conditions are instrumental in helping diverse individuals unite in tight bonds. Sex, class, and race differences are conditions that can be consciously utilized to create a powerful political base.

The concept "sisterhood is powerful" was an attempt to ground feminism in a strong group identity. It didn't catch on as widely as was hoped, primarily for the reason offered by the San Diego Women's Studies Program:

> It (sisterhood) came from women in the movement who were mainly white, middle class women. They believed that all women were our sisters. Seeing the commonality of their oppression for the first time, they realized that what they had gone through was not unique or crazy but had a common social base. This made them gloss over differences that were real differences in women's social realities (class, race, sexual preference). Given the fact that this idea came from white, middle class women, it is reflective of their attempt to gloss over differences rather than to deal with them.[3]

It was just too simple.

Consciousness raising and feminist therapy groups were two tools that might have provided roots for group identity in the movement, but they were successful with only a small number of women. They, too, overlooked some important considerations: not only should they be planned politically but they should provide and encourage space to act *out* of one's group identity, and their reasons for existing needed to be more apparent.

Some groups of women have a group identity, and more important, have succeeded in utilizing it. Out-of-the-closet lesbians have created strong bonds of group identity based on their sexuality. Their solidarity comes from the need to depend upon one another for survival, because coming out is a political risk. This provides them with a closer understanding of woman's class identification in general. Genuine love and passion for women helps strengthen the lesbian's self-concept and give her a deepened respect for and trust of women.

Black, lower- and working-class women, as a result of pressing economic problems, are likely to establish roots for identity with one another out of common necessity. This form of group identity is potentially powerful: the necessities they're after are *nonnegotiable*. Survival demands watching out and caring for their families, neighbors, and friends; these shared responsibilities strengthen group identity.

These two groups illustrate that if feminism is to strengthen a sense of group identity in women, it must allow for flexibility and work with the *differences* among women rather than ignoring them to get to the similarities. Women who work on race and/or class demands should not be criticized as "not feminist enough," but supported for being strong women at work on change. If the women's movement doesn't recognize these differences, it will never acquire a large basis for group identity. If it does, it has the potential to be a revolutionary coalition of organized, strong groups.

Accountable Leadership

Leaders are visible representatives of ideologies to the public. They are also images of strength, direction, and enthusiasm for those working around that ideology. However, the public view of the women's movement has been greatly affected by its lack of acknowledged leaders. Since the movement has stifled the development of leaders, denied their importance, and condemned some visible personalities, the media have created feminist leaders to satisfy media audiences. The majority of these are researchers, authors, and other professionals whose primary relation to the movement is their vocal or written observation. Others are women working on single-issue reforms or government programs designed to improve life within the capitalist system. Most media-created leaders reinforce the white middle-class stereotype of the movement.

Real leaders of an *effective* feminist organization must be able to combine diverse issues and make them relevant to many different women. In addition, they must deal accountably with issues that affect some women, but not necessarily all, such as the needs of lower- and working-class women, lesbians, and nonwhites, as well as those of the straight, white, middle class. Leaders are needed who begin with the assumption that everything must change, including governing social institutions, if everyone is to be free.

Accountability to and identity with a broad spectrum of women, and practical experience in utilizing and gaining power, are essential for leaders. In certain respects, nonwhite and poor women have a head-start in these areas. For example, they understand the relation between money and power—a vital quality for good leadership. Contrary to the bourgeois myth that welfare mothers mismanage money, ". . . an AFDC mother's probably got a better head for money than Rockefeller. She has to. She has so little to begin with that she's got to make every penny count if she and her kids are even going to survive."[4] This kind of confrontation with the system forces poor women to see how society operates. Once they are politicized, these women offer new perspectives on how things should be redistributed, providing visions for future alternatives.

Since understanding one form of oppression usually makes it easier to analyze others, the movement should support leaders who are accountable to class and race issues as well as feminism. As Margaret Sloan, a founder of the National Black Feminist Organization, puts it:

> It would be very easy for me if the oppressor would split up the week and say from Monday to Wednesday we are going to mess over her because she's female, and the rest of the week we are going to put her down because she's black . . . but it doesn't happen that way.[5]

The issues of feminism are too closely bound with class and race issues for some strong women to set one aside in favor of the other.

Consequently, a comprehensive political analysis will most likely come from nonwhite lower-class women. As Geraldine Rickman puts it, the black (poor) woman

> has the necessary adaptability, sense of self, and reality orientation. The high risk involved for the black woman as a functioning change agent is equal only to the high stakes to be gained by her. Economically, she is at the bottom of the barrel, and as a group, there's only one way to go—up.[6]

It's no wonder that those of us from lower- or working-class backgrounds, or those who are black, once involved with the women's movement, have taken responsibility for bringing to feminists the issues of class and race.

What We Need to Correct

Rather than list all the shortcomings of the movement, I will point out a few attitudes that have resulted in the exclusion of black and poor women: the "women-as-one-class" analysis; concentration on middle-class-bound demands within the existing system; and socialist feminists and reformist feminists acting out of a bourgeois position.

Much of the movement's political analysis has been developed around a false sense of women's equality: all women are equally oppressed, have an equal number of problems, and can change existing conditions by equal amounts of effort and participation. Rather than attacking the power structure, the women's movement has dealt primarily with sex-role oppression, consciousness raising, and supportive services. When exposed to the public, these often get lost between the feminists who express them and the women who hear them:

> With one exception, nobody I talked with has articulated an understanding of the socialization process and sex role stereotyping that the women's movement is fighting against. Beyond the job sphere, the

movement is perceived as "kookie" or "man-hating" or "women who wish they were men" or "bra-burners."[7]

The movement has been bogged down in abstractions and personal confrontations. There is a lack of organizing around solid economic demands applicable to lower-, working-, and even middle-class women.

For example, Ellen Willis points out that the movement's biggest employment concern has been the lack of career opportunities for *educated* women.[8] Economic demands are coming from the already privileged, requesting the legal authorities to grant them more privileges. Educational reforms have been geared to the college and university levels: higher admission rates, especially to medical and law schools; more programs for women; the establishment of women's studies programs; and so on. But the majority of nonwhite, lower- and working-class women *don't have the power to utilize these benefits because their primary, objective economic conditions haven't changed.*

Socialist feminists are developing a class analysis within feminism. (For analysis and criticism of women's movement, see the *NAM Bulletin*.[9]) Many still relate to mixed socialist groups that instruct them to create feminist caucuses. Even those who organize independent socialist feminist groups maintain Marxist analyses, viewing women as "laborers" in the proletarian sense only. Little consideration is given to lower-class women—particularly welfare recipients, the demands of black women, or the working-class wives who are hard to organize. Many socialist feminists romanticize, but don't understand the daily life experiences, perceptions of society, cultural determinants, and levels of struggle that shape lower- and working-class women. These aren't found in Marxist books of the Left nor are they understood in terms of twentieth-century, highly technological American society.

This oversight stems from the primarily white, educated, middle-class experiences of many socialist feminists. The gap between their daily lives and the lives of women of the other classes makes it difficult for them to act out their theories. Nevertheless, some discussion groups have politicized socialist women around feminism, and vice versa. For example, women in San Diego wrote a good piece on how to identify and combat their own classist and racist attitudes. They stated that though many feminists have "politically correct" ideas and motivations, in daily life they are capable of attitudes oppressive to black, poor, and working-class women.[10]

Reformist women have organized projects around economic demands but lack an overall analysis that includes class issues. These feminists, also primarily middle class, educated, and white, work with the objective of winning minimal concessions from the power structure. Because they have benefited from the system, they merely try to extend its benefits to some of the needy, instead of questioning the validity of capitalism itself—a condescending attitude at the least. Most of their programs concern single-issue demands—ones that the government can meet without flinching.

The majority of reformist women (such as those in NOW's Task Force on Poverty or on various Status of Women commissions) aren't concerned with eliminating classism and racism; they simply help gloss over some "differences" (inequalities). These women haven't felt the necessity for an ideology that settles for nothing less than revolution. In fact, reformist middle-class women may feel threatened by the concrete economic demands of black and poor women because they have some privileges to lose.

What We Need to Do

The feminist movement must commit itself to the absolute *necessity* of an economic and social revolution if it is serious about adequately meeting the needs of nonwhite lower- and working-class women. This, of course, would affect everyone. A majority of feminists still fail to understand the importance of continuous struggle around broadly based issues within a revolutionary context.

Most of the work to determine and activate programs and theories applicable to black and poor women lies ahead. I will mention a few general concepts and specific questions I feel are important in the effort to link class and race issues with the women's movement.

Many women organizers directly affect the lives of women by organizing primarily around economic issues. Beverly Fisher, in a series of radio programs, stated that community women who wouldn't define themselves as feminists actually have a "feminist approach to their organizing."[11] They recognize the strength of women and the issues that will be of greatest concern to the community. Yet many won't affiliate with the women's movement, primarily because of the media's emphasis on the male-female confrontation and because there is no organized structure through which women can state what they need and want from the movement. We need to develop those structures.

Many of the political divisions among women's groups are simple differences in style and not necessarily ideology. Studying the styles of various organizations should strengthen each group and open communication channels; differences in strategies can serve as a basis for sharing and learning more skills. Feminists should assess what groups are organized around which issues and work with those that get things done. Parts of the new feminist ideology we seek may already exist in various forms in other organizations.

Reevaluate Our Demands

We must become conscious of those demands that are either harmful or irrelevant to black and poor women. A push for women's studies in higher education, for example, isn't going to reach those it should unless it opens its doors to women in the community and gives them free access (or offers a sliding scale) to skills building and continuing education. This would help working-class, black, and poor women raise their standard of living and carry out more effective organizing. As the San Diego women noted:

> . . . we know of women's issues that are not anti-capitalist, which in fact hurt rather than help women. Such demands might be increasing the number of women in the military, the police force or in managerial positions. Oppressive institutions are oppressive no matter who staffs them. It is not in the interest of women to participate in the injustice of arresting other women for shoplifting, prostitution or forgery when capitalism has forced women to these things in order to survive.[12]

This puts another challenge to the women's movement—how to secure decent-paying jobs for those who need them, without being forced to oppressive institutions for employment. Some middle-class women can afford to choose their jobs according to morals (and also to be downwardly mobile), but this isn't true for poor women.

Professional women in jobs oppressive to lower- and working-class women must begin to take risks. Social workers, probation officers, and administrators in health, psychiatric, and penal institutions must make demands and use their leverage if they believe they are there in the interests of women. They must expose oppression in these institutions, make demands for change, use their skills and position for women, and urge others to do the same. Unless there is struggle and agitation within, the professions—prison guards of the class system—will not voluntarily change.

For those women who cannot take many political risks, there's the option of sharing financial resources. If women don't have the time or energy to actively participate in feminist organizations, their financial contributions, preferably on a regular basis, should be pooled into a community women's bank, supervised by representatives of women's groups that organize around class- and race-related issues. It is criminal that now (thanks to progressive capitalism) a single woman may make up to $25,000 (not to mention what a man can make) while an AFDC mother is *allowed* to struggle with her family on less than $4,000 yearly. If women are serious about eliminating class inequities, then they had better *start acting out their honest intentions now, not after the revolution*.

Select Tactical Specifics

Lots of issues are actually "women's issues" (e.g., welfare) that the women's movement hasn't acted on. One such issue is public housing. The majority of people forced to live in housing projects are welfare recipients, most often women and children. The government is just as bad as private slumlords. Public housing usually doesn't meet government housing standards: it is the most susceptible to break-ins; women and children are vulnerable to attacks and rapes, and if they protest, evictions are easy to process. Since finding other housing is nearly impossible, many women tolerate unlivable conditions rather than live on the streets. Yet middle- and upper-middle class women haven't paid much attention to housing issues. They are in a position to make demands, contribute resources, and work around community programs in coalitions with other projects (tenants' unions and welfare rights, etc.), and therefore have a great deal of potential for producing change.

Public transportation is another important issue to lower- and working-class women, who usually cannot afford cars. Most cities have inadequate mass transportation: no subways, irregular and expensive buses, unsafe stops, and so on. Many working poor women are subjected to these unsatisfactory conditions. Again, feminists haven't acted on this issue because they don't have to contend with public transportation as part of their survival. Organized women's groups could demand improvements, such as more bus stops and frequently running buses in areas where public housing projects are located. Women in these projects are especially dependent on public transportation to get to government agencies, health clinics, and so on. Women in isolated workplaces should demand that their employers provide transportation to and from their jobs—especially when night shifts are involved. Strong coalitions of various women's groups could gain influence in decisions made about public transportation, and set a precedent for organization around other citizens' issues.

A final problem for women from the lower classes, black and white, is the division between those of us who are feminists and those who aren't. Many of us got involved in the movement through situations not always open to our sisters: decent jobs, upwardly mobile marriages, political participation in overtly sexist groups, or higher education. Our "nonfeminist" sisters feel the difference. Roots must not be forgotten, no matter how painful the memories or how critical of us other feminists may be. It is our responsibility to share any resources (skills, money, property) we may have gained from newly acquired privileges—particularly since it will be a while before most middle- and upper-class women share their resources without feeling they are being used.

These constitute only a few suggestions. There are many others forming in women's heads, and their ideas, courses of action, and programs must be discussed and expanded. This is only the beginning in reevaluating the directions of the women's movement, its class composition, and its inherent relationship to self-concept, forms of power, and new structures of organization.

NOTES

1. Kathleen McCourt, *Politics and the Working-Class Woman: The Case on Chicago's Southwest Side* (Chicago: National Opinion Research Center, July 1972), p. 11.
2. Johnnie Tillmon, "Welfare Is a Woman's Issue," *Ms.* preview issue, Spring 1972, p. 111.
3. San Diego Women's Studies Program, "Working Draft-Socialist-Feminist Paper," in *Three Years of Struggle: A History of the San Diego Women's Studies Program* (San Diego: SDSC, May 1973), p. 14.
4. Tillmon, "Welfare," p. 112.
5. Quote by Margaret Sloan appeared in "Words on Women," *Civil Rights Digest*, p. 55.
6. Geraldine Rickman, "A Natural Alliance: the New Role for Black Women," in *Civil Rights Digest*, a quarterly of the U.S. Commission on Civil Rights, Spring 1974, p. 58. This issue is titled "Sexism and Racism: Feminist Perspectives" and contains valuable material. Copies—in bulk or singly—are available without charge by writing to Office of Information and Publications, U.S. Civil Rights Commission, Washington, D.C. 20425.
7. McCourt, *Politics and Working Class*, p. 13.
8. Ellen Willis, "Economic Reality and the Limits of Feminism," *Ms.*, June 1973, p. 91.
9. Women's Caucus, New American Movement, "Notes From a Workshop on Socialist Feminism," *NAM Bulletin*, March–April 1974, p. 48.
10. San Diego Women's Studies Program, "Racism in the Women's Movement," pp. 32–33, and "Ways Petit Bourgeois Women Can Struggle with Biases," pp. 33–36, in *Three Years of Struggle*.
11. *Radio Free Women*, WGTB-FM, Georgetown University. Series on class and the women's movement, leadership, cultural differences, and future visions. Included Beverly Fisher, Karen Kollias, and Dolores Bargowski. Rita Mae Brown on the leadership tape. Series taped in Spring 1973. Tapes available through The Feminist Radio Network, P.O. Box 5537, Washington, D.C. 20016.
12. San Diego Women's Studies Program, *Three Years of Struggle*, p. 13.

Class Attitudes and Professionalism

Mary McKenney

I come from a working-class family that became sub-working class when I was eight. My father became completely disabled by multiple sclerosis in the mid-1950s and the government "supported" our family of five on $66 a month. Before he got sick, my father had worked in a foundry; in fact, all my relatives had working-class jobs. But not understanding anything about social class (we thought we were poor only because of my father's illness), I grew up believing I was part of the middle-class affluent America I read about and saw on TV. I was so out of touch with my real life that in a creative writing class, I portrayed myself as having a businessman for a father, a cocktail-drinking bridge player for a mother, and the problems of a middle-class suburban child. Ironically, this subversion of my real experience helped me escape the life of poverty my parents had led.

I always knew I would go to college; it was my mother's life dream for herself, instilled in me. Living in a small town in the Midwest, and having had a good academic record, I found it wasn't hard for me to be noticed and propelled along the college prep/scholarship/student loan route. Now I have a B.A., a Master's in library science, and a semiprofessional job as a medical copy editor.

Mine is the typical success story that is supposed to make poverty and discrimination sound like excuses for a lack of personal initiative and hard work. The ruling class provides "escape valves" for a small percentage of working-class children to go to college and get low-level managerial, semiprofessional, or even professional jobs—but it ensures that our thinking is changed in the process. The higher we rise economically, the less likely we are to identify with the people we left behind. So we serve two purposes: we can be pointed to as successful products of the democratic system (Diana Ross was born poor, black, and female, but *she* made it), and we can be coopted into putting our energies into that system.

Professionalism

Many educated working-class women who rise into a middle-class income bracket by working in the professional or semiprofessional fields take on middle-class ways and values as well. In my work experience, I have found that one of the major middle-class values—and the one that operates most insidiously in the workplace—is professionalism. As an ideal, professionalism—and the middle-class attitudes that go hand in hand with it—is used to justify the higher status of professionals and other middle-class workers. Professionalism promotes the idea that middle- and upper-class people are entitled to more "challenging," responsible, and rewarding work because they are more intelligent, dedicated, and individualistic. Their jobs seem to bear this out: Doesn't it take brains to be a lawyer? And conversely, if it doesn't take brains to collect garbage, garbage collectors must be unintelligent, or at least lazy. People in San Francisco are outraged that some street sweepers make $17,000 a year (by occupying the crafts category); their fury derives not from simple taxpayers' thrift but from the worker's social position. The amount is only a fraction of top city salaries.

Not all middle-class workers are professionals. But the ideology of professionalism keeps both low-level white-collar workers and semiprofessionals upwardly identified and divided against blue-collar workers. Even skilled laborers gain status from the ideology that says they are better than common workers. Professionalism, then, determines more than the internal dynamics of professions like medicine and law; it ranks the entire hierarchy of jobs according to a status system, ensuring upward identification and "class climbing."

The middle-class "pride of professionalism" is supposed to be an idealistic commitment to others or to the world. But professionalism, ostensibly service-oriented, still provides the means to control others and maintain privilege over them; few people, especially those who are poor and working class, have any control over the services professionals offer or the cost of those services. And we have little opportunity to change this pattern because the professions are closed to those who cannot or will not abide by middle-class rules.

The professions differ from other occupations not only in wages, working conditions, and related factors but also in the degree they are mystified, and consequently in their social rewards and apparent value. The mystification centers around both what professionals do and who can be part of the group; knowledge and skills are closely guarded, and credentials are jealously meted out. Professionals all have "larger questions" that they mull over in their professional journals and at annual conventions. This public but closed discussion sets professionals off as concerned with the more important things, and excludes nonprofessionals from the realm of morality and decision making. The real function of professionalism is further obscured by defining it as doing the best job one can. If this were really the case, all jobs—if well done—would have equal value. Thus a cook in a cafeteria may take pride in her work, but her dedication is not rewarded like that of an upper-middle-class professional. "Doing the best you can at the level you are" (like taking pride in doing housework for love, not money) is part of the ideological justification for economic inequities.

Professionalism is a big issue in the semiprofessional fields (teaching, nursing, librarianship, social work, and so on), where women predominate. The battle cry of the semiprofessionals is "Upgrade!" Their dangerous proximity to clerical or menial work makes them especially susceptible to the syndrome of mystification. In the name of feminism, women in the semiprofessions fight for equal rights, opportunities, and salaries both within their own field and in comparison with the male professions. This tendency extends the feminist message to all women: become doctors, not nurses; businesswomen, not housewives. Middle-class skills are seen as desirable, not strictly because they pay better, but also because they have better value in middle-class terms.

But subprofessionals are fighting a losing battle by aligning themselves with higher-level professionals and trying to upgrade their image. Attempts to upgrade only ensure that the values of the present economic system will be preserved. While semiprofessionals gain higher status and salaries, in the long run their interests are not with the rich and powerful. They don't often control their own working conditions, and their power over the workers they do supervise is limited. So in the end they tend to have the consciousness and ideology of the more powerful sectors *without* their power. Their interests rest with nonprofessional white-collar and blue-collar workers.

Middle-Class Norm

Class lines in the United States are deliberately obscured. Few, especially in the middle class, will believe or admit the degree to which our society is stratified along class lines. While the values and attitudes promoted among us by the higher classes do not in themselves create unequal economic conditions, they do play an invaluable role in rationalizing and disguising the class system.

Ruling-class ideology says we're all middle class, except for certain groups like ethnic minorities. Working-class people are described as "middle class" (or "lower middle class"), "middle income," "middle American," and other terms implying an adequate, stable standard of living. Working-class people, even those below the poverty level, often describe themselves in the same terms, unwilling to take on an identity considered undesirable (just as blacks once denied their blackness).

The idea that the majority of white Americans is economically comfortable is far from the reality. In 1974, 33 percent of white families and 58.7 percent of Third World families were living below the *lowest* of three hypothetical family budgets proposed by the Bureau of Labor Statistics. Fifty-eight percent of white—and 77.7 percent of Third World—families were living below the bureau's very modest "Intermediate" budget.[1]*

I stress the income of whites because liberals and leftists are conditioned to attribute Third World poverty solely to racism, but tend to categorize the white working class as paunchy, contented Archie Bunker types or high-paid union manipulators who've literally bought the American Dream. In fact, workers in higher-paid working-class jobs—carpenters, electricians, mechanics, plumbers, etc.—who are at the lower end of a "middle-class" standard of living ($20,777 for an urban plumber's family of four in 1974), comprised only 1.5 percent of the total work force in 1969 (1.7 percent of the white work force, 0.5 percent of the Third World work force) and only 1.9 percent of the working class itself (2.2 percent of the white working class, 0.5 percent of the Third World working class).[2] In other words, this tiny fraction of workers is portrayed in the middle-class media as "typical."

But despite the statistics, the myth of solidly middle-class America remains. When an image doesn't jibe with reality, there must be a reason. The twin ideologies of the middle-class norm and professionalism obscure real economic differences and allow distinctions between classes to be made on other grounds. If we are all in the middle class economically, each with an equal chance for advancement, then observable differences in status and wealth must stem from other causes, like differences in intelligence, talent, culture, creativity, usefulness, and morality.

---

*Every year, the Bureau of Labor Statistics issues a hypothetical budget for an urban family of four, divided into three income levels. In 1974 the "Lower" budget was $9,198. (A sample item was $146.50 a month for housing; food was $13.28 per week per person.) The "Intermediate" budget was $14,333 with housing $269.67 a month and $17.05 for food per week, per person. In 1974, 33 percent of white American families had an income of less than $10,000; another 25.1 percent lived on more than $10,000 but less than $15,000. For Third World people, 58.7 percent were earning less than $10,000, and another 19 percent made below $15,000.

A middle-class woman said to me that those who rise from the working class to go to college and get good jobs are "the intelligent ones." Although this statement would be obviously racist if directed toward an ethnic minority, it is the prevailing view of the white working class in all social institutions: media, schools, libraries, churches, government.

When confronted with the issue of class, most people point to the hypothetical $20,000-a-year plumber and $20,000-a-year professor, saying that one's income will buy as much as the other's. But financial security and economic potential involve more than annual income. The cultural differences (and economic fringe benefits) between the plumber and the professor are far-reaching, just as the social status and economic potential of a white woman or a minority woman or man is not equal to that of a white man, even when they earn the same salary.

Middle-class people tend to believe either that working-class people are no different, just underprivileged—just as men believe that women are weaker, less fortunate versions of themselves—or that they *are* different but would rather be middle class. Although the working class is certainly upwardly mobile to the extent that they want to have decent things, an education for their children, and a secure retirement, they do not necessarily hunger for the middle-class life. Working-class life is demeaning not because its culture or values are inferior but because of the lack of money, lack of opportunity, lack of job responsibility, lack of respect, lack of power—that is, because of oppressive treatment of the working class by the higher classes (cf. "penis envy").

Working-class people do resent those with money and power; they do know that the middle class is born with a better chance; they do feel pride in doing "hard honest work" rather than pushing papers and controlling people. But at the same time, they believe the myth that economic insecurity is an individual problem, the result of the personal inadequacy of one who doesn't work hard enough, and the myth that working with the mind is more important than working with the hands. There is apology, defensiveness, and contradiction in white working-class people because nowhere is their culture validated, their opinion solicited, or their effort rewarded.[3]

Class Snobbery

Any middle-class attitude that is seen as superior (class snobbery) acts in the same ideological capacity as professionalism and the middle-class norm by disguising the real differences between classes. Professionalism could not exist without class snobbery; but whereas it is often defended, class snobbery is denied even as it is practiced.

Implicit in the view that workers are culturally backward oafs who squander their riches on color TVs, class snobbery has its basis in the belief in the "superiority" of the upper classes. And this snobbery exists not only in the "establishment" but also among the forces that consider themselves "alternative" and supportive of "the workers"—that is, among younger, hip professionals influenced by leftist, feminist, and countercultural beliefs.

We Are More Dedicated

Professionals are supposedly more dedicated, more idealistic than others—not just working for a buck, but people who are truly concerned. Naturally, those who make plenty of money can pursue ideals beyond mere money, while those unimaginative file clerks just do their work and take home their paychecks. A clerk-typist making $500 a month may care less about social programs or intellectual freedom than about her annual raise, but then she's never consulted about these issues. She is no less "dedicated" for being dedicated to survival.[4]

Radical teachers, social workers, lawyers, and other professionals often raise valid issues that affect us all, but it is unreasonable to expect clerical or other workers to rise above their place in the hierarchy to join in a political struggle with people who don't recognize their own material privileges and class biases. Similarly, middle-class women in lower-level jobs often identify with broader issues; their background makes them more willing and able to risk "shit jobs" over political issues. Frequently, they can't understand why their co-workers seem to want to preserve the status quo; they interpret as reactionary certain attitudes they don't understand.

We Are Less Bourgeois

One of the contradictions in our society is that the working class gets dumped on for being "bourgeois"—materialistic, security-conscious, and conventional—all classic definitions of middle-class behavior. Feminists, liberals, and other hip people are opposed to everything that's "straight" or "plastic." But without a class perspective, this approach lumps the working class in with those who actually run the system. Here are some examples of "rejections" of bourgeois values that actually support those values:[5]

- Middle-class feminists often feel superior to women who want to or must wear dresses, makeup, bras, and other survival gear. Middle-class women can often flout dress rules or can afford the more masculine attire that is currently fashionable; working-class women frequently have to work harder to maintain an acceptable feminine image—a "liberated" working-class woman may be considered a slut.
- The romanticization of poverty—and the resulting downward

mobility—is common not only among those who actually drop out of the system but among working professionals and semiprofessionals who disguise their earnings through a downwardly mobile life style (old clothes, communal living, etc.) or find "meaningful" part-time work that offers a comfortable wage.

• Those who think they are defecting from the middle class are always on guard against bourgeois tendencies in themselves and others. It's a form of puritanism. Among most radical and countercultural adherents, one must rationalize (or not get caught) enjoying any kind of mass culture. Depending on the political or esthetic consciousness of the peer group, there is pressure not to watch big league football, eat junk food, play cards, go bowling, watch TV except for "serious" programs, or go to the movies except for "heavy" films. I share the legitimate objections toward what big business tries to shove down our throats, to "plastic" American culture, "consumerism," and so forth. But self-righteously judging the masses of people for not having one's good taste is simply another form of middle-class elitism.

We Are More Liberated

Professional and semiprofessional feminists almost invariably confuse their "liberated" life style with some kind of personal or political choice rather than view it as a privilege of their economic security. In this way, "feminism" becomes just another indicator of middle-class supremacy. Liberation defined as personal freedom from sex roles is a purely middle-class phenomenon. Middle-class women gain by getting some of the jobs their husbands or fathers once monopolized. Middle-class men gain still more by increasing their options to include expressing their feelings, working part-time, or taking nontraditional jobs, and becoming more passive in relation to women and family responsibilities. Working-class women have long been "liberated" to work, but their jobs are not of the responsible, rewarding variety. Working-class men have much less economic and cultural leeway than middle-class men for making changes in the traditional family (like part-time jobs for husband and wife) and giving up the little power they have in this world. The idea that working-class men are more sexist than middle-class men is based on the truism that the more money and/or power you have, the less obvious and crude you have to be to fuck over women. Although sex roles certainly exist in the working class, they are more visible there precisely because of economic oppression.

We Are More Liberal

Many feminists emerged from the white male Left where workers are romanticized, like nineteenth-century proletarians coming out of the factories with fists raised. "Workers" are almost always men who work in factories or drive trucks; their wives aren't workers unless they work in factories too; and their daughters are never workers, especially if they go to college. But the Left's view of class is confused and romantic. "Rednecks," for instance, are despised for sitting in front of the boob tube, voting for George Wallace, and being disagreeable when young male revolutionaries come to work in the factory. The working class, engulfed in its contradictions, is dismissed as counterrevolutionary, even as its fictional or historical counterpart is exalted.[6]

The ruling class encourages this portrayal of the working class because it further divides middle-class liberals and leftists from their traditional allies. Most middle-class people have no firsthand knowledge of the working class because their living situations and often their jobs are completely segregated. Their ideas about the working class are governed by media images like "All in the Family" and by commentators and academics who expound on the working class as the new reactionary force in America.[7]

That the working class is the last bastion of racism in this country is a popular view among many observers. Because middle-class people don't themselves have to deal with changing schools and neighborhoods, they can afford to be terribly "tolerant" and abstract about race relations: to be against busing is automatically to be a racist; to be afraid of one's neighborhood turning into a slum is to be a racist. I am not denying that racism may be an important motive, and that there might be a tendency for poor or struggling whites to fear and hate blacks even more for being just below them on the social scale and therefore threatening. But working-class people control only their own feelings, not institutions. It is those in positions of power—the politicians, the bankers, the real estate brokers—who use racism to further their own ends, who profit from containing the rage of black people to certain parts of town, to certain groups of whites. For example, through "redlining," banks can restrict housing loans for blacks to any areas they choose, controlling the racial composition of a neighborhood. Through "blockbusting," real estate agents encourage white residents to sell "while they can" and inflame the fears of people who in many cases have lived in a close-knit ethnic neighborhood all their lives. These people don't want their neighborhood to "turn"—not because they have a particular aversion to black skin but because they know city services will decline, their children will confront racial tensions in the schools, and they—not the bankers, politicians, or intellectuals—will have the consequences of years of racism, poverty, and neglect dumped on their doorsteps.

We Will Define Class

If an educated working-class woman tries to confront middle-class women about class, they tell her that she is not working class any more, so what's the fuss? According to the stereotypes, she can't be working class if she went to college, seems intelligent, cares about larger issues, has good table manners, or likes the arts. If she acts and talks middle class, she must have "become" middle class.[8] But education and a good job don't turn a black person white and they don't negate a white working-class person's background or her continuing financial needs. A working-class woman who borrows money to go to college, then gets a $10,000 teaching job and buys a new car and a new wardrobe, may pass for middle class, but her life experience and outlook are still different, and her economic security is more tenuous than that of a middle-class women in the same apparent (or "poorer") circumstances. Among other things, they may differ in financial responsibilities (especially as relatives age), sources of financial help during unemployment or illness, sources of loans, favors, or gifts (including inheritance), desire for material possessions, and need for security.

If ruling-class ideology says we're all middle class, leftist ideology tends to say we're all working class (except for the bosses). Though it is important for middle-class people to understand that their interests are not with the ruling class but with all working people, it is irresponsible to pretend that common interest is the same as common oppression. To be "for the workers" without examining one's own class background and attitudes, and to claim to be working class by virtue of an abstract "consciousness," leads only to obfuscation of real issues.

Class and Professionalism

By combating both traditional professionalism and the more "progressive" ways of dividing people along class lines, some healthy alliances might be formed between more privileged and less privileged workers. Among working-class women who go to college and enter semiprofessional fields, there is at least a dormant understanding of class and an impetus for changing elitist attitudes among their co-workers who have middle-class backgrounds. The combating of professionalism at this level would do a great deal toward exposing the economic (class) basis of cultural attitudes and realigning the interests of semiprofessionals with the working class.

NOTES

1. U.S. Bureau of Labor Statistics, "Autumn 1974 Urban Family Budgets." For more thorough examinations of the incredibly confusing statistics that relate to class, see Judah Hill, *Class Analysis: United States in the*

1970's (1975), available from P.O.Box 8494, Emeryville, Calif. 94662; and Andrew Levison, *The Working-Class Majority* (New York: Penguin, 1974).

2. U.S. *Statistical Abstracts*, 1975, p. 390.

3. *Class Analysis*, p. 39.

4. For an entire book on the subject, see Richard Sennett and Jonathon Cobb, *The Hidden Injuries of Class* (New York: Random House, 1972).

5. See Charlotte Bunch and Nancy Myron, eds., *Class and Feminism* (Baltimore: Diana Press, 1974), especially Rita Mae Brown, "The Last Straw," and Tasha Petersen, "Gimme Shelter."

6. But see Hill, *Class Analysis*, for an extremely useful breakdown of the class system today, a leftist analysis that takes women, minorities, and the media-inspired image of the "reactionary" worker into account.

7. In one important area—sociology—the trend is finally beginning to change. See especially Lillian Breslow Rubin, *Worlds of Pain: Life in the Working-Class Family* (New York: Basic Books, 1976).

8. See "Ways of Avoiding Class Consciousness," *Women: A Journal of Liberation* 2, no. 3, (1971): 49; and Bunch and Myron, *Class and Feminism*, especially "The Last Straw" and "Revolution Begins at Home" by Charlotte Bunch and Coletta Reid.

Race and Class: Beyond Personal Politics

Beverly Fisher-Manick

Contributing editor: Jackie St. Joan

In this article are segments from a taped discussion among three women active in the National Congress of Neighborhood Women in Brooklyn, New York. The discussion took place in the apartment of Marie Casella, an Italian-American woman with three children. Marie works as the office manager with a community organization in Brooklyn, but was then at home, laid up with a broken leg. Diane Jackson is a black woman with two children, who is working primarily on creating a shelter for battered women in Brooklyn. Maria Fava is a Chicana with four children. Each is enrolled in the community college program offered through the Congress. Often their words speak more directly and clearly than any objective analysis of race and class. I wish to thank them for allowing me to use their experiences to illustrate my thoughts.

Have you ever tried staring at a black dot with a blue ring around it and then shifting your gaze to a blank gray background? You see a greenish ring and sometimes a dot on the supposedly blank background. Your eyes cannot adjust fast enough; they carry over something that isn't there, creating a false image.

This phenomenon, called "negative afterimage," reminds me of what happens with the "politics by experience" on which much of our feminist analysis of race and class is based. We have discussed the class and race attitudes, values, and behavior affecting our interrelationships within the feminist movement. But when we attempt to look *outside* our movement, we carry with us the "afterimage" of our personal experience. We have difficulty seeing the different relationships among people, groups, institutions, and systems. While our personal experiences are valid and may be the best starting point for analysis, we have gotten stuck in them.

Because of this phenomenon, we need to review what we as a movement have been doing on race and class issues—how the scope of our vision of race and class has been limited by our reliance on our personal experience—and look for some ways for evaluating and changing our direction.

Tools to Approach Race, Class, and Culture

Most of this analysis is directed at how feminists have been dealing with the *effects* of racism and classism rather than at the basic causal factors of race and class oppression. I start with the recognition that patriarchy and capitalism are the source of these oppressions. I am not building a case that one or the other is the primary contradiction, but acknowledging both as enemies which must be destroyed. "A class society is, by definition, a society where people do not have equal opportunity, power, security, and access to resources. Oppression is the basis of a class society." Race and class attitudes, values, and behavior "are a product of class oppression, not the cause."[1] Our task as a movement is not to attack people who show the effects of a class and race system, but to attack the causes themselves. In developing theory and strategies for our movement, we must always ask whether we are dealing with the causes or the effects. Answering this question will help determine our priorities and our futures.

Any attempt to integrate analysis concerning race and class faces the danger of making analogies or drawing comparisons that are not always accurate. The class position of black and other minority women, for example, is sometimes problematic. "Black women are keenly aware ... that this society is comprised of haves and have-nots."[2] In other words, by virtue of being black, a woman is also very probably poor or working class. However, we should not overlook the existence of the black middle class. Black and poor are not necessarily synonymous but are often correlative. While I do not believe race and class are intrinsically linked, in the context of this article the same considerations usually apply to both minority women and working- and lower-class women. However, I try to make the distinction between them when appropriate.

Another dimension to treating class and race together is that though class is not immutable, race is. It is possible for women to change their class and/or their class identification, but not their race. Often this difference between race and class can distort discussions of them. We must be careful to distinguish between class-identified and race-identified behavior, oppression, values, and attitudes.

Culture is an additional dimension in an analysis of race and class. Culture is the "belief, thought, speech, action, artifacts, and material traits of a social group."[3] The verb "to culture" means to grow in a prepared medium. Thus, one's culture is the medium in which one grows. My approach is to integrate questions of race, class, and culture. What is black culture? What is a ghetto culture? Does ethnicity affect culture more than class? A social group's culture often is a line of defense against the oppressive majority society. We have developed subcultures within the women's movement to protect us in this way. But as I point out in the next section, our subculture not only protects us but also *isolates* us.

My analysis is based particularly in economics but also in life styles, habits, social tastes, education, family structure, relationships, and types of work as cultural aspects of class and race. A real strength of feminist politics is that we integrate experience rather than isolate it. We view women as whole selves. Our approach challenges patriarchy's divisions of mind and body, heart and head. Neither race nor class exists as an isolated aspect of one's existence. Both affect many aspects of our lives and cannot be separated from our general experience.

The Nonaligned Experience

How have the various sectors of the women's movement dealt with the complex relationships of race, class, and culture? In the nonaligned feminist sector,[4] this process has occurred primarily around class rather than race. Lower- and working-class women began voicing their feelings of alienation or exploitation within the movement after having kept quiet for a long time, unaware that their anger and frustration had anything to do with an issue as supposedly "unfeminist" as class. As women began to come out of their class closets, they found other lower- and working-class women who felt the same way. They gained strength from each other and articulated more loudly and clearly the differences between their own class experiences and those of middle-class women. Throughout this process—which is still continuing—they often had to force the issue, and were sometimes outrageous and self-righteous in their demands that feminists face this conflict. Working-class women felt good in their newly discovered class identities, but middle-class women often were hostile and arrogant, and others were defensive and reactionary. The most common response of middle-class women was guilt, which was usually immobilizing. Some had thought feminist process would be different from typical confrontational process, and asked, "Will the movement survive? *Should* it survive if it can't deal with our differences?"

"To be perfectly honest, women's liberation was not important. I don't appreciate some middle-class woman telling me to get out of the kitchen who didn't know if there was a kitchen there, and didn't know if the struggles of her home related to the struggles of my home. I don't know who they are, they sound far-out and far-fetched. I happen to like my kitchen. I like being a mother and happen to like being a wife. I don't think you have to give up those things to be a liberated person. I think it's just a matter of juggling books; of keeping everybody happy; of knowing there's a place for your husband and there's a place for you in the world. . . . I came from a very proud heritage. I know I'm Italian. It was drummed into me what Italian people are: they keep their home; they keep their husband; they keep everything. It was just a proud thing for me."

Marie Casella

Lesbian Feminist Subculture

In addition to facing newly recognized class "cultures," nonaligned lesbian feminists developed a subculture of their own. Like any oppressed group struggling to assert its power and opposition to the mainstream, lesbian feminists developed a group identity and lifestyle that reinforced them individually and collectively. This subculture is essential for sustenance yet it also contributes to making radical feminist politics a closed system. The subculture's mode of dress, appearance, way of talking, sticking together, insulation from the mainstream, alternative jobs or alternative living arrangements both empower us personally *and* cut us off from other women.

The movement subculture has forged tools to energize, renew, support, and protect its members. These tools are "the beliefs, thoughts, speech, action, artifacts and material traits," which comprise the lesbian feminist subculture. While it protects individuals from the outside, dominant male culture, *in itself it is not political action*. It seldom brings radicals into contact with women as yet unreached by feminism. And, too often, the subculture has not seriously challenged patriarchal institutions. In fact, it often provides a buffer or escape hatch for feminists.

The nonaligned lesbian feminist subculture does not seriously legitimize *political* action to the same extent that it legitimizes action such as music and the arts, which nourish the subculture itself. Political action necessarily requires dealing with the world outside the subculture, often on *its* terms rather than on our own. As a result, even the political theorizing done in the nonaligned movement often suffers from a limited experiential basis that is limited only to the lesbian subculture.

"I started to think that I had to keep my family together. I saw
what happened to my own friends when they were growing up,
in all the homes where there were no fathers. These were the
kids that were junkies; these were the girls who turned out to be
prostitutes. I just thought that if I want an education and any
kind of a future for my children, that I had to keep this man in
the home. How am I gonna raise a son without a father image in
the house? I just felt that I had to take a whole lot of shit,
literally shit, that was happening. I had to take it all in order for
my children to have a family together."

Diane Jackson

Choose Among Your Selves

By ignoring the intricacies of race, class, and culture, the nonaligned
women's movement has often pressured us into choosing among our
various identities. For instance, some are uncomfortable with black
women who won't put the women's movement before the black
movement, or distrustful of lesbians who prefer to work in mixed gay
groups.

The feminist movement has been particularly insensitive to the
feelings of minority women. How many times have we heard white
women get up at a meeting and bemoan the fact that there aren't any
Third World women there? It may be that when they can choose
where and with whom to spend their free time, like us, they may
prefer to be with people of their own cultural identity. After all, most
Third World women have to deal with white people all the time.

The feminist movement often fails to acknowledge the differences
between the power relationships of black and poor men and those of
white, middle- or upper-class men to the system. By ignoring this
power reality, feminists ignore the real experiences of women in these
same groups. They, however, know the differences in power that their
men have compared with white men or middle-class men. Thus, because of our blindness to these political realities, it is difficult for all
women to bridge the gap created by race and class divisions. Most
black and brown women will see a feminist's white skin first, and
then her sex.

The enthusiasm and defensiveness of the lesbian subculture has
alienated many of the very women our movement needs. Both our
actions and our theories reflect their absence. The time has come to
move beyond our subculture. We have to deal with issues we have
previously avoided because they weren't "women's issues" as we defined them—issues that concern the everyday lives of poor, working-
class, and minority women—issues like schools, community control
of child care, police and courts, housing, food stamps. Some of us

"When I had my son, my mother always kept him. She felt that I was young and wild, and I was. I didn't have time for the kid. I used to bring him home on the weekends sometimes. I used to come over to see him when she wouldn't let me take him home with me. Then, two years ago, my mother died and I had to make a decision. We were very close as a family, and I had to decide whether I was gonna move in with my two younger brothers or stay with my husband. And I decided to move in with my younger brothers. That was like a whole big trip, and that was when the fighting started. All my friends were telling me I was really crazy. 'How'd you give up your husband for your family?' But nobody understood like the way we were raised. My mother always told us that we gotta stick together—no matter what. Eventually, my husband moved in with my brothers and me."

Diane Jackson

have to leave the self-created ghettos of women's centers, coffee houses, and project offices to meet women in *their* neighborhoods, homes and jobs. We have to listen more carefully to women who talk differently, and who don't have our "consciousness." Those of us who have lost touch with our personal roots as a result of education and "becoming a feminist" have to reclaim some of our past and bridge the gulf between our old selves and our new selves. We need to remember who we were before we changed, analyze what made us change, *and determine whether it has potential for spurring change in other women*. We must find ways to break down the walls between us and those women who cannot understand us by the language we now speak.

The Socialist Feminist Experience

Socialist feminists have addressed class and race with an emphasis different from the nonaligned feminists, but we share some of the same problems. (While my personal knowledge of socialist feminism is limited, I am aware of some of its weaknesses and of some of its developing strengths in trying to integrate race, class, and culture.) The socialist approach to class is too often abstract and theoretical. It uses terminology that alienates many women—terms such as "masses"—and defines people in relation to means of production. Its politics seem to come from textbooks rather than from experience.

Socialist feminists have failed to explain what dialectical materialism and Marxist theory of capital and wage labor mean in our everyday lives and struggles. In this way, socialism has been as much a failure as "politics by experience" in giving people concrete ideas of what to do next. Where nonaligned feminists have dwelt on a personal, experiential approach, socialist feminists have dwelt on the opposite impersonal, abstract approach.

> "I went to Albany to fight for day care even though I don't believe in day care for me, but for the people who do need it. There's so many people who do need it. I think if somebody needs it, they should get it. I didn't believe in day care for myself, for my children. I felt they should sleep late until they go to kindergarten. They have to get up early most of their lives, to school, to work. I felt it's important that they have a home, to play for a while. I took them to parks; I took them to my friends. I used to have my friends' kids over. I believe in babysitting for the whole neighborhood because I feel it's important that they should have friends. But I also believe in doing everything myself."
>
> **Marie Fava**

On the other hand, socialist feminists have given the women's movement an appreciation of the role of history and of the usefulness of some parts of Marxism to women's struggles. In addition, socialist feminists have added important dimensions to internal movement dialogue on such important questions as feminist businesses, state power, and reformist strategies.

The Reformist Experience

Ironically, reformist groups often focus on issues relating to race and class experiences but stick almost exclusively to seeking reform legislation concerning them. The scope of these reforms includes minimum wage, welfare reform, child care, and household workers' benefits. All these are issues that could have direct results in the lives of lower- and working-class women. However, the weakness of the reformist approach has been the lack of an overall analysis relating these reforms to long-term goals. For example, in Karen DeCrow's "Women's State of the Union Address" in January 1977 she called for federal programs and legislation to end women's oppression. Demands of this kind are received with skepticism by many poor, black, and brown women—women who have already been on the receiving end of social services and programs and have learned to have no faith that these kinds of solutions will produce any lasting improvements in their lives. Federal programs may provide some relief, but they are not the cure. In addition, reformist feminists ignore the fact that the direct dispenser of the services or aid is usually a professional women, who (to the recipient) appears to be the person benefiting most from the program. The client gets a handout with strings attached, and the government worker gets a well-paid job.

When reformist groups advocate "equality with men into the mainstream" as their primary goal while also making bread and butter demands, they undermine their potential support from lower- and working-class and Third World women. They fail to recognize the obvious contradiction inherent in advocating both goals at the same time. It is easy to see why a woman who is the wife of a doctor or lawyer may want into the system on terms equal with men. But to a working-class woman, this idea may not be so attractive. A middle-class woman can hope for the same status, control, comfortable income, and fulfillment she sees the middle-class men around her achieving. But a working-class or minority woman most likely can hope only for what she sees her husband or brother doing: hard, dirty work over which he has little control, a job with little or no status, with meager wages, and probably motivated only by the paycheck rather than by the work itself.

For example, Marie Casella doesn't want her huband's job: "I don't want to do the dirty, shitty job that he does. I'd rather stay here at home and have to struggle to make ends meet, take care of the kids, and take care of the hassles in the neighborhood. I *don't want* to do what he's doing."

Another example of contradictory reform goals is the recent campaign for educational and job training programs for displaced homemakers, carried on at the same time as demands for better pay and job benefits for household workers. "Displaced homemakers" are women "who have lost their jobs through a spouse's death or divorce, and their sense of self-worth and dignity after years as homemakers, economically dependent on their husbands."[5] To advocate job training for one group of women so that they will be able to hire household workers is a slap in the face to a lot of black and brown women, who have seldom been in the position of being "just homemakers." Minority women have usually had to work at the same time as keeping a home and raising children. In fact, often their work (26.9 percent of minority women are employed as household workers)[6] has been cleaning homes for white women who could afford to pay someone to clean for them because they had well-paid husbands.

These examples indicate that white middle-class women fighting for reforms that would improve the lives of lower- and working-class women produce a one-dimensional approach to reforms with complex race, class, and cultural implications. A strictly reformist ideology is not comprehensive enough to analyze the impact of those reforms outside the dominant middle-class culture from which they were developed.

Last year's National Black Feminist Organization–Sagaris Conference on Racism and Sexism was one attempt at struggling in a substantive way with race divisions within the women's movement. The concept of a "mandatory presence" of an antiracist consciousness presents a challenge to our movement: If there aren't women willing and able to confront racism in our movement, then how will an antiracist consciousness be promoted? Can white feminists who have not directly experienced the effects of racism change their racist attitudes, behavior, and values? Will they recognize them as racist, and know how black, brown, red, and yellow women perceive and receive them? Even if they can do that, how does changing our individual values, attitudes, and behavior relate to producing overall societal change?

> "A lot of time I thought that the women's movement was just middle-class white women. Here they are struggling to have equal opportunities with men—to get the same pay as the man. I can't get involved with that. I gotta struggle to get a job, number one. Why should I struggle to get equal salary and equal status as a man? I can't identify with a group that is for middle-class white women. What would a black woman look like saying, 'I'm a women's libber; I believe in equal pay for equal work' when she can't even get a job?"
>
> **Diane Jackson**

Biases of Feminist Ideology

In addition to dealing with race and class as "issues," feminists have developed *concepts and methodologies* that also relate to race and class. These more indirect responses to race and class differences are equally important, because how women perceive what we say and do will affect our view of feminism. If we perceive classism or racism in an idea or process, we will assume it is part of feminism's overall disposition toward other subjects. In other words, we must examine how our political actions and ideas reflect bias. Although this is a topic much written about and discussed at conferences and meetings where black, working-, and lower-class women have articulated their perception of the race and class biases of feminist politics, it is an area in need of more thorough examination. I include it here to stimulate further analysis and development.

Consciousness raising is a valuable cornerstone of feminist theory and practice. But as a verbal exercise in self-examination and group sharing, it is also an approach with a class and race bias. White middle-class women are comfortable with a form that relies mainly on verbal skills. Women of other races and classes are not as comfortable in situations that stress group process. I'm not saying that Third World women and working- and lower-class women can't express themselves verbally. I'm saying that the formality of using CR as a technique for communication is stifling and intimidating to women who are accustomed to expressing themselves in many less defined and directed forms. In addition, many black women see it as typical for white people to make a big deal out of something they do (talking) and call it by some fancy name (consciousness raising).

How we approach issues that we see as affecting women of all races and classes can also demonstrate a lack of awareness of the differences in our lives and theirs. The struggle for abortion and contraception was often criticized by Third World women for lacking demands for maternity care, an end of forced sterilization, and better health care in general for poor women. Although the ideological demand has been "control of our own bodies," the movement's focus was on abortion primarily and birth control secondarily. Racial genocide and population planning by the ruling class is a reality in the lives of Third World and poor women. Many of these women could not trust a movement whose priorities appeared to feed into that reality. Issues such as rape and battered women do cut across race and class lines, but as long as our programs and solutions rely on the police and the courts, we will not have the support of women who have suffered repeatedly at the hands of those very institutions.

The feminist analysis of sexism has placed great emphasis on our being passive and weak as well as exploited and regarded as sex objects. Often, this passive image is an inaccurate description of lower- and working-class women who have "seldom been able to depend on someone else for their decisions and maintenance. The process of taking active control over their lives, and of influencing those close to them, has given them a lifetime of experience with decision making of the most basic nature—survival. This decision making is part of what makes a strong self-concept."[7] It would be self-degrading for a lower-class woman to relate to a movement that characterizes women as weak and dependent. In addition, feminists have dwelt on how the housewife and mother roles oppress women, but have overlooked how those roles often are fulfilling and important to many women. Raising children can be much more rewarding than doing a repetitive, stultifying job for low wages. Many writers have often said that childrearing is how the values and culture of a society are transferred and learned. Certainly this function could be viewed as an important source of power for women to use to affect the future of society.

Feminist analysis of the family has been narrow, with its focus primarily on the *middle-class nuclear* family. It has overlooked the family as perhaps the last barricade between minority and lower-class people and the oppression of the state. The family is often the "soul" of minority and lower-class culture. It provides a shelter for the abuses of a classist, racist, sexist society. It is a place where one knows she can go when she's in trouble or needs help; most often, the mother is the backbone of that shelter. Feminists have examined in detail the oppressive aspects of that role, but have seldom analyzed the function of home and family as a positive force. Minority and lower- and working-class women are sensitive to this feminist imbalance. They feel excluded and put down by our theory on the family.

> "I never felt that I couldn't do anything. I did what I wanted to. I was raised with boys and with girls, and my father never treated the girls as women. I mean he never treated us like the little nanny-pammies in nice little white dresses. We carried bundles; we knocked out walls; we carried plaster. We were treated like boys, too. There was nothing like, 'You were a girl and you did that,' and 'You were a boy and you did this.' We were treated equally.
>
> "Now that I'm laid up with my broken leg, my son has been making beds, vacuuming, dusting, preparing supper. My husband has been pitching in to do the cooking, going to wash and hang up clothes. They try. They're men. I still don't want a man to do my job. Just like I don't want to go out and do his job either. I don't mind. Maybe because we came from a family where men and women do the same things. There were no big, tremendous differences."
>
> **Maria Casella**

Conclusion

In this article, I have tried to define the terms "race," "class," and "culture" in order to present some analysis of how the feminist movement concerns itself with these ideas. I have given some examples and criticisms of race, class, and cultural effects in various sectors of the women's movement over the past ten years. And finally, I have discussed a few of the actual strategies of the women's movement that reflect the barrier between ourselves as political feminists and ourselves as products of a racist, classist, sexist society.

By looking at the shortcomings and limitations of our theory and strategies, perhaps we can see where we should go next. My hope is that this analysis will help us get there.

> "I'm only getting used to people saying 'middle-class.' Being raised in the South, having to work on farms, moving to a basement full of rats, I always thought I was gonna be poor the rest of my life. That I was destined to be poor."
>
> Diane Jackson

NOTES

1. Editorial, "Critique-Class and Feminism," *Women's Press* (Eugene, Oregon), January 1976, p. 8.
2. Brenda Daniels-Eichelberger, "Voices on Black Feminism," *Quest: a feminist quarterly* 3, no. 4 (Spring 1977): 34.
3. *Webster's New Collegiate Dictionary*, 1973 edition.
4. For a definition and discussion of the nonaligned feminist movement, see Charlette Bunch, "Beyond Either/Or: Feminist Options," *Quest: a feminist quarterly* 3, no. 1 (Summer 1976).
5. Karen DeCrow, "The First Women's State of the Union Address," Washington, D.C., 13 January 1977. (Mimeographed.) Speech delivered for the National Organization for Women, Inc., p. 8.
6. U.S. Department of Labor, Employment Standards Administration, Women's Bureau, *1975 Handbook of Women Workers*, Bulletin 297: Government Printing Office, p. 106.
7. Karen Kollias, "Class Realities: Create a New Power Base," *Quest: a feminist quarterly* 1, no. 3 (Winter 1975): 34. Note reprinted here.

Patriarchy and Capitalism

Linda Phelps

In the last few years, the attempted convergence between feminism and socialism has been an important new development within the women's movement and the radical movement as a whole. After a murky period in which the women's movement was divided between various forms of Marxism, radical feminism* and liberal feminism, the idea of socialist feminism has emerged as a hopeful, positive sign of a new level of understanding and synthesis.

To tell the truth, socialist feminism is still very murky. It feels more like the beginning of a new sense of direction than an arrived-at position. Nevertheless, it is an accurate and timely description of where many women find themselves politically: in the tension between socialism and feminism, which is expressed organizationally by the scattering of women calling themselves socialist feminists in separatist groups and mixed organizations with both Marxist and non-Marxist perspectives.

In the recent discussion about the relationship between socialism and feminism, the sexual division of production has emerged as the major theoretical link. Sara Evans described the concept in a NAM discussion bulletin:

> Socialist-feminists understand that the forms of sexism today are rooted in the sexual division of production between the home (women's realm) and the outside workplace (men's realm). The home is the arena of privacy and personal life. The woman at its center embodies the qualities of emotion, nurture, cooperation, submissiveness, and

---

*By radical feminism I mean that form of feminism which defines sexism as the major contradiction and the cause of all other forms of oppression.

morality. The outside workplace provides the arena for public and political life, and men should embody the qualities which it demands: rationality, dominance, competitiveness, and amorality. The ideology which undergirds the sexual division of production thus defines women and men as different kinds of human beings and sexuality as an attraction of polar opposites. In this sense the heterosexual norm is built into the structure of capitalism.[1]

In *Socialist Revolution*, Eli Zaretsky analyzed the split between the personal and the public (political) that has grown out of the capitalist organization of production:

> The overall tendency of capitalist development has been to socialize the basic processes of commodity production—to remove labor from the private efforts of individual families or villages and to centralize it in large-scale corporate units. . . . With the rise of industry, capitalism "split" material production between its socialized forms (the sphere of commodity production) and the private labor performed predominantly by women within the home. In this form male supremacy, which long antedated capitalism, became an institutional part of the capitalist system of production. . . . Just as capitalist development gave rise to the idea of the family as a separate realm from the economy, so it created a "separate" sphere of personal life, seemingly divorced from the mode of production.[2]

This divided structure of capitalist society has been paralleled by a similar division of labor between the socialist and feminist movements. Feminism developed as a separate movement partly because Marxists have largely confined their analysis and their organizing to the "outer" areas of life, like the state and the economy; feminism, and in particular radical feminism, has tried to change the "inner life" while largely ignoring the economic structure. Both movements, Zaretsky argued, failed to understand that the proletarianization of the population and the isolation of women and children from the mainstream of society were twin results of the development of capitalist society.

The idea of the private/public split is a more sophisticated restatement of the popularly understood notion of the separation of work and home. It brings us back to the understanding that women's oppression, as well as working-class or other forms of oppression, are a function of an entire social system, different viewpoints from which to survey the entire society; and it is only with their convergence that a higher and more complete revolutionary synthesis will be achieved.

I consider myself a socialist, but like many other women I am uncomfortable with any mixture of socialism and feminism that takes its departure, a priori, from the assumptions and methods of Marxism,[3] or that assigns the "real" social and economic causal variables to the Marxist analysis of capitalism and leaves the "cultural" sphere to the feminist treatment of sexism. My major objection, however, is that to incorporate feminism into Marxism obscures the crucial task of understanding what sexism is, how it operates, how it is unique. After all that has been written and said, I still do not think we can adequately answer these basic questions. At this point a marriage between Marxism and feminism would be a typical union in which the female partner, lacking a firm identity, gets swallowed up.

The task of socialist feminists therefore becomes doubly difficult: on the one hand to develop a feminist analysis that can delineate the unique character of sexism; on the other hand, to help us understand the whole picture that emerges in an organic fashion for the interaction of many different structures of oppression. A Marxist would argue, of course, that both understandings can come only through the use of the Marxist method, but I say that the Marxist's conceptual apparatus is too tied to a partial understanding of modern society. I would like to offer an alternative model to draw our attention back to some of the crucial questions.

Power and Authority

Every new revolutionary point of view faces the problem of finding concepts adequate to describe its new perceptions. When women began looking at some old familiar experiences from a feminist point of view, such a new set of perceptions was generated; but, like other newly born perspectives, feminism has been operating largely with borrowed concepts. As women, we have been trying to understand our own situation and our own history through a series of analogies: women as caste or colony, women as slave or worker, and (the greatest analogy of all) women as black. We still have no adequate descriptive concepts to help us understand women's roles or the power relations between women and men. *We still do not know what sexism is*.

The relationship between women and men cannot be derived from any other authority relationship: capitalist-worker, white–Third World, master-slave. Of course individual women make up roughly 50 percent of all these categories. But the experience of being oppressed as a female cannot be made to fit any of these. Nor is the experience of female subordination a uniform one. There is not just *one* relationship between women and men. The problem is rather to develop some descriptive concepts that can help us better understand the range of relationships that do occur.

One problem in understanding the variety of relationships between the sexes has been the women's movement's treatment of history. The movement has put forward an image of universal and timeless male dominance: women have always been oppressed. While this may be true, it does not mean that women have never had any power. We know of many societies, including our own, in which some women wield a great deal of power, from owning property to controlling the behavior of others.

To understand this paradox of women's history—apparent universal male dominance but some real female power—it is necessary to make a distinction between "power" and "authority." While power is the simple ability to elicit from another person a behavior not necessarily of her/his own choosing, authority is legitimate power, power that is accepted as valid by those subjected to it. Nonlegitimate power—the kind usually exercised by women—is uncertain, disjointed, and often disguised; legitimate power or authority is continuous and formalized, institutionalized in power arrangements and also in thought patterns.

The distinction between power and authority can be seen in the old sexist joke about the woman who "wears the pants in the family." When we use such an expression, we grudgingly acknowledge the power that a woman temporarily holds and at the same time we remind her that the structure continues to be male. The distinction between power and authority seems essential for any analysis of relationships of dominance and subordination.

We must remember that power and authority are not mutually exclusive. In fact, female power has usually existed within the framework of male authority. In examining universal male authority, we are also dealing with a wide range of behavior in terms of the extent and severity of male dominance. It is a range of behavior whose lower limits make women almost beasts of burden and whose upper limits approach (though never reach) a kind of equality.

Building on these concepts, we can arrive at a working definition of sexism as *a social relationship in which males have authority over females*. If we define sexism in this way, that is, not only as a power relationship but one that is accepted for the most part by females as well as males, then we can understand the basic paradox of women's history without violating its complexity. We can establish the fact of universal male authority, but in understanding the variety in female power, we can search for the dynamic variables of change. By defining sexism as the authority of males over females, we can also incorporate into the term all the social-psychological attitudes, traditions, self-perceptions, and meanings whose acceptance by women has kept them in their place and which have been such an important part of feminist analysis. We can integrate social-psychological reality as part of power relationships instead of removing them to some other plane as "superstructure" or "false consciousness."

If sexism is a social relationship in which males have authority over females, *patriarchy* is a term that describes the whole system of interaction that arises from that basic relationship, just as capitalism is a system built on the relationship between capitalist and worker. Patriarchal and capitalist social relationships are two markedly different ways that human beings have interacted with each other and have built social, political, and economic institutions. Thus, the oppression of women, while shaped in its present form by the rise of capitalism, must be understood first in its precapitalist origins *as a separate, distinctly different form of domination and subordination.* This dual character of sexism—as a precapitalist form and as a capitalist form—makes it quite complex and difficult to analyze. We must first understand the historical roots of sexism and then understand its present form.

Types of Authority

Sexism and capitalism are representative of two larger systems of authority, different in their power dynamics, sources of dependency, types of interaction, ideology of legitimation, and economic underpinnings. These two larger systems are a "traditional" system of authority and a "rational-legal" system of authority. According to Max Weber, a rational system of authority rests on "a belief in the 'legality' of patterns of normative rules and the right of those elevated to authority under such rules to issue commands"—a kind of legal authority. Traditional authority rests on "an established belief in the sanctity of immortal traditions and the legitimacy of the status of those exercising authority under them." "Obedience is owed to the *person* . . . who occupies the traditionally sanctioned position of authority and who is (within its sphere) bound by tradition." The obligation of obedience in a rational legal system is impersonal—something owed to offices, while the obedience owed in a traditional system is personal loyalty defined by tradition.[4]

In this chapter, I am using the terms "patriarchal relations or relationship" in the same way that I defined sexism as the authority relationship of male over female. "The patriarchy" refers to the whole system of male authority and will be explained in more detail later. I use "traditional" relations to describe those status and authority relationships that are organized along patriarchal lines but occur (primarily in preindustrial society but also in part today) between many different types of people and on all levels of society. An example of this kind of relationship in a traditional society would be the relationship in European feudalism in which a landlord or a king would grant either land or partial rights in land to subordinates in exchange for obligations and services that the lord could call upon when needed; a type of relationship that bound two individuals together and went beyond the impersonality and limited nature of the modern business contract. I indicate some of the differences between traditional and rational-legal systems of authority.

Marx analyzed one type of power relationship and the authority patterns that grow out of it: class relationships which come from the ownership and control of the means of production. Marx, by pointing to class relationships, reformulates the concept of rational-legal systems of authority and explicitly recognizes the distinction between rational-legal authority—in which individuals seem free—and traditional, more personal systems of authority—in which personal dependence is clear.

Capitalist relations and the class roles arising from them develop out of a situation where economic resources (along with political and military resources) are far enough developed, in size and density, so that they can be easily appropriated. Patriarchal relations, on the other hand, arise out of the opposite situation, where power resources are varied and dispersed, and where people are in close personal contact, with face-to-face interactions—as in most preindustrial societies and in the structure of resources characteristic of a household.

In contrast to the class roles Marx described as arising from capitalism, relationships in a traditional society are defined and experienced as "status roles." A status role is a complex of rights, obligations, and behaviors conferred on groups over time; it is a social role whose main function is to maintain legal and/or prestige distinctions in the actual relations between people. In modern democratic societies, status can be legally conferred or, as is usually the case, maintained by custom and unspoken rule.

High status tends to coincide with high class position, as those with access to the most resources find themselves able to maintain, or rather create, as standards change, the clearly defined and often exclusive life styles that often make up status. But status is a different concept from class, and except for the highest and lowest positions in a society, class and status are different types of social organization. The position of women is perhaps one of the best examples of the difference between class and status. In the United States today, women have a special status, which takes both a legal form (in terms of jury duty, protective legislation, etc.) and a customary form (in terms of traditional definitions of women as wives and mothers). Different class positions cut across this general "status" of women.

The status relations characteristic of both patriarchal and traditional organization become institutionalized on every level, so that in most preindustrial societies people step into status patterns of interaction established long before they were born and that have little to do with the individual traits of the persons involved. Similarly, today, men and women often interact according to customary roles.

American society for the most part is characterized by a lack of formal behavior patterning. Yet American culture seems to have incorporated along with customary relations between the sexes a strange mixture of traditional deference patterns (wife gives the husband the best place, the best food, is not supposed to contradict him in public, etc.) with a form of romantic chivalry in which men nominally defer to women (man stands when she enters, opens doors, walks on the outside). The difference would seem to be that in chivalry, men "protect" women or through some gesture like raising their hats acknowledge women's frailty or purity. In deferential behavior, the woman acknowledges the superiority and precedence of the man, his work, his goals. Such female behaviors in American society are not formalized deference patterns, but somewhere along the line most women pick up a set of learned behavior through which they are always giving way to men. Patriarchal relations are thus hard to get at because they exist almost unconsciously.

Uses and Limits of Authority

A traditional society encompasses a system of relationships in which people of unequal power and resources and clearly accepted unequal status work and live closely together. By contrast, a capitalist authority system is one where people of unequal resources are separated and segregated, each developing their own subculture and sometimes laboring under the ideological illusion that they are all equal or at least have the inherent opportunity to be so.

Capitalism represents one type of organization within a rational-legal system of authority, just as patriarchal relations are a type of traditionalism. In order for the capitalist economy to function, economic relations had to be abstracted and set free from the mesh of personal ties, rights, and obligations characteristic of traditional society.

Like any system of authority, rational-legal authority is in part an ideology that legitimates existing power relations. In the United States this legitimation is tied to the impartial rule of law. Americans accept authority (when they do) if they understand the rules on which that authority is based and believe that the game is played fairly and is (potentially) open to all.[5] The rules of a workplace or the laws of government characteristic of a rational-legal system of authority are supposed to be universalistic, applying impartially to all persons who come within their domain. A rational system is a leveler, disregarding all special status, in theory at least, giving civil rights to all groups. Of course, in a rational capitalist system, behind the facade of equality for all is the reality, not only of special status groups that are oppressed, but also of a class system.

Rational-legal authority is more than an ideology to mask class oppression, however. It is also a way that power is experienced and carried out and a way that people relate. Rational authority is familiar to us because it is the type of human interaction characteristic of much of modern industrial society—impersonal, objective, rational. It is the set of rules and understandings in terms of which groups, classes, and sexes come together for specific, limited tasks—work, education, "politics," and so forth. It marks not only the way that large groups of people can interact impersonally but also the boundaries attached to the power exercised in these larger arenas. The capitalist exercises authority over the workers, for example, only under specifically defined conditions—as they work in a designated workplace, for specified wages, during certain hours. The workers' private lives are certainly affected by their roles as workers and their experiences on the job, but the capitalist has neither personal rights nor responsibilities for them. This fragmentation of the individual and of authority is an important aspect of the social relations of a rational-legal society and is in sharp contrast to the bonds in a traditional system.

It is this fragmentation that has given rise to the separation of the personal and the public, to the development of "personal life" as an area of fulfillment perceived as being outside work or public life. The impersonality and fragmentation of rational-legal relations leaves people unsatisfied and often unanchored personally. It causes two different responses. Some people preserve and strengthen what remains of patriarchal family and love relations and/or create and cling to "new," sometimes hereditary types of traditional statuses, such as the system of private schools among the ruling classes. A second response to the impersonality of rationalism has been the counterculture life style, which is seen by its participants as existing outside the "system."

While the source of legitimacy in a rational system is law, legitimacy in a traditional system is the sanction of time—not mere habit but the sacredness of time-honored ways. This kind of thinking is hard for most Americans to understand until we realize that it describes the unthinking justification for women's roles. Common-sense thinking about women's roles is particularly characteristic of traditionalism: it is taken for granted—one of the few things in our society accepted in this way—because "it has always been that way." Its origin is unimportant, lost in time. It is simply that way, "natural" (which becomes a biological argument only when pushed to become rational).

Authority in a traditional system has its own dynamic. It is by no means unlimited; rather, it is not clearly specified. In contrast to a "position" in a rational system where authority is confined to specifically designated areas, traditional authority covers all areas where it is not specifically restricted. Those boundaries are, first, the traditional rules and regulations that govern the acceptable conduct of members. Custom puts limits on how far power can go, for example, in wife beating.

In traditional relations, people are seen as unequal but at the same time the relationship is more clearly reciprocal, involving an exchange of services on both sides.* Unlike capitalist relations, higher status in a traditional system carried with it increasing obligations. In illness or during a bad harvest, for example, the upper classes had responsibility to take care of and guide the working people who were part of their sphere of power, just as they did their womenfolk and children.

Power and authority in a traditional system are organized as a system of statuses, designating who can legitimately exercise authority. This hierarchical system of statuses puts another boundary on traditional authority. The severity and contours of male authority differ depending on how it is limited or supported by other authorities in the hierarchy—in the past by the authority of the feudal lord or king; today, by the authority of the state, the educational system, and so on.

Another characteristic of traditional power is a certain amount of arbitrariness, which states that if there are no traditions limiting it, power is exercised by the person in authority by virtue of his superior status, a system that survives today as "male prerogative," or the unbounded contours of the "male ego." In such a system, power is more immediately and personally experienced. Loyalty is due not to the order, the position, or the office but to the person of the master. We often have failed to do justice to the complexity of female-male relations by ignoring this characteristic of patriarchal authority. Much of the power that men have (particularly in precapitalist days, but also in part today) derives from the status of maleness, a hard-to-define but clearly present social reality that cannot be understood by reducing it to the economic function of breadwinner or protector.

Finally, we can understand the difference between the oppression of women and that of workers by noting that the working class passed from traditional to rational authority relations while women underwent a transition within traditional relations. It is this different his-

---

*Because patriarchal relations in the household involve some benefits on both sides (although unequal ones), lesbians and other women not in traditional father-headed families are in a slightly different position, failing to derive the benefits of male-female relations (heterosexual privileges) but also free to be more mobile (insofar as they are allowed to by sexism in the world outside the family).

torical experience with capitalism and its consequences today that is the key to the split between socialism and feminism.

Sources of Patriarchal Authority

What are the sources of male status and female dependency in the patriarchy? While the source of power and authority of the capitalist class is their ownership and control of the means of production, males derive power in patriarchal social relationships from their ability to have greater access to and mediate the resources, rewards, and gratifications of authority structures outside the context of the household. The household is the setting of the economic provision of daily life, but it is not the nature of productive activity either inside or outside the household that is the crucial factor. Studies that have attempted to explore the correlation between women's contribution to productive activity and their status have shown that there is no clear relationship.[6]

The crucial variable in distinguishing men's status from women's seems to be the demographic fact of childbearing and childrearing. It is not only the fact that women give birth but also that they provide nursing and child care that imprisons women as mothers, or potential mothers, within the household's demand for everyday routine. Men, therefore, have greater mobility and range of movement than women, and this mobility lies at the base of male dominance. Christy and T. A. Caine, in a recent paper on the subject, describe the many facets of this difference in power, a power that relates to economic resources, but is more broadly based than that:

> It is the man who can occupy the interface between groups. It is men who discover novel people and goods, renew old acquaintances and control many of the networks of communication. . . . The human pattern of interfacing is such that it is the source of a great deal of power over the distribution of surplus commodities. Not only are men able to seek out surplus commodities, they can also create value in surplus commodities by having the means of converting them into something else. Occupying the interface, males also have access to the different and innovative, again another source of power. It is axiomatic that the capacity to control the distribution of rewards tends to generate a consolidation of power.[7]

It seems a reasonable working hypothesis, then, that the base of women's dependence is contingent on the demands of everyday life as institutionalized by the wider society within the context of the household and that require a tremendous amount of labor, primarily in regard to children and secondarily in terms of everyday maintenance.

I have constructed a model of patriarchy as a structure of authority relations between women and men. What does it tell us about our position as women today and how we got to where we are? It directs our focus first to the nature of our relations with men within the context of the household and then to the ways outside authority structures have influenced that basic relationship, either by reinforcing it or by providing women with alternative sources of power. Women are not oppressed only by the family or household, because the household does not function in isolation from the rest of society. Rather, patriarchy is the whole system of male authority that develops as a result of the interaction of all the structures of a society. As a result, women's secondary status is built into every institution.

Oppression in Two Worlds

The development of capitalism and the differentiation of new rational structures outside the household did not eliminate, but did change, the nature of patriarchal oppression. Capitalism's destruction of traditional society *strengthened* the patriarchy by placing the major resources within the household in the hands of men and by diminishing women's access to resources outside the home; it *weakened* the patriarchy in the long run because it created new structures outside the home that would later enable women to find a place to stand on their own outside the family.

Understanding the contradictions between capitalist and patriarchal spheres (and the contradictions within each sphere) can help us sort out the complex situation of women today. The status of the American woman changes, for example, as she moves back and forth between the conflicting definitions of the rational and the traditional world. How else can we explain why motherhood is both exalted and despised in our culture? Motherhood is one of the highest expressions of devotion in the traditional world, ridiculous in the rational world where its ascriptive status has little to do with rationally measured achievement. In this sense, women are all right as long as they stay in their place. They are tolerated elsewhere. They are tolerated in particular if their activities in the real world are combined with traditional female behavior. The servicing nature of women's traditional roles has become a necessary part of modern society, a sort of social lubricant that makes rational society run more smoothly. In this sense traditional female behavior has itself become rationalized. It is rationalized in the concept of private charity, which is really mothering writ large, involving as it does thousands of organized women volunteers ringing doorbells in their capacity as caring individuals. It is rationalized into "women's jobs" in the role of the secretary, for example, who must be wife and/or mother to the boss as well as employee, as also in the low pay and high expectations for caring placed on teachers, nurses, and social workers.

The contradictions and interactions of capitalist and patriarchal spheres may have strategic implications particularly in terms of the old dilemma of reform versus revolution. In some ways, women are two steps back, oppressed by both capitalist and patriarchal forms of male supremacy. We are imprisoned in traditional definitions of ourselves and for many of us a rational style is the only immediate alternative—whether it be in work, sexual relations, or education. The women's movement should give critical support to rational reforms that help women transcend traditional identities, increase their mobility, and provide room to change. We should withhold support from reforms which rationalize traditional behaviors. Using these criteria, for example, the proposal that women be paid wages by their husbands for work they do in the home would be a backward step because it would rationalize and further institutionalize women's dependence in the home. An alternative proposal—that women receive social security benefits from the government for the work they do at home—carries some of the same dangers but should be supported because it would give women an independent income. Similarly, the ERA will at last secure for women, at least on the books, their equal place in a rational society. Women will be able to experience—and benefit from—the equality of a rational order at the same time that they experience the limits of that equality.

There is always the danger that we will not go far enough, that our roles as wage earners will be just another adjustment or rationalization of our primary patriarchal identities; or that the alternatives we have created in the form of communal living may backfire and be nothing more than a nostalgic return to a simpler, more traditional life where people know their neighbors and women are oppressed as the mothers again.

Our new vision must extract what is good and healthy in both the traditional and the rational world and combine these with hope for what human beings can become. This will be difficult, because we have all been socialized into the hierarchical structures of these two systems and do not know what an alternative would look like. But we are taking the first steps by understanding more clearly what we are trying to change. Through the insights of socialism we began to understand our subordination through large, impersonal structures. Through feminism, we are beginning to grasp the more intimate dimensions of power. Both understandings are necessary for creating a new vision of the future.

NOTES

1. Sara Evans, "Socialist Feminism and NAM: A Political Debate Whose Time Has Come," *NAM Discussion Bulletin*, no. 8 (July–September 1974): 36–37.
2. Eli Zaretsky, "Capitalism, the Family and Personal Life," *Socialist Revolution* 3, nos. 1 and 2 (January–April 1973): 83–84.
3. See Juliet Mitchell's statement that "we should ask the Feminist questions, but try to come up with some Marxist answers," in *Woman's Estate* (New York: Vantage, 1973), p. 99.
4. Max Weber, *The Theory of Social and Economic Organization*, ed. Talcott Parsons (New York: Free Press, 1964), p. 328.
5. Robert Lane, *Political Ideology: Why the American Common Man Believes What He Does* (New York: Free Press of Glencoe, 1962).
6. See Peggy Sanday, "Toward a Theory of the Status of Women," *American Anthropologist*, 1973, p. 75.
7. Christy and T. A. Caine, "The Evolution of Male Dominance Patterns" (paper presented at the 39th Annual Meeting of the Midwest Sociological Society, April 1975).

Do Feminists Need Marxism?

Jane Flax

In the past three years, a tendency has emerged called socialist feminism. Many feminists have argued that it is the most progressive position in feminism today.*

Socialist feminism is not a precise term. Those who consider themselves socialist feminists include female socialists, women who consider imperialism to be the primary contradiction, socialists who see feminism as a way of organizing women into the class struggle, and women who see patriarchy† and class as equal and (to varying degrees) independent sources of women's oppression. The minimum area of agreement seems to be that Marxism has something to teach us about the sources and maintenance of women's oppression and about ways to overcome it. On a theoretical level, this assumption has led to attempts to integrate feminism into Marxism or to reconceptualize one in terms of the other.[1]

Feminists have received strong criticism from both male and female leftists for "dividing the working class," making bourgeois "personal" issues central to political struggle, and so on.

Perhaps the turn to Marxism is to some extent an attempt on the part of feminists to show that they too can do "real" political work and "real" theory. It may be a way of showing that it is "correct" to organize women because they do produce surplus value (through housework), or at least reproduce labor power, which is the precondi-

---

*The most visible organizational manifestation of this tendency was the Socialist Feminist Conference held at Antioch College in July 1975 and attended by 1,600 women.

†Patriarchy means here a system of power relations whereby men dominate women.

174

tion for extracting surplus value. Alternatively, since women constitute an expanding segment of the working class, they can now be seen as significant in the organization of a socialist movement (as workers). Or, socialist feminism allows women to argue that feminism, because it focuses on process, is a valuable *tool* for building revolutionary organizations or revolutionizing the working class.

All these positions implicitly assume that women's lives in and of themselves have little or no revolutionary potential, that women's experience becomes meaningful only when it is related to the class struggle, and that patriarchy is not a relatively autonomous historical force that also determines the character of social relations and human history. In short, socialist feminism suggests that feminists have raised interesting questions and developed forms of organization that must now be integrated into ongoing class struggle.

These issues are considered subordinate to class struggle and have not been taken seriously as a fundamental challenge to the way Marxists understand politics and political change. The real question is whether we accept Marxism as the correct (if flawed) paradigm for comprehending women's oppression or instead call for the development of a new mode of analysis. What, if anything, can Marxism as it stands now teach us about women's oppression, and what is the utility of the Marxist method for feminist analysis?

Problems of Orthodox Marxism

A careful examination of Engels' writing can point up the weaknesses of orthodox Marxist theory* in regard to the analysis of women's oppression. I will not restate Engels' argument in *The Origins of the Family, Private Property and the State*,[2] but rather I will list seven basic problems with his argument and discuss how these problems are related to the general nature of a Marxist approach. Furthermore, I will show that Engels' own theory can be fully comprehended only by integrating an analysis of patriarchy with his work. By relying solely on a history of changes in the mode of production, Engels ignores the specific history of women.

First, Engels takes a sexual division of labor for granted.[3] He assumes that labor has always been divided on the basis of sex and that women have always done household labor. He provides no explanation for why this is the case, and moreover, does not do justice to the fantastic variety of the *content* of work done by women and men; as recent anthropological work shows, child care seems to be the only type of work women do almost universally.[4] A more concrete analysis

*The term orthodox here means a simplistic or mechanistic use of Marx.

of the sexual division of labor in different societies would have high-lighted one crucial fact: whatever women do is considered less valu-able than whatever men do.[5] The orthodox Marxist approach has not explained this fact. Nor does Engels explore the consequences for men, women, and children of the primary responsibility for child care falling on women.

Second, Engels argues that wealth was owned by the gens* and that the gens was matriarchal. But then, how can he argue that cattle became private property of men because they were "heads" of these families?[6] According to more recent anthropological work, agricul-ture and herding developed about the same time, so that the de-velopment of private property in cattle could not in itself be such a radical transformation that it would lead to the overthrow of mother-right (if it ever existed).

This is merely one concrete instance of the larger difficulty of as-suming the existence of a matriarchal society and the primacy of changes in property relations. Engels needs a matriarchy so that it can be overthrown by men—not as men but rather as owners of pri-vate property, or the instruments of labor.[7] That is, the course of history depends on changes in the mode of production and the con-sequent property relations, not on (or as well on) sexual-power rela-tions or the mode of reproduction. For Engels, the family becomes part of the superstructure rather than part of the base. He recognizes the centrality of the "mode of reproduction" but fails to carry out the exploration of sexual politics required to understand it.

Third, also along these lines, if cattle and slaves were such clear signs of wealth, how did the presumably male heads of households claim them? Why did they not belong to women? "Custom"[8] cannot explain why these sources of power could so easily be appropriated by men.

I am led to two possible conclusions: either there never was a ma-triarchy (in which case one cannot explain the oppression of women solely on the basis of changes in production-property relations), or the overthrow of matriarchy was a political as well as economic revo-lution in which men as men subdued or destroyed the privileged (or perhaps equal) position of women for a number of historically possible reasons (such as men discovering their role in reproduction and/or asserting control over reproduction).

Fourth, why should inheritance be such a crucial issue?[9] Engels is reading the present into the past. In gens society, is there any danger to children themselves (would they be outcast, or not be taken care of), or is illegitimacy and/or individual inheritance even a meaningful concept in a matriarchal society? Men must already have been feeling

---

*As used by Engels, "gens" refers to a circle of blood relations in the female line.

excluded from the gens and/or from reproduction, since, as Engels states, in premonogamous marriage systems, only the mother of the child could be known with certainty.[10]

Thus, men might attempt to use children as a means of claiming power and overcoming exclusion, promising protection in return. (As feminists have pointed out, this is one of the oldest protection rackets around—women and children are guaranteed protection by the aggressors—men.) Furthermore, in most cultures, only *sons* can inherit property, not daughters; thus inheritance can be seen as another way of keeping power and property within male control.[11] Alternatively, inheritance could point to the possibility that women and their products (children) were already regarded as property. Indeed, Lévi-Strauss suggests that women were the first form of property and were traded out of their clan to cement relationships between *men* in differing clans. At least initially, such a system must have been instituted and maintained by force.

Fifth, Engels suggests that men wanted their own children to inherit and that this was a reason for overthrowing the then traditional matrilineal order of inheritance. But what is wrong with a sister's children (or anyone else) as inheritors? There must already have been a property/patriarchal system in which children and women were seen as a special sort of property.

This is where the concept and reality of patriarchal privilege become important. Men, according to Engels, would want to retain the power and privilege they held as a result of the original division of labor. Women's natural interest in a restricted birthrate (because childbearing is dangerous and tiring) would oppose men's interest in increasing their power by increasing the amount of property for trade or labor available to them. Restricting births would also reduce men's control over women since women would have more energy for activities other than childbirth and childrearing. In addition, as long as women have children at home, service to children spills over into service to the man (why cook, sew, clean, for example, only for children). Why would anyone want to give up these personal services? So men have an interest in controlling reproduction. At this point, the sexual division of labor becomes an instrument of oppression.

Sixth, Engels argues that the overthrow of mother-right could take place through a simple decree.[12] Wouldn't women be disturbed by being transferred out of their gens upon marriage, thus losing a crucial source of their power? How and by whom could a "simple decree" be issued that descent would in the future be patrilineal? Why would women obey it? Certainly legal doctrines had little meaning in this era and would have had to be backed by other forms of power. Again, the very structure of early social systems seems to point to force being used by men against women, originally for control over scarce resources (children) and later to maintain the privileges the initial system created.

Finally, why did shifts in inheritance of property bring total supremacy to the male? Doesn't this view transfer the present centrality of private property back to "primitive" times? Moreover, there is no reason to think that property owned *by families* would necessitate or lead to male-dominated families. The existence of male domination and private property cannot be explained unless we postulate a whole structure of society in which power derives from and is exercised by *males* as well as by a property-based ruling class. All men are kings in *their* castles, no matter what or who they are in the King's castle.

In short, the dynamic Engels sees centered in property and inheritance must also be grounded in a struggle for power, in the dialectic of sex. Changes in the mode of production are not a sufficient explanation for the overthrow of mother-right. On another level, even though it is doubtful that a matriarchy ever existed, Engels nonetheless needed to postulate one so that he could paradoxically avoid following out the implications of his statement about the modes of production and reproduction. *Women* (communal property) are overthrown by *men* (private property): Engels only examines property relations, not relations between men and women, and hence does not carry out a thorough analysis of the mode of reproduction. In fact, the mode of production and the mode of reproduction are not necessarily in harmony, and contradictions can be overcome by force, by the maintenance of patriarchy, and by realignments of the family, and realignments within the family.

Marx acknowledges this when he discusses "the natural division of labor in the family."[13] Marx means "natural" in a very specific sense (i.e., "uncivilized"). "Natural" is the opposite of "social." So the "natural" division of labor in the family must be based on the capacity of women to bear children, and since they bear them, it is "convenient" (Engels) for them to also raise children. Marx explicitly acknowledges that the distribution of labor and its products is unequal *within* the family and that it is unequal because the man has control over the woman and children and can do with their labor and reproductive power what he wills.

Property is the power of controlling others' labor.[14] Marx does not explain how/why men got this power. Furthermore, he says that the slavery latent in the family is the "nucleus" of later forms of property, which are just higher forms of essentially the same relation. Although the question of how men got this initial power is still unresolved, its existence permits men to gain other, more extensive and elaborate forms of property and power. Thus we can argue that "patriarchal privilege" is both a foundation for ("primitive accumulation"?) and basis of men's economic power. Once the initial act of expropriation (women and children as property) is carried out, men can use their differential power bases to subordinate other men through giftgiving, wifetrading, and the like. To destroy men's privileged position in the family means to take control over our own labor power, and thus it is analogous to removing the privilege of appropriation of surplus value from the capitalist.

In fact, Marx himself seems to be making a similar analogy in his next paragraph when he says

> the division of labor offers us the first example for the fact that man's [woman's] own act [childbearing, labor for the man] becomes an alien power opposed to him [her]—as long as man [woman] remains in natural society, that is, as long as a split exists between the particular and the common interest, and as long as the activity is not voluntarily, but naturally divided. For as soon as labor is distributed, each person has a particular, exclusive area of activity which is imposed on him [her] and from which he [she] cannot escape.[15]

Translated into feminist terms, Marx's argument means that patriarchy is a form of individual expropriation that constricts the possibility of developing a communal form of society. The man's private possession of women and children leads to the antisocial form of private and privatistic families. Nonetheless, the man has an interest in maintaining this form of property; he benefits directly from this inequality. Furthermore, women will remain enslaved as long as they are subject to a "natural" as opposed to "social" division of labor.

Marx does not point out, however, that the division of labor has different consequences for men and women. Men go outside the home; the family is the base from which they can move out. Women remain embedded in the family, and the split which results from the sexual division of labor (particular/common, private/public), reinforces the powerlessness and exploitation of the woman.[16] While historically neither men nor women can escape their exclusive areas of activity, men's sphere has expanded and increased in importance while women's area of activity (the family) has decreased in importance. Men, having committed the first act of expropriation and having accumulated their first property, are free to expand their holdings and power. Women remain slaves.

In addition, Marx has an ambiguous view of the family. He states that "the third circumstance entering into historical development from the very beginning is the fact that men who daily remake their own lives begin to make other men, begin to propagate: [they create] the relation between husband and wife, parents and children, *the family*."[17] Since the two forms of activity to which Marx refers—the production of material life (food, clothing, shelter), and the creation of new needs that arise once the old ones are satisfied—are constitutive of human history, we might assume that the mode of reproduction is just as important as the mode of production itself. Indeed, in the paragraph following, Marx calls the production of persons and the mode of cooperation that accompanies it a "productive force."[18] Marx implies that the family could be treated as the "mode of cooperation" with which the production of persons is allied. At the same time, however, Marx says that the family becomes a "subordinate" relationship as society becomes more complex. This would imply that although historically the family was one of three aspects of historical development, it no longer retains any independence and can only be understood as a subset of some more central, autonomous aspect. However, Marx does not tell us here *what* the family becomes subordinate to or how this occurs—a typical failing of Marxist discussions of the family.

Finally, any mention of women as *women*, or of how their historical development might have proceeded differently from men's, is glaringly absent from Marx's discussion. Indeed, this absence points to the dangers inherent in any analysis of women's oppression that relies solely on a history of the changes in the mode of production. *Without an analysis of patriarchy, women as historically specific beings disappear.*

This is where socialist feminist theory must begin. We must trace the history of the mode of reproduction and its changing forms of social cooperation. We must work out the relation between the mode of reproduction and the mode of production, with special attention to the different experiences of women and men within this history (the dialectics of sex as well as the dialectics of class).

In order to carry out such an analysis, we must overcome the simplistic determinism we have inherited. (Marxists have their equivalent of the Holy Grail—the search for *the* contradiction from which everything else follows.) An analysis of the mode of reproduction requires considering psychological and sexual-political dimensions that remain almost untouched in Marxist literature.

Patriarchal Ideology and Feminist Theory

Georg Lukacs shows us the interaction between self-interest and theoretical unclarity:

> The hegemony of the bourgeoisie really does embrace the whole of society in its own interests (and in this it has had some success). To achieve this it was forced both to develop a coherent theory of economics, politics, and society (which in itself presupposes and amounts to a

"Weltanschauung"),* and also to make conscious and sustain its faith in its own mission to control and organize society.[19]

His words apply to men's protection of their interests as well as to the bourgeoisie. Any ruling group protects its hegemony by making universally valid rules out of currently existing relationships. In addition, however, the ruling group must develop a clear enough grasp of reality to be able to control and manipulate it. A ruling group thus claims objectivity but only elucidates those aspects of relations that are in its interest to know. For example, bourgeois economists could develop laws of the market but could not develop the Marxist labor theory of value or the concept of surplus value. The self-interest of any ruling group must necessarily lead it to ignore the deeper contradictory aspects of reality that underlie the immediately given, and that provide possibilities for revolt and liberation.

Lukacs contrasts the bourgeoisie's need for mystification to the proletariat's need for an analysis of the real social relations underlying the production and exchange of things.[20] He adds a warning that is as relevant to feminists as it is to socialists:

> When the vulgar Marxists detach themselves from this central point of view, i.e., from the point where a proletarian class consciousness arises, they thereby place themselves on the level of consciousness of the bourgeoisie. And that the bourgeoisie fighting on its own ground will prove superior to the proletariat both economically and ideologically can come as a surprise only to a vulgar Marxist.[21]

Feminists must understand that in order to maintain their hegemony, men will attempt to deny or obscure the experiences and insights of women who challenge their privilege and power. Men will deny that they have any special self-interest because in order to maintain hegemony, they must insist that they are speaking for and acting in the interest of society as a whole. If we deny the lessons of our own experience and/or try to fit that experience into categories established by men, we will lose both the meaning of that experience and our struggle for liberation (men cannot be beaten on their own ground).

This means we have to stop "acting like women," by justifying our theory and practice to men. We must stop seeking their approval of what we do. In particular, we must stop proving we are more socialist than they.

Men do not have a monopoly on truth. Indeed, their self-interest keeps them from seeing the totality. The "personal *is* political" because our *experience* drives us both to understand and to transform the present (indeed the two activities must be aspects of each other,

---

*"Weltanschauung" refers to a world view.

integrally connected). If we deny our own experience, if we decide a priori to fit those experiences into categories others have decided are politically correct, we lose the very possibility for comprehending and overcoming our oppression.

In summary, it is the orthodox Marxists who have been insufficiently dialectical, and who have never adopted the standpoint of women. They did not adequately deal with the "woman question," in part because they never really explored reproduction as a crucial moment of history—both in its internal relations and in its relation to the other moments of history. An overly deterministic methodology which focuses exclusively on production in the narrowest sense, will, of necessity, ignore women and the dialectic of sex because women's labor often takes place "outside" the market. Moreover, determinism leads one to focus on things rather than on relations, and patriarchy is above all a social relation.

One cannot ignore the fact that most socialist theorists are men. It is not in their interest to acknowledge the existence of patriarchy. Engels' work is a clear example of the distortions and omissions typical of orthodox Marxists. After the opening chapter of the *Origins*, the book becomes an analysis of the changing nature of production. Reproduction and the family disappear, "hidden from history" indeed.

Historically, socialists have put off women's demands until "after the revolution," or have defined women's demands as particularistic, divisive of the working class, not central to socialist revolution or society. Again, we must ask: Who defines what is central and what is not? On what grounds? Working-class demands are defined by Marx as both particular and universal: this is precisely what defines it as the revolutionary class. Working-class demands as traditionally defined by Marxists speak to transforming the social relations of production. We women must speak to the question of reproduction because in that realm, as well as in production, our labor is being expropriated.

Marxism can help us understand women's oppression only if it is radically reconceptualized. Specifically, we must develop a theory of social relations, and analyze history as the development of social relations.

Marxism can help us understand *one* aspect of social relations: that between the exploiters and the exploited in the realm of production. (It was to understand these relations that Marx developed categories such as surplus value, commodity fetishism, and class.) Furthermore, Marx (and Hegel) developed a method—dialectics—one of the most flexible and richest modes of social analysis. But there are other, equally important aspects of social relations, among them, relations centering around reproduction. Despite his insistence that all history is rooted in concrete human beings, Marx had little to say about these other relations. The categories adequate for comprehending the realm of reproduction have yet to be developed; though reproduction and production are separate but interrelated spheres, it is a mistake to impose categories developed for the comprehension of one directly onto the other.

In developing these new categories, we need to look beyond Marxist theory. Psychoanalysis, structuralism, and phenomenology have provided many valuable possibilities for comprehending the reproduction of social persons, but they often lack a historical dimension. Freud enables us to begin to understand how sex/gender comes to constitute a central element of our very being as persons. Under patriarchy we do not become *a* person but a male or female person. In many ways our gender *is* who we are and this identification goes far deeper than sex roles understood in the sense of socialization or intentional (and easily changed) choices of roles and behavior. The theory of the unconscious, the role of sexuality, and the Oedipus complex, which traces out on an unconscious level the consequences of the domination of the father—all provide a starting point for the analysis of the social relations of reproduction. Structuralism and phenomenology are excellent tools for examining ongoing social relations without falling into the simple determinism characteristic of orthodox Marxism.

We can conceptualize production and reproduction as two spheres of human life and history, constituted by the social relations within them and by the relations of persons to their own biology and to the natural world. These two spheres have historically been related to each other through the family. For this reason, the organization of the family reveals *information* about both spheres, and shows us the attempts people are making to bring these spheres into some sort of harmony. The study of the family can also reveal the contradictions between the demands of production and reproduction. The more disjunctive the nature of production and reproduction become (conceptualized by Marx as the difference between use and exchange value, and by Freud as the conflict between the pleasure and reality principles), the more possible it is for the family to retain an aspect of autonomy and uniqueness. The categories we employ must do justice to these disjunctions, not submerge them.

Conclusion

As feminists, we must not assume that there are Marxist answers to feminist questions. Our history is not the same as men's—neither on an individual nor a collective level. Until we understand the mode of reproduction more thoroughly, we cannot begin to bridge the often discussed gap between Marx and Freud. To comprehend reproduction, we must continue to explicate our experience with the help of psychoanalysis, structuralism, and phenomenology. This is not to deny the interrelation of the world of production and reproduction, or to ignore the fact that we are shaped by both—indeed, we need to retain consciousness of this interrelatedness while carrying on our explorations. We must come to understand how and why men obtained and kept power over women and how this power relation varied historically. We must explore the consequences this relation has for the ways we are constituted as persons. We must learn how power relations interact with and affect relations of production. Finally, we must discover the most effective sources for change.

Marxism alone cannot answer our questions. But if we retain and expand our original insights into our experience as women, we will be operating within the spirit which originally motivated Marx—that history is rooted in human needs and social relations. By confronting Marxism with feminism we require an overcoming, a retaining of the old within the new. What we will create will be neither Marxism nor psychoanalysis, but a much more adequate form of social theory. The concepts used by Marx, Freud, and others are only guidelines along the way, to be retained in a new form within a more integrated and inclusive theory. For now, we have only glimpses of the necessity and possibility of such a theory, through the frustration we encounter in trying to answer feminist questions.

NOTES

1. Juliet Mitchell, *Woman's Estate* (New York: Random House, 1971); Margaret Benston, "The Political Economy of Women's Liberation," *Monthly Review* 21, no. 4 (1969); Eli Zaretsky, "Capitalism, the Family and Personal Life," *Socialist Revolution* 3, nos. 1–3 (1973); and the articles on women's labor in *Radical America* 7, nos. 4–5 (1973). All insist that *in the last instance* contradictions *within* the sphere of production are the crucial determinant of women's status. The radical feminists emphasize patriarchy as either equal to class or as the first form of class oppression, which still underlies all forms of oppression. See Shulamith Firestone, *The Dialectic of Sex* (New York: Bantam, 1971); and Kate Millett, *Sexual Politics* (Garden City, N.Y.: Doubleday, 1970); as well as Barbara Burris, "The Fourth World Manifesto," *Notes from the Third Year*.
2. Frederick Engels, *The Origins of the Family, Private Property, and the State*, ed. Eleanor Burke Leacock (New York: International Publishers, 1972). All citations from Engels refer to this edition.
3. Ibid., p. 119.
4. See, for example, Claude Lévi-Strauss, "The Family," *Man, Culture, and Society*, ed. Harry Shapiro (London: Oxford University Press, n.d.) for the varieties of work done by women in primitive cultures.

5. See Sherry B. Ortner, "Is Female to Male as Nature Is to Culture?" in *Women, Culture, and Society*, ed. Michelle Rosaldo and Louise Lamphere (Stanford: Stanford University Press, 1974), pp. 67–73.
6. Karen Sachs, in Rosaldo and Lamphere, *Women, Culture, and Society*, pp. 211–12.
7. Engels, *Origins of Family*, pp. 119–120.
8. Ibid., p. 119.
9. Ibid., pp. 119–120.
10. Ibid., p. 106.
11. Suzie Olah, "Impolite Questions about Frederick Engels," *A Feminist Journal* 1, no. 1 (March 1970): 4.
12. Engels, *Origins of Family*, p. 120.
13. Karl Marx and Frederick Engels, "The German Ideology," in *Writings of the Young Marx on Philosophy and Society*, ed. Lloyd D. Easton and Kurt H. Guddat (Garden City, N.Y.: Doubleday, 1967), p. 424.
14. Ibid.
15. Ibid. My comments in brackets.
16. For an elaboration of this point, see Michelle Rosaldo, "Theoretical Overview," in Rosaldo and Lamphere, *Women, Culture, and Society*, pp. 23–42.
17. Marx and Engels, "German Ideology," p. 424.
18. Ibid., p. 421.
19. Georg Lukacs, *History and Class Consciousness* (Boston: MIT Press, 1971), pp. 65–66.
20. Ibid., p. 68.
21. Ibid.

PART FOUR

Organizations and Strategies

Our section on Organizations and Strategies considers the many strategic and practical problems that arise in building and maintaining feminist organizations. Underlying all the writing is the question of our need to revise organizational theories to meet the needs of feminist practice. Some specific problems discussed include issues of race in the women's movement, the possibilities and limitations of using reformist techniques to bring about radical change, and the contradictory demands faced by feminist leaders and in feminist workplaces. One article proposes feminist principles for evaluating the financial obligations of women to our movement. A description of the Beguines, a medieval women's community, and a consideration of the feminist possibilities of science fiction provide both historical contrast to these contemporary questions and a vision of alternative worlds.

The Reform Tool Kit

Charlotte Bunch

In recent political discussions among feminists, the question of reform continually comes up. One "revolutionary veteran" states flatly: "What is there to do today that isn't reformist?" Another woman who has worked on women's reforms for four years declares that they are a dead-end and that she has to get out, to go beyond. There is a lot of concern, confusion, and rhetoric about reform and revolution, about our survival as women, and about our fears of cooptation. Often, however, it is hard to discern in these discussions what is really at stake, what is essential for feminists. Some women want to abandon the old terms of "reform," "revolution." I welcome language that clarifies those questions. Until we create the new language, however, we must sort out the old language, examine what has happened, see what the basic issues in the debate are, and determine how we can resolve them.

In this article I begin with a discussion of terms, explore the history of both reform and radical wings of the women's movement, examine the relationship between reform and our long-term goals/strategies, present some criteria for evaluating which reforms are most useful, and discuss conditions necessary for feminists to work on reforms. Certainly there are other ways to approach these questions. Women with different experiences will undoubtedly continue this debate. This paper is an initial probing of the topic, not the final answer.

Reform and Reformism

What is reform? What is reformism? What is revolutionary? Stereotypes for these words abound. Common stereotypes of what is reformist are white middle-class professionals and politicians working to get a bigger piece of the pie for themselves, organizations lobbying for new legislation, or university women creating a comfortable niche called "women's studies." Stereotypes of what is revolutionary tend toward one of two extremes: either bombing and violent takeover of the government or complete withdrawal from the system in order to create a totally separate feminist community.

When we probe these stereotypes, we find that they primarily reflect *style* (how one lives or the comparative virtues of lobbying vs. shooting) and *surface content* (how far out or different it sounds from the way things are now) rather than *substantive content* (how the activity affects different classes of women and what happens to the women working on it) or *ultimate goals* (where the action leads in the long run and how it will get us there). Style is not irrelevant to the processes of change, but it has become too important a factor in our attitudes toward reform. To get beyond these initial stereotypes, we must define reform and examine it in terms of substantive content and goals.

A reform is any proposed change that alters the conditions of life in a particular area, such as within the schools or throughout the legal system. It *re-forms*, or forms anew, the ways things are. It can alter them in a way that is helpful or destructive. A reform, simply put, is a change or a program for change. It can be a change that alters existing male-dominated institutions directly, such as Equal Rights Amendment legislation, or a change through the creation of women's alternative institutions, such as a record company or a health clinic. Reforms or proposed changes can be part of any group's program, whether conservative or revolutionary in ideology.

Reform*ism*, on the other hand, has come to mean a particular ideological position. That position is that women's liberation can be achieved by a series of changes that bring us equality within the existing social, economic, and political order of the United States. Reformism assumes that the interests of women are not in fundamental conflict with the American system and that therefore, through a progression of changes (reforms), it will grant us freedom through equality. By contrast, a radical analysis sees American society rooted in patriarchy, capitalism, and white supremacy and therefore in fundamental conflict with the interests of women; freedom for oppressed groups ultimately does not come through reforms or equality in those systems, but through a total restructuring of the ideology and institutions of the society. I will use this definition of reformism as an ideological position within the women's movement. It is crucial to separate the word "reform"—a change or strategy that might be used by women of varying politics, from "reformism"—a particular politics. The failure to make this separation has been a problem in the women's movement.

Radicals and Reforms

"I thought getting a good job was immoral until I ran out of money," remarked one middle-class feminist as we discussed reforms, class, and feminist revolution.

Generalizations about the history of the women's movement are always controversial. The following observations have been discussed with others but are based on my own experiences in the New Left, women's liberation, and lesbian feminist movements in the past ten years. In the middle and late 1960s, women's liberation grew from two different directions. The National Organization for Women (NOW) and similar groups were explicitly reformist; NOW stated that its purpose was "to bring women into full participation in the mainstream of American society."[1] Such organizations developed programs to bring about this equality.

Meanwhile, other small groups began meeting to discuss female oppression and define goals quite different from equality in the American mainstream. These groups, first called "women's liberation," sought a politics that questioned the whole structure of society. The groups were generally composed of socialists who focused on capitalism, or radical feminists who focused on patriarchy, and sometimes those who tried to combine these two approaches.

Over the past six or seven years, both the reformist and radical trends have developed and changed in many ways, altering and sometimes confusing both their ideologies and their programs. NOW and some reformist groups were forced by the radicals' analysis, by women joining their groups, and by women leaving their groups to deal with more than just "equality." They were challenged to take up issues that originally had been avoided as too controversial, such as abortion and lesbianism.[2] They adopted some radical rhetoric (including the term women's liberation) and a broader program of reforms. But, generally, they continued to operate with an ideology of reformism, not challenging the premises of the whole society and only occasionally moving away from their initial goal of equality within the American mainstream. More conservative women's groups, such as the Business and Professional Women's Club, have worked for reforms that would explicitly bring privilege within existing systems to *some* women, usually white heterosexual middle-class professionals. Such reformist groups aim to get a few women integrated into higher echelons of society; groups such as NOW, because they are more diverse and sometimes responsive to radical ideas, are more ambivalent.

Meanwhile, those feminists who challenged the whole system, with visions of a very different society, splintered in many directions in search of an elusive political clarity. (I am using the term "radicals" for all those, including myself, who have rejected a reformist ideology and who share a belief that more basic changes in society are necessary. Obviously, such groups as socialist feminists, radical feminists, lesbian feminists, or cultural feminists differ from each other and have divergent strategies, but they usually share the desire to go beyond reformism. Most of the following observations apply to all these groups in varying degrees.)

Radicals found ourselves caught up in an effort to develop a new kind of politics that could not be coopted by the system. This involved numerous struggles over ideological, organizational, and internal issues fundamental to the future of feminism: collectivity, leadership, lesbianism, class, power relationships, and so on. With few exceptions, however, these struggles did not lead to organizational or ideological coherence or to programs that involved large numbers of women.

One reason radicals have difficulty developing programs is our fear that reforms will coopt us or pacify too many women without overthrowing male supremacy. The American system coopts our visions by incorporating radical rhetoric while distorting the original meaning of the words and ideas; it coopts our leaders by offering token prestige, power, or money if we cooperate, and by isolating and destroying those who won't be bought. It coopts our people by adopting some reforms that improve our lives but leave intact, and often even improve, the structures of patriarchy, capitalism, and white supremacy. Some women also fear reform because it means involvement with power (seen as male) within the slimy institutions we want to destroy. They ask whether we can keep our souls and not be corrupted by such involvement.

Such fears of cooptation are justified, but sometimes they have resulted in the attempt by many to remain pure, to be uncorrupted by association with *any* reforms. For example, radicals who consider working on the ERA, in women's studies, or in women's trade unions can become immobilized by uncertainty about whether we can keep our politics and souls alive. As a result, we often neglect the creation of conditions that could make these actions more progressive, as well as keep us honest. Purism taken to its extreme results in immobilism and cynicism; if we cannot achieve the final good now, then we feel we cannot do anything at all because it might be cooptable.

Radicals of various ideologies push the hard political questions and project visions of what we could do and what we could be. This process is a source of vital ideas and changes. But we have failed to create the tangible programs or organizations that could show women our potential for power or that could provide concrete steps for involvement in change. For example, some have accurately challenged the white middle-class bias of most women's reforms, but too often the alternative has not been a better program but no program at all. Our strength has been the willingness to raise basic questions, but it has also led to our weakness. Our questions often are so basic, such as those examining power relations in all parts of our lives, that we are unable to move far on them. Not knowing what to do with the immensity of what we question, we often become isolated, discouraged, and immobilized.

Enter Reformism. Where radicals have failed, reformists have flourished. Reformist groups and activities attract many women primarily because such groups are well organized and provide involvement in programs of action that can produce immediate results and tangible—though limited—successes. Women working on reformist programs often have a radical analysis of society but find few places to work concretely on that analysis. For example, a lesbian may be, ideologically, a lesbian feminist, but if she wants job security in order to "come out," she may well put her energy into the organization working on the reform that will guarantee that security, no matter what its overall ideology. Most radical groups fail to develop concrete reforms as a part of their program and direction, because they have not realized that such reforms need not be tied to a reformist ideology.

Other problems have grown out of our focus on internal change— the effort to make our lives and groups reflect the same changes that we advocate outside, such as collectivity, equality, and so forth. Again, this is important, but it cannot be achieved quickly or be separated from the struggle to change the structures of the whole society. The failure to transform ourselves and others more completely has left some women feeling defeated and cynical, or consumed by efforts to achieve that change. Similarly, many service and cultural activities, while providing concrete activity, have come to a dead end because they do not confront society directly and are not integrated into an overall ideology or program for liberating women.

At present at a crossroads in the question of reform, large numbers of women who call themselves radicals are asking, "What is the role of reform in our movement?" Simultaneously, women who work on reforms or in service projects are asking, "What is the political framework for the future that goes beyond reformism and can be used to evaluate our work?" From our different places, we can look anew at women's reforms and political ideology.

Reform and Long-Term Goals

Between social reforms and revolution there exists for the social democracy an indissoluble tie. The struggle for reforms is its means; the social revolution, its aim. . . . Formerly, the activity of the Social Democratic Party

*consisted of trade-union work, of agitation for social reforms and the
democratization of existing political institutions. The difference is not in
the what but in the how. At present, the trade-union struggle and parliamentary
practice are considered to be the means of guiding and educating the
proletariat in preparation for the task of taking over power.*
—*Rosa Luxemburg*

Those interested in fundamental social change or in revolution
have long debated the role of reforms. As Rosa Luxemburg put it, the
point is not the opposition of one to the other but the relationship
between them. The primary issues are What is our long-range goal?
How does a specific reform aid or detract from that goal? How should
the reform be carried out to advance our goal best? To state it another
way, reform is not a solution but a strategy toward a larger goal.

In using these points to evaluate reforms in the women's movement, we must first ask, what is our goal? We want an end to the
oppression of all women. What does that mean? What is our analysis
of why and how women are oppressed? Women's oppression is rooted
both in the structures of our society, which are patriarchal, and in the
sons of patriarchy: capitalism and white supremacy. Patriarchy includes not only male rule but also heterosexual imperialism and
sexism; patriarchy led to the development of white supremacy and
capitalism. For me, the term patriarchy refers to all these forms of
oppression and domination, all of which must be ended before all
women will be free.

Stated positively, we need a new social order based on equitable
distribution of resources and access to them in the future; upon equal
justice and rights for all; and upon maximum freedom for each person to determine her own life. How will we bring about these
changes? What is our long-term strategy? What kind of process does
this involve? What types of power must women have to make these
changes? *These* must be our questions.

The socialist tenet that the first phase of revolution required the
taking of state power by the proletariat and the destruction of
capitalism guided Luxemburg's discussion of reform. Following her
framework, I will sketch initial goals and strategies for our discussion
of reforms. In order to end patriarchy and create a new society,
women must have power. We must have power in all spheres—
political, economic, and cultural—as well as power over our own
beings. Since we seek power as a means of transforming society, we
must also transform power or find new ways of exercising power that
do not duplicate the oppressions of today. We must discover how
women can build our own strengths, create these new forms, prepare
for, and gain such power. Since all this cannot be accomplished
within American society as it now exists, my long-term goal is not the
achievement of piecemeal reforms but a feminist revolutionary pro-

cess that alters the entire social order. Reforms, therefore, are not an end in themselves but an important *means* toward reaching this larger goal. They must be evaluated in terms of it.

Some argue that a revolutionary women's goal is the end of power—to create a world not based on any power dynamics—and that association with male power will necessarily corrupt us. Perhaps, ultimately, we can dream of an end to power. But before we can accomplish that, women must first gain enough control over society today to end patriarchal domination and destruction of the world. In that process, we hope, we can change the nature of power, but we cannot avoid or ignore it.

Radicals often debate when people can be expected to act: when the situation is most unbearable (intense repression or economic depression) or when reforms are making things better and raising expectations. I would pose the question differently. Most people are willing to risk basic change when a movement (or party) has done three things: 1) raised their hopes by pointing to concrete visions of ways in which life could be better; 2) provided organization and strategy for how to achieve those visions; and 3) demonstrated that the existing system is not going to make those changes willingly. As we gain more power both through our visions and our institutions, we will encounter more opposition from the system. We can mobilize more people to fight with us at that time if they can see and believe in what we have done. I would never favor making the conditions of people's lives more difficult just to "raise consciousness." But if repression comes, then we must adapt our strategies to use it.

The crucial point here is not whether the government is liberal or repressive. What *is* crucial is that we are able to demonstrate that we can organize society anew in a way that is better for people and that we have a chance of winning in a battle with traditional forces. If women are to achieve political power, we must convince large numbers of people that we can do all this. We are far from that point.

Programs of reform, including the institutions that we build, are part of the means, the strategy, by which we demonstrate what we can do. The effect of those reforms depends not only on what is done but also upon how it is accomplished. The "how" includes questions about the ideology, structure, approach, and type of group carrying out a reform. This leads us to a discussion of the criteria to be used in evaluating specific reforms.

Criteria for Evaluating Reforms

We oppose the utopian position which argues against any change until the perfect solution is possible. On the other hand, we also are not for working on any and every reform action that presents itself. Our strategy allows us to

define priorities and timetables to lend structure to issues in terms
of particular situations.
—"Socialist Feminism: A Strategy for the Women's Movement"

To say that radicals should reevaluate the importance of reforms does not mean that we should rush out and accept every women's reform as progressive. Criteria depend on goals and strategy. To say that we must evaluate reform in terms of goals and strategy does not mean that our analysis is complete and our direction is set. We begin with what we have. Those who differ with my questions and goals outlined above will differ some on criteria, but the following framework should still be useful.

The primary goal is women gaining power in order to eliminate patriarchy and create a more humane society. We must determine what is necessary in order for women to obtain power and use it for these purposes. We must also look at the class, race, and sexual preference base of that power, if we are to create real change and not just acquire power for a few privileged women. I have outlined five criteria for evaluating reform that correspond to these goals. The criteria often overlap and are ordered somewhat arbitrarily, according to process more than priority: 1) Does this reform materially improve the lives of women, and if so, which women, and how many? 2) Does it build an individual woman's self-respect, strength, and confidence? 3) Does it give women a sense of power, strength, and imagination as a group and help build structures for further change? 4) Does it educate women politically, enhancing their ability to criticize and challenge the system in the future? 5) Does it weaken patriarchal control of society's institutions and help women gain power over them?

1. *Does it materially improve the lives of women and if so, which women, and how many?* Reforms that alleviate immediate pain and economically improve our lives are important because they give us space to breathe, work, and plan; they make it possible for more women to act politically. This is particularly true where reforms center on daily problems like child care, job and housing discrimination, or sexual abuse. Many working-class women of all races have not supported women's actions because these did not directly improve their lives. Some women's reforms even appear to worsen their situation, for example, when middle-class women are given jobs ahead of the working-class men whose income supports the working-class woman. When we can show that our programs meet women's survival needs, not just advance the position of a few, then more women will join us.

All women are oppressed, but some have more privilege than

others. Reforms that focus on enhancing the status of white heterosexual middle-class women with the most privilege often divide us further. To give an example, working to move women into oppressive executive positions supports the structures of patriarchy and exacerbates class differences among women. Reforms that aid the least privileged, that is, force distribution of resources to women at the "bottom," such as a decent income for welfare mothers, begin to close some of those gaps. Reforms that benefit a wide spectrum of women, such as the Equal Rights Amendment (even with its dangers), also have potential for bringing women together. Women are all vulnerable, and each of us is only as secure as those women that society puts on the "bottom," not as powerful as the token top. Material reforms should aid as many women as possible and should particularly seek to redistribute income and status so that the class, race, and heterosexual privileges that divide women are eliminated.

2. *Does the reform build an individual woman's self-respect, strength, and confidence?* A movement is only as strong as the women in it. Self-respect is basic to the success of our own work, to respecting other women, and to believing in the power of women. Reform activities that help women find a sense of themselves apart from their oppressed functions and which are not based on the false sense of race, class, or heterosexual superiority are important. This is not to encourage individualism or tokens who are personally liberated. It is to encourage women who see their strength and future tied to the liberation of all women.

Consciousness raising, feminist counseling, and women's skills programs can help build self-respect; so too, successful work on reform activities can build self-confidence. But it is vital that these activities not be done in isolation from a political perspective. By helping women understand why we lack respect in this society and how the society will continue to destroy our confidence until we gain power as a group, these activities can build women's political as well as personal motivation.

3. *Does working for the reform give women a sense of power, strength, and imagination as a group and help build structures for further change?* Women need to win. We need to struggle for reforms that are attainable. We need to act where it is clear that the changes achieved are the results of our efforts—not a gift from the system—but victories won by our pressure, our organization, and our strength. The greater variety and larger numbers of women who benefit from this victory—and who participate in its accomplishment—the better.

To take one example, we need to make clear to people that changes in abortion laws were won by the combined efforts of many women, not given to us by the government. Still, we can't stop with any one reform. Changes in abortion laws, while important, did not bring us control over our bodies. That victory should be used to spur us on to fighting for more changes, such as an end to forced sterilization, better and free health care for all, and the like. These specific reforms should also help us build structures and organizations that can work for more changes and use each separate reform to gain power. Victories and programs, especially when linked to specific organizations, give us a clearer sense of what we can win and illustrate the plans, imagination, and changes that women will bring as they gain power.

4. *Does the struggle for reform educate women politically, enhancing their ability to criticize and challenge the system in the future?* Working on reforms can teach us about our enemies and about the systems we oppose. Winning a reform such as the right to enter "men only" accommodations shows women that ending superficial signs of our oppression changes little. Even reforms that fail, such as the efforts to ordain women in the Episcopal church, can reveal the limits of the system and raise the consciousness of those who once believed in reformism. I do not propose working on unattainable demands or superficial issues just to educate. Rather, when many women are interested in any issue, we can enhance its educational possibilities through political discussion. Since winning one reform is not our final goal, we should ask if working on that issue will teach us new and important things about ourselves and society. Particularly when a reform fails, political education is important to motivate women to continue, rather than to become cynical about change.

5. *Does the reform weaken patriarchal control of society's institutions and help women gain power over them?* As women, we want to improve the conditions of our daily lives. In order to do this, we must have power over the institutions—the family, schools, factories, laws, and so on—that determine those conditions. One way to build power is through creating our own alternatives, such as health clinics that give us more control over our bodies or women's media that control our communication with the public. Alternative institutions should not be havens of retreat, but challenges that weaken male power over our lives.

Some reforms directly challenge the power of existing institutions, such as hospitals, welfare systems, and schools. In confrontations with such established powers, we seek to change what they do; but above all, we should demand that those most affected by each institution have the power to determine its nature and direction. Initially, these challenges and reforms help to undermine the power of patriarchy, capitalism, and white supremacy. Ultimately, these actions must lead to the people's control of all institutions so that we can determine how our society will function.

Conditions for Reform Actions

Every reform will not necessarily advance all five criteria, but no reform that we undertake should be in opposition to any of these points. If we seek power for a feminist revolution, we must develop an overall program and organization that links these reforms together, that goes beyond them, and that builds women's power more coherently. Until that coherence is developed, the initial criteria help us evaluate our present activities and potential reforms. Once we are working on a reform, however, we need not only criteria but also conditions that will prevent its cooptation or dilution, that keep the reform consistent with our long-term goals, and that help us know when to move on. Otherwise any reform activity can become an end in itself.

In discussing conditions for working on reforms, it is helpful to summarize some of the problems and pitfalls of reforms. Unless we are determined to prevent it, reforms most often enhance the privilege of a few at the expense of the many. Unless good political education accompanies work on a reform, success can lead to the conclusion that the system works or failure can lead to cynicism about women's ability to bring about change. Reforms should be judged by how they actually affect women; some sound good in theory but work against women's material needs. For example, "no-fault divorce laws" sound like equality, but since male and female incomes are not equal and many women have worked for husbands for years, these laws cut off some women's badly needed and justified rights to alimony. If too much is staked on any one reform, as happened with getting the vote, we are cut off from other vital areas for change. Finally, if we do not make it clear that women made a reform happen, it can look like the result of a benevolent establishment. Therefore, we should maximize women's direct participation in bringing change, emphasize the power of our combined efforts, and avoid backroom styles that tend to obscure where ideas came from and who forced them into reality. Otherwise, devious politicians can take over our reforms in ways that disperse our momentum and pacify rather than politicize masses of women.

There are many types of reforms and ways to work on them—through women's reformist groups, inside male-dominated institutions, by building alternate institutions, through mass actions or coalitions. The conditions required to keep a perspective on the reform will vary in each. Let us take one situation as an example.

Sally Gearhart once described how a feminist might evaluate whether or not to work for reforms in the church. First, she outlined reasons to leave the church: it is totally patriarchal in attitude and structure; remaining may falsely inspire others to believe that it can

be changed within itself and within the existing system; it can separate you from your sisters, especially if you move into a higher position that makes you more a part of the system; you and your support
group waste lots of energy. She then outlined reasons why one might
stay there: it is a job providing some economic stability for a woman;
it can be a place to focus on the spiritual questions and needs of
women; you can gain certain skills, contacts, and experiences and
make similar resources available to other women; you can make
room for and help politicize large numbers of women who are at
present in the church, giving them a sense of their power and outlin-
ing possibilities for women to make change. Finally, she emphasized
the minimum conditions that would be essential if you chose to stay:
1) a feminist community outside the church to whom you are accountable and which helps you to stay in touch with why you are
working in the institution; 2) a feminist group for support and
strategy inside the church with whom you work regularly to build
something there; and 3) a clear personal sense of how necessary it is
to risk and what the strategies and motives are and must be behind
each risk.[3] Similar conditions could be described for women working
in women's studies/universities, business, politics, law, trade unions,
or any other established institution.

A radical who works on reforms within a women's reformist group
faces similar questions. She must also work out the relationship between her own ideology and the dominant reformism of the group.
She must define clear objectives for what she does and does not expect to change about the group and what she hopes to accomplish by
working there. She would also need feminists who share her politics
outside the group to provide ongoing support and criticism of her
work.

Feminists in groups who share a common radical analysis may also
work on reforms, either on their own or in coalition with other
groups. In determining what to do, the group should consider the five
criteria, the particular skills and interests of their group, and the
needs and interests of their community. Ongoing criticism must be
built into the group so that the reforms can be kept moving in a
progressive direction and so that improvements can be made or a
project ended if it is not serving its purpose. Feedback from feminists
who share their goals but are not working on the same activities
would also be useful.

Most feminists are, or will be, involved in various reform activities,
no matter what their ideology. The questions we face are "Which
ones?" "How?" and "With whom?" Since I believe that women must
work toward gaining power to end patriarchy, capitalism, and white
supremacy, and to create a new society, I have outlined criteria and
conditions for determining which reforms to work on and how to

approach them that correspond to that goal. The next evaluations of reform will come out of our ongoing experiences as feminists.

NOTES

1. National Organization for Women, Statement of Purpose, Washington D.C., 1966.
2. These issues were considered illegal or outlawed in 1968; NOW was primarily involved with job equality and legal issues at that time.
3. Sally Gearhart, "The Miracle of Lesbianism," in *Loving Women/Loving Men*, ed. by Sally Gearhart and William R. Johnson (San Francisco: Glide Publications, 1974).

Put Your Money Where Your Movement Is!

Beverly Fisher-Manick

Money is harder for women to talk about than orgasm. The much flaunted concept of collectivity in the women's movement has not reached into the bottom seams of women's pockets. Feminists have discussed nearly every topic imaginable, but rarely do we discuss what we do with our money, as individuals and as groups.

We must recognize the importance and potential power of money for us as a movement committed to challenging power relationships. Money is leverage for gaining the power to be self-sufficient and autonomous in both the short and long run.

Money and Attitudes

To sound a horn in this money silence, this article begins by examining how our attitudes and behavior about money often reflect our class backgrounds as well as our present economic situations. A woman who has learned to live on an income that just barely allows her to pay for essentials—rent, food, and utilities—considers any additional money as extra. On the other hand, a woman with a more substantial income may also see car payments, gas, charge accounts, insurance, clothes allowance, and gift allowance as essentials; she will spend twice as much yet see herself as having no extras.

This basic difference manifests itself in many ways. When a woman says, "I haven't got any money," she may mean she doesn't have cash because she hasn't cashed a check or she may mean she doesn't have any money at all, not even in the bank. What constitutes "pocket money" can vary as much as $5 to $55 a week. Going out to lunch and dinner three or four times a week is a life style that many professional women practice, without considering how much money they consume above and beyond normal food spending.

While visits to doctors and dentists are included in many women's budgets, for others it is rarely possible. Teeth go bad, illnesses may get better by themselves, and preventive medicine is an impossibility. Women who never had credit or charge accounts have no concept of spending more money then they have at any given moment. Their ability to buy is only immediate. Planning often is impossible because next week's living expenses will eat up any extra they have now.

Women who make enough to save money out of their regular income have options for planning vacations and buying investments toward their future. They consider this planning essential to their psychic survival. But women who have no extra money after living expenses have no choices about planning or buying. They live from paycheck to paycheck. Life takes on a very different perspective with no escape or release to look forward to.

Being able to live on past privilege is another asset for some women. Those who have accumulated goods over the years, such as clothes, household furnishings and appliances, typewriters, cameras, and TVs, are way ahead of women who had nothing to start with and often never get these things or have to purchase them out of their present incomes.

During my four years in the women's movement, I have observed many friends move from typing and secretarial pay to professional salaries. Along with an increased salary there is an inevitable rising spiral of economic need. New categories of needs inevitably arise; air conditioning and a car become necessities where once they weren't possibilities. What at first was a huge increase in income is soon eaten up by galloping consumption.

The different economic experiences of women are acted out in the politics of the movement. For example, while equal pay for equal work is practically a holy principle to feminists, the principle is often forgotten when a woman is doing work for the movement. There is an unspoken expectation that women can and should work for pure political satisfaction. This assumption may have originated out of a predominance of women in the movement who were not faced with the necessity of work for survival; as such, it is an important manifestation of individuals' economic situation being reflected in movement politics. Similarly, the heavily emphasized campaign for promoting women to high-level, well-paying positions overlooks the widened gap created between them and lower- and working-class women.

The Movement's Need for Money

The women's movement often idealistically assumes things will happen without attending to the practical aspects of accomplishment, particularly when it comes to money. To change this assumption, we must define our goals and their relationship to money. If our goal is ending the oppression of women and creating a humane society for all people, we must develop and undertake strategies for achieving this. Confronting and eliminating the institutions of capitalism, sexism, racism, classism, heterosexism, and imperialism requires a powerful social, political, and economic movement. We have to develop strategies and institutions on many different fronts. On all fronts, we need movement resources to achieve these ends. We cannot expect traditional funding sources to underwrite us.

Money is important. It can buy survival for movement projects and the individuals who give their time and energy to them. Money enables us financially to support leaders, organizers, thinkers, writers, printers, office workers, and the like who are essential personnel of any social movement. By providing them with decent salaries they can put all their energy and time into the movement rather than having to split themselves into several chunks in order to survive. As salaried personnel we can develop structures and systems for accountability of all our work. No more "tyranny of structurelessness."

Money to pay for movement work could also help alleviate the class bias of the movement. For example, at present, only those who have accumulated savings or are supported by husbands can afford to work full-time in movement activities. We must be able to offer women jobs in the movement as a means of support at a reasonable level. We need women of all backgrounds and experience, including those whose salary must support children or a household.

Money and other resources are basic to the survival of and control over our programs and projects. Lack of financial resources should not be the deciding factor in determining our priorities. If we decide that it is essential to begin a new publication, we should be able to do so without jeopardizing our purpose and politics in order to make the publication financially feasible. For example, advertising income, often essential to continued publication, can be canceled at any time, as a feminist newspaper learned when a publisher that did not appreciate a bad review of one of its books canceled its ad.

As the development of a women's culture and its institutions becomes a reality, the necessity for equipment and capital resources becomes more crucial. We need to purchase major equipment that will make us more self-sufficient and bring us more capital for further growth. Buying buildings and houses provides a permanent base of operation and ensures our existence beyond the expiration of a lease.

Control of communication resources is key to building mass support for feminism. Owning our own media and communication resources increases our visibility and impact; we can reach women who never go to underground bookstores or listen to movement radio stations. Radio, television, film, and publishing all require capital investment and technical skills.

As we create feminist institutions we will provide jobs for women. This is vital for women's economic self-sufficiency. Yet, too often the old maxim holds true—"It takes money to make money." If we do not have the resources to purchase new equipment and expand our operations, we will not be able to provide these jobs. To the extent that the present system provides women with economic survival, most will resist the destruction of capitalism. Only when we can offer women an alternative system with new principles and actions, which also guarantees economic survival, will we have generated a substantial source of power.

Changing Our Attitudes and Politics

Once we recognize that money is essential to our movement and examine our attitudes toward it, we can analyze how to change our values and action about money in order to build a new political perspective on money and feminism. We must acknowledge that as long as money is solely in individual feminists' control, it divides us. It creates privileges and security for a few, thereby leading to conflicting ideas about movement priorities.

We have been dealing with money in capitalist ways by *not* discussing it as a movement issue. We have allowed it to remain an individual's right, as sacred as the right to religion or free speech. It is time to create programs and strategies growing out of a common political ideology that develop means for controlling money collectively and redistribuing privilege and security.

We must discuss money openly and honestly, not just in abstract discussions of the ruling class and their money, but in real gut discussions of who has what in our particular groups. We should be aware of each other's resources—including money and property—as well as whether we can type or prepare incorporation papers. We must examine our values and see how we deal with money as well as talk about our financial backgrounds.

Too often women react with guilt or downward mobility whenever a discussion of economic differences arises. Neither reaction gets us anywhere. Guilt only immobilizes; quitting a $15,000/year job wastefully denies money to all women. What is essential is understanding our economic differences so that we begin to develop ideology and strategies which take these differences into account. We must realize that our money is going to make a vital difference in the movement. Without it the movement will rise, then fall, as the money runs out. It is not necessary to become lower or working class—in fact, that can't be done. What can be done is to recognize that our individual money can make the movement something that is important to each of us and to all women. Put your money where your movement is!

We need to develop strategies for acquiring money as well as for using it. Our strategies should rest on these assumptions: 1) Money is a necessary resource for building a revolutionary women's movement. 2) Money is a means to an end. 3) There is a reasonable living standard that can be established and adhered to by all. 4) No individual should have more money than is needed for her to live at this reasonable level. 5) Any individual whose income exceeds that reasonable level shares the excess. All these assumptions challenge the values of capitalism.

As a movement dedicated to eradicating inequities, building new systems that correct the present ones is essential. Experimenting with new ideas and programs which incorporate these assumptions will lead to new economic relationships and will prepare us for our task of creating a new economic system.

Some Proposals for Redistributing Money

Movement activities fall into roughly two categories—projects that can be done in a financially self-sustaining manner and those that cannot. The approaches for financing the two categories vary according to this essential difference.

The majority of projects within the women's movement are not at present self-sustaining but can and should be. For example, our women's centers offer free services to women with little planning as to how we will pay for the operating expenses, such as salaries for staff. Story after story of women's centers folding because of lack of funds should be lesson enough. Usually such centers wait too long to get financial backing and when they do, too much time and energy is devoted to it to the detriment of the quality of the services.

Women's centers usually consist of a loose association of autonomous service projects. If these projects operated as "feminist businesses," offering the same essential services for reasonable fees, they could pay for their staffs, and at the same time, continue to grow.

I suggest that we offer services at a standard pay and fee scale that both permits low-cost services and provides a reasonable income to the women supplying the services. In setting a pay/fee scale, groups should evaluate carefully what constitutes a reasonable standard of living, taking into account their own geographic area and the special needs of individuals, such as health and dependents. Department of Labor statistics on what constitutes an adequate income for an individual may be a helpful guide. In this area, a figure between $3 to $4 per hour would represent a reasonable wage.

We have worked hard within the movement to provide *free* services for women, and yet, anytime we seek a woman's professional service, we can expect to pay the same rate that we would pay a male professional. Defensive statements from the women professionals range from "I paid to get the degrees to do this work, why shouldn't I charge these rates?" to "This is the first time I've had an opportunity to make money." This kind of blindness, which ignores the perpetuation of the class system, is an intolerable practice for anyone who professes to be a feminist. Therefore, one strategy to be considered involves the commitment of feminists to give up their professional salary privilege and live on a reasonable wage. Since the pay scale would be equal no matter what the particular job performed, this policy involves a considerable reduction in income for some women, while for others it means an increased standard of living.

If the group providing the service sets a pay scale at this reasonable level, they in turn will be able to offer their services for a reasonable charge. This system is one way in which feminists can begin to make money work for each other.

Another advantage of such a proposal is that it begins to free feminist projects from the hold of male money-granting institutions. So far these institutions have demonstrated that they will fund only those projects that are not threatening to the status quo, that is, those groups espousing goals of equality rather than power for women. Projects relying on such funding must keep their politics and activities acceptable to the funder. This reliance on male-controlled funding exercises a conservative influence on the entire women's movement.

Political Action Groups

Not all the necessary projects and organizations of the women's movement can become entirely self-sustaining. These include those groups that engage in political organizing and action, the ideological and strategic core of our movement. With this financial support, they could carry out mass and grassroots organizing, act as the political education branch of the movement, and plan and execute actions that confront the institutions of patriarchy and capitalism. If we examine existing political organizations for women, we find that most are primarily reformist groups that seek equality for women within the existing system (e.g., groups such as NOW, National Women's Political Caucus, and the Women's Equity Action League). There are few organized groups with radical or revolutionary ideology; what exists are mostly city-wide coalition groups and socialist feminist action groups.

One reason that more radical groups have not formed is that many feminists have disdained money and believe they will destroy capitalism by totally avoiding it. Meanwhile, reformist groups have grown and survived because they have dealt with money. Early in the radical women's movement, I remember repeated derogatory remarks about NOW's $15 membership fee. Since then, NOW has changed its position and makes provision for women who cannot afford to pay the fee; the radical movement sits in the same place. Membership dues can provide some basic income for a political organization as well as a definitive membership. Still, unless the dues are prohibitive or the membership in the millions, dues do not guarantee viable financial security for any political organization that has paid organizers and staff, and the expense of printed and other media propaganda. While the sale of some publications and literature can be another source of income, here again the income is limited.

Radical political organizations are necessary, but given their inability to be self-sufficient, how can we fund them? And how can we develop a system of income sharing and redistribution of privilege within them? I propose a personal income tax on each woman's income in excess of the reasonable standard of living described earlier. Taxing ourselves provides a means of ensuring political commitment with our money as well as our lives. This proposal particularly is directed to those career women, often single, who comprise the movement rank and file, both the feminist and radical. These women have been sufficiently aware of female oppression to join feminist groups and volunteer time and energy to projects, but rarely consider giving their money to the movement as well. This proposal provides a mechanism for doing so.

Such a tax should be paid not only by the individual woman. Female-owned business as well can pay taxes, and have a responsibility to do so. Feminist businesses that cannot produce excess income can benefit by receiving tax revenue. Services rendered should be part of a political program determined by a feminist political organization.

Political Organizations: The Redistributing Agent

Eventually we must develop political organizations to which we entrust the important task of redistributing income through a tax, as well as establishing a system of accountability for those projects and businesses that practice on a standard pay/fee scale basis. We can begin by establishing the political goals and principles for such an organization. Then, decisions about how money is used and redistributed can be made on the basis of these principles and goals. The following questions provide a guide for evaluating an organization's political principles and goals and its money values and strategies.

1. Does the organization include an analysis of how the program or project will affect power relationships in our society, both personal and institutional?
2. Does it contain elements that make it an instrument for eliminating sexism, racism, and capitalism?
3. Does the program understand and examine its relationship to other movement programs and strategies and have an analysis of how its goals relate to them?
4. Does it support the development of the feminist community?
5. Does it build mutually supportive systems among women and not promote further class divisions and distinctions?
6. Does it promote economic self-sufficiency for women?
7. Does it provide experience for women in management of resources for feminist interests?
8. Does it disperse control of money among women of different economic, cultural, and social positions and provide accountability for uses of money?
9. Does it encourage women to grow in their feminist commitment and level of participation?
10. Does it lead to a new economics based on shared resources?
11. Does it reach out to women who have not yet been involved in or touched by the women's movement?
12. Does it examine the relationship between its strategies and its goals?

There are many difficulties facing us in implementing these proposals without initially developing correlative organizational structures and systems of accountability for members and leaders. They are vital areas to explore before undertaking any proposal as radical as an income tax or standard pay/fee scale. However, since my principal concern in this article is money rather than the formulation of political organizations, I have limited this discussion. Many women must do the thinking, discussing, planning, writing, and experimenting in other areas, keeping this article's proposals in mind.

As one approach to the interlocking questions for the coordination, administration, and implementation of these two proposals, I would like to look at Feminist Credit Unions as a possible resource.

Feminist Credit Unions are new to the movement; women in Detroit established the first one and many women elsewhere are now forming their own, based on that model. In order to obtain federal insurance, a federal credit union must establish membership through a common bond. The Feminist Credit Union's bond is based on women's organizations, which become the charter subscribers. For an individual woman to buy shares in the credit union itself, she must be a member of one of the charter subscriber organizations. These organizations could be the same political organizations this section of the article discusses. The FCUs could administer the income tax and standard pay/fee scale by acting as a conduit for collecting and distributing funds between individuals, businesses, and organizations.

In addition, they could provide financial counselors to women. The training of these counselors should be carried out jointly by the credit unions and the subscriber political organizations.

This training should be viewed as both a political and a practical task. Training programs should be developed by women from all class backgrounds with clear principles and goals much in line with the questions outlined above. With trained financial counselors from the FCU, women could develop budgets and comprehensive pictures of their financial status. Having "extra" money for feminist groups generally is not going to happen without careful budget planning and practice.

Local FCUs with the experience of handling many different women's budgets could aid in ascertaining what "reasonable" expenses are and in developing a reasonable budget for all salary levels. From these figures, joint committees of representatives from the FCUs and the respective political organization could determine fair tax percentages and a reasonable pay/fee rate. These figures could be discussed between each woman and a feminist credit counselor. In the case of the tax, an agreed upon percentage would then be deducted by the credit union from each regular deposit, and transferred to the organization designated by the woman. The possible role of the feminist credit union speaks to the necessity of women in every city and area organizing their own financial institutions controlled by their membership.

A Transition: Privilege Sharing

While aspects of both these approaches can and should begin right now, essentially they are long-range strategies that require further development. I would like to urge immediate attempts at privilege sharing among defined groups to serve as a transition to these long-term plans. Privilege sharing is based on a basic commitment to one another's survival, and to the survival and building of a strong women's movement. Groups, whether existing project/program groups, living collectives, or defined communities of women, can institute various ways to pool individual money and resources. Too much of present privilege sharing is tied only to personal relationships, such as between friends or lovers, rather than to political goals or groups. In addition, if the proposals I have made are going to be instituted, they will require some women getting used to living on less and others readjusting to having more than they have ever had. Transition attempts at privilege sharing will be encountered in the long-range proposals—such as who makes the decisions of allocation and by what means?

On an individual level, a woman's decision on how to use her money is not in the control of the group. If one woman spends it on art objects and another for going out to the bar, that is her choice. On an organizational level, however, we must determine how it is going to be spent, and there will be no simple formula for these decisions. The work before us is immense, but I feel anxious to begin so we can get to the future we are setting about to realize.

Confrontation Black/White

Interview with Ginny Apuzzo and Betty Powell

The National Black Feminist Organization was formally established on August 15, 1973, to "address the specific needs of the black female who is forced to live in a society that is both sexist and racist." Sagaris, an independent institute for the study of feminist politics, held its first two extended sessions in the summer of 1975. The following summer both organizations formed a coalition to sponsor an intensive three-day conference of workshops, lectures, and discussion sessions to explore the links between racism and sexism. Betty Powell and Ginny Apuzzo participated in the event as facilitators and as leaders of a workshop on forming coalitions. Interviewer Dorothy Allison is on the staff of *Quest*.

A brief excerpt from the conference brochure outlines the design and scope of the session: "We will explore the linkage between racism and sexism, its importance for political change and how to move towards that change. Our intention is not to provide quick and easy answers but to provide training to eliminate the kinds of unconscious racist or sexist blocks within ourselves that prevent the building of a multiracial woman's movement that really moves."

DOROTHY: How were you invited to participate in the racism and sexism conference?

GINNY: For over a year before the conference was scheduled, I had been working on a concept of coalitions, so when Betty became interested in facilitating the conference, she approached me and we decided to hold a joint workshop around the topic of coalitions.

BETTY: I was invited to participate as a facilitator by members of the

National Black Feminist Organization (NBFO). There were to be twenty facilitators, evenly divided between black and white, and prior to the conference we were to have a series of meetings where we would literally "walk through" the entire conference. We engaged in workshops and exercises that we were to involve the participants in, with the result that we all had a total perspective of what the goals of the conference were and what our roles were.

DOROTHY: The conference itself was a remarkable coalition between two very different groups—the Sagaris Collective and the National Black Feminist Organization. How did that come about?

BETTY: There were a number of criticisms of the first Sagaris Institute. One of the criticisms was that it was extremely theoretical and that there was little concern with the issue of racism. At the same time, the women of NBFO had the feeling that while black feminists might be very much in touch with the phenomenon of racism because they experience it every day of their lives, they are probably not as strong in terms of feminism, even though they might consider themselves feminists. NBFO could see a need for helping First World women really get in touch with feminism and Sagaris could see the need for non-First World women to get more deeply in touch with racism.

I had better explain what I mean by "First World women." So often we see the term "Third World women." Since we need to start looking at our racism, we can begin with the language. Who decided who was first and who was third? What does it mean anyway? After asking these questions, many of us are starting to use the term First World women as an affirmation of ourselves as nonwhite women choosing our own definitions.

It was Jane Galvin Lewis who emphasized the idea of the linkages between sexism and racism during the organization of the conference. She helped to design the conference so that the dominant idea was trying to see those links from each perspective. From the black perspective, it's a matter of having racism as an integral part of your life but rarely seeing its relationship to sexism. For the white feminist, it's a matter of emphasizing sexism while being less sensitive to racism.

Throughout the conference we used Jane Galvin Lewis's suggested definition of the linkage between racism and sexism. Both "isms" assume superiority of one group over another based on biology; this phenomenon is manifested throughout the society, in theory and practice. It is also the case that the allegedly inferior group is always challenging this assumption in theory and in practice. This was the central concept that we focused on.

GINNY: Most of the exercises we went through were designed so that we as women, sometimes as white women and sometimes as black women, would experience the fact that the allegedly inferior group was constantly challenging our oppression. The exercises were broken up into small groups with white and black co-facilitators. The questions led the participants to deal with the broad issues of racism and sexism in their everyday lives, in a very personal way. There were questions that forced the women to deal with our own racism, our own self-hatred, on the level of one-to-one relationships. The attempt was made to set up a situation of direct confrontation between individual women, asking, "Why do we behave in the way that we do? What are our reasons and what are our excuses?"

I had the feeling that this particular aspect of the conference was designed in such a way that confrontation was evidence of success of the interaction. Personally, I had an enormous sense of confidence in what would happen if confrontation took place in the context of those workshops. I agree with the women who have been saying that we have gotten too damned polite; we've gotten so polite we tend to say, "Well, your group has this value and our group has that value, so we'll just make our base all the broader." What has happened is we've so diluted our objectives and our values that confrontation never takes place. It's only when confrontation does yield conflict that a consequent change can take place.

The Bottom Line

BETTY: One of the exercises we did the first day was on the question, "What is your bottom line?" It was a two-part session asking, "What is your personal limit; how far can you go with a person of a different race?" and in part II, "How do you go about working on your limitations?" The situation really pushed you to be absolutely honest and so when a woman said it would be very difficult for her to bring a person of a different race to her home, the other people began to draw her out in terms of why, not just saying, "Isn't that horrible!" It was all in terms of confronting racism rather than just revealing it.

GINNY: In that workshop I really saw some women facing their own responsibility for their racism. One woman in particular said she couldn't send her child to a public school because, in her area, it is predominately minority-populated. I watched the expression on that woman's face when she was confronted; she started to give her reasons and found that so many of them didn't belong to her. It was the family, her father, her mother, or her husband. I could see the woman struggling with the idea of her own responsibility, "You, why won't you send your child to that school?" In a sense she got to see the poverty of her own lack of reasons for taking that stand.

DOROTHY: I would think that the overriding tendency in any situation like that would be a lot of very subtle pretense and shielding of feelings. I don't mean actual lying, but still trying to be "nice" to avoid saying those obviously offensive things. How did the workshops break down that tendency?

BETTY: What we did was break up first in racial groups. Then we came back together and reported the statements, positions and experiences recounted in each group without, at first, identifying individuals. Initially, there was hesitancy on the part of the women to speak out, but the longer we went on the more people began to speak more freely. That gave a kind of space for people to become more honest.

GINNY: The sexism element was very interesting around that question because you had lesbians who said they wouldn't sleep with a black man because they wouldn't sleep with any man. But the big discussion was around the definition, what was meant by "bottom line." I've found that one of the most common tactics used in the beginning of any significant dialogue is to debate the validity of the question. The white women in my group all started to debate that definition. When you don't want to deal with something you tend to make-believe that you don't completely understand the question. So before we could get down to the nitty-gritty of what each of us meant by the bottom line, an enormous amount of time was wasted on semantics. The women were conscious of what that question would bring out. There was great difficulty in recognizing that no matter how much we want to respond out of a growing consciousness, we have been here for too many years and are still encumbered with prejudice.

BETTY: The black women and other First World women were much more comfortable in stating what their bottom line was because it is a part of their daily dialogue. There are just so many occasions for us to express those feelings, because we are constantly talking about THEM and the world out there and what happened last. The black women's response to the question really differed from the white women's. There were responses like, "I couldn't join a white-dominated organization," mostly talking in terms of feminist organizations, or, "I could join one but couldn't tolerate it if there were any manifestations of the power play where the white women make sure that they remain the ones in power." The white women would not only tolerate but would want the black women to join their organizations, but because of their conditioning just would not see themselves being led or directed by a black person. There were a lot of questions brought up around the issue of nonwhite women working with white women. There was a general assumption that "when I am aware of overt racism in a situation then I would not be able to continue my efforts to work in it."

NBFO, in making its statements about who it was, why it existed and how it relates to the white feminist movement, makes it clear that the need for such an organization was because the experiences of the black feminist are somehow obliterated or just not at present conscious in the white feminist movement. It is not so much a matter of overt racism as the need for space to deal with our own priorities and our own visions.

NBFO provided a list of questions and answers about black feminism to the facilitators and it proved very valuable, particularly where it clarified some of the questions that arose around black and white feminists working together. For example, on this issue there was a statement: "It is very difficult to get anyone to work on issues that are not close to their experience. The areas of welfare, domestic workers, reproductive freedom, the unwed mother, and many other areas are things we feel are not being addressed, as well as the professional black woman, sexuality, unemployment, and a host of other issues that affect us as black women. ... Many of us come out of the women's movement, but we feel that the duality of being black and female made us want to organize around those things that affect us most. It is very important that we set our own priorities, but we will lend support to feminist organizations and will work in coalitions in areas that affect the majority of women in this country.

GINNY: This conference took all the assumptions regarding black and white feminists working together and smashed them. I was in two groups where there were more black women than white women.

DOROTHY: How did it change the interaction to have that kind of composition? You know it's definitely not the usual thing at feminist conferences where it's typical to have only a few black women among many more white women.

BETTY: It made everything just so much more real for me. There were enormous numbers of black women even on the third day when so many women had to go back to work. We still had an incredible racial and ethnic diversity. The physical setting was such that we were together the entire time and the topics kept reinforcing that whole business of interacting, of relating personally. There were some people who left, particularly after the first day when there was such a level of confrontation that some women went home enraged, embarrassed, and turned off to the whole thing. But most women came back and there was a completely different feeling once the fear and mistrust had been worked through.

DOROTHY: I'm really interested in the fact that the workshops were designed to go beyond just asking the initial question. For example, you mentioned how the workshop on the "bottom line" also asked how to go about working on the limitations the initial question drew out. That's the step past analysis into strategy. I know that one of the other workshops dealt with the first experience of racism. In that case too, the discussion moved on to how that situation has changed.

BETTY: The end result of that workshop was that we saw that nothing much was changed in terms of how those feelings and attitudes are still prevalent in this society. There is still such fertile ground for racism and sexism to grow. It was a phenomenal experience for people to really get a grip on where that kind of feeling comes from, to see that society has been nurturing the negative self-image of First World people or nurturing the anti-life postures that white society is conditioned and socialized to take.

GINNY: When the first woman spoke in that workshop, the room became terribly quiet, the kind of silence that makes you think that nothing can be more quiet. Then the next woman spoke, and the room got even more quiet. It was just an incredible feeling of people letting something echo deep inside them. That silence spoke eloquently to the way women were attending and responding to each other.

There was a third exercise that took us back to the definition we were discussing earlier, particularly the idea that the allegedly inferior group is constantly challenging the assumptions of the dominant group. It examined attitudes by asking, "What do minorities think of whites? What do whites think of minorities?" and, "What do women think of men? What do men think of women?"

BETTY: For that workshop we broke down into mixed groups and everyone just rattled off everything they could think of; then we came back together and put the four questions up on the wall where the facilitators could list all the responses. The entire group then examined each of the statements to say whether each one was, in fact, true or false. The object of that exercise was to get people to make connections, to see the linkage between the oppression of one group by another. It quickly became very clear that the oppressed group has a much more accurate picture of the dominant group than the powerful have of the oppressed. The point is that the oppressed have to know the oppressor in order to survive.

GINNY: That's a rule that applies to both racism and sexism. As women and as minority people, the obligation is imposed on us to know what we are plus who the oppressor thinks we are, especially if we have a particular goal to achieve.

DOROTHY: That reminds me of lessons from my college psychology classes about the "me as others see me." We get confused between who we really are, who we are seen to be and a kind of mock identity when we have to play to the man in order to be seen at all. So often when dealing with a more powerful group, our behavior isn't understood at all.

GINNY: The fact that the group in power has determined the boundaries of acceptable behavior is an extraordinary advantage in protecting the status quo. Unacceptable behavior can be readily disregarded as eccentric or downright deviant.

BETTY: When we looked at those lists of perceptions, the idea that came up was that we are really enemies, that those words have to come from enmity. There just seems to be no in-between there, and clearly we are destined to remain enemies unless we change the whole system that perpetuates these ideas. I saw an interview with Lois Gould recently where she was asking how there could be any love between men and women when we are raised as enemies. How do we expect little boys to come out of their camp at thirteen years old loving little girls, or for that matter, blacks loving whites? No, we came out slugging, fighting—so the only answer is to retool, to change the whole system that creates these viewpoints.

DOROTHY: It is when I think about how we develop our perceptions of ourselves and others that leads me to think in terms of class. Sex and race are in a way, prime determinants, what defines us in terms of this culture; but equally important is the economic and social class that conditions so much of our later behavior and expectations. I'm curious about how the issue of class was examined in the racism and sexism conference.

GINNY: There was not a particular workshop or exercise directed at the issue of class, but it came up in many of the exercises we have been discussing. Women came to grips with the fact that their reasons and their values came out of their experience, the x number of years they had lived, what they were bound to and what was either holding them up or opening them up. I think that's the way they got in touch with certain realities of class experience for themselves and for others. You are not only who

you define yourself as, now in this room, but all the things that
have happened to you before and all the values that have been
accumulating—I am the particular product of my experiences.
Much as I'd like to be, I am not culture-free. Nor do I have to be a
victim of my experiences and culture. The process of raising my
consciousness involves factoring out values, experiences, and
attitudes that may predispose me to certain behaviors. The
more aware I am of the elements involved in my predisposition,
the more I can work to balance them with the factors I have
determined are significant.

BETTY: I want to say something about more concrete notions of
where we go from here, how we begin to actualize some of the
experiences and the knowledge we have. I think a very important thing that came out was this whole notion of mandatory
presence. I had a sense that people were aware at the conference
that, realistically speaking, as rich and powerful as the experience was for us all, we were not all going to go out and start
working together as minority and white women in any kind of
situation. The idea of mandatory presence was brought back
into sharp focus as the understanding that a black does not have
to be a member of the organization, a Native American doesn't
have to be present at the meeting or conference, for the issues of
concern to blacks and Native Americans to be part of the
agenda. I think the women went away with the idea that in
whatever activities and endeavors they would be involved, they
would be conscious of the need to raise these issues, whether a
minority person was present or not.

DOROTHY: Then it also becomes the responsibility of the white
women to develop their own consciousness of these issues and to
raise the questions.

GINNY: I completely disagree. I came away from there and sub-
sequently have had a large number of experiences that say to me
that mandatory presence is still necessary. I feel that if there
weren't lesbians there and if we didn't call for a lesbian caucus
to meet, that the conference could very easily have overlooked
the issue of heterosexism, and in fact it did. I think the lesbians
had to come together, had to make a statement, and had to open
up the issue, to focus on that for the straight women to say, as
Charlotte Bunch has said, "No woman is free until all women
are free to be lesbians."

DOROTHY: It seems that the idea of mandatory presence can be
applied to class and lesbianism as readily as to race. It's extraordinary to me that the two issues that seem to have been
pretty much neglected at the conference were the issues of class
and heterosexism. I am familiar with two analyses that might

have contributed to that. One is the idea that you cannot apply a class analysis to the lives of black women that centers on the definition of the term "working class," that minority people are the real working class of this society. Another is the idea that you cannot make demands on black women to deal with the issue of lesbianism because lesbianism threatens the solidarity of black men and women, and is in some ways more threatening to the cultural concepts of the black woman.

GINNY: I think there was one black woman who spoke during the lesbian caucus who spoke to that. She got up and said, "People all my life have accused me of being a dyke, because I am aggressive and I have always had to be out there functioning this way but I am not a lesbian and I don't know any." She was so angry because the larger society saw all those characteristics as the stereotype of the lesbian, and those were the characteristics she had to develop to survive. In a sense she was giving the most marvelous statement of the oppression of the lesbian, but she didn't realize it.

BETTY: She was not able to carry it a step farther in terms of an analysis; she just took it where she needed to take it. I think the notion of lesbianism being less acceptable to black women just isn't true. It has validity for some black women and certain experiences, but in terms of a general posture, I would tend to think exactly the opposite, that more black women would be inclined to accept lesbianism.

GINNY: I would disagree with your point. I think that for those black women for whom the church represents a basic social institution, lesbianism would be most difficult, if not impossible, to accept. For them, the church and the social life built around it is a survival structure and I think that would determine a lot of their perceptions and attitudes.

BETTY: A lot of that would depend on the particular culture that different black women come out of—it's a different situation for a black woman active in her church who lives in a nonurban southern community than for one in a more urban setting where a very different notion of homosexuality prevails.

DOROTHY: What about the question of whether black women must support black men as a group and therefore lesbianism is a dangerous concept?

BETTY: It's a complex question. In an urban setting like New York, there would be black women who would have to look on the notion of homosexuality as destructive to the building of a black nation and that stance would be supported by black men. There's a question like that in the NBFO material. It goes: "Shouldn't the black woman be behind her man, giving him support? After all, he has been discriminated against since being in America." The answer is: "We would never deny the injustice or abuse put upon the black man in this country. But, because we live in a patriarchy, we have allowed a premium to be placed on *male* suffering. Black women have also faced enormous hardship and pain, and rather than getting behind someone, we should be supportive of each other. Rather than being the day of the black man, it is the day of the black people."

I think it just really depends on how far along a woman is in terms of her own sense of self as a woman. If she doesn't feel that necessity to respond in the same way that the black man does, then she may be able to deal with lesbianism and homosexuality in a much more understanding way.

DOROTHY: What was the response to the lesbian caucus that organized during the conference?

GINNY: The responses were as diverse as the women there. We simply made a statement relating to heterosexism and the fact that one cannot look at sexism without looking at the implications of the normative status of heterosexuality. There were women who then said they had never realized that talking about sexism meant talking about heterosexism. But then there was a woman who came into the workshop on coalitions that we directed, who, despite the fact that she had expressed an interest in coalitions, literally backed out of the room saying, "I just can't be here, this is disgusting." She couldn't be in the same room with us after she knew we were lesbians.

Still, I would say that the consequence of the caucus was positive. It did open up dialogue; it got people talking to each other; and it brought the issue out on the table with all the pain and accompanying difficulty that racism had had for women who were there.

DOROTHY: As participants and facilitators you saw the entire event through from the training sessions to the last criticisms. If you were to design another such event with similar goals, how would you change what was done? Particularly, how would you incorporate the issues of class and heterosexism?

BETTY: The only way I could see incorporating class and heterosexism in a more vitalizing way within the session would be to extend the length of time of the conference. I think the structure served it perfectly—the basic structure of presentation and workshops, small-group encounter, and really focusing on trying to elicit confrontation. I would resist changing the definition that specified the links between sexism and racism. I would suspect that another statement would have to be added, and that might be that the consequences of acting out the alleged superiority of one group, economically and culturally, would bring about the kinds of class differences that are perpetuated by a racist, sexist society. In the day-to-day world perpetuating the status quo we get the kind of rigid classist attitudes that cannot be separated from the economic reality.

What I would not want to do would be to dilute the importance of these two issues—racism and sexism. They need to be looked at in just the terms that they were addressed at that conference, with a balance between introducing attitudes and feelings and letting people work them through, as well as translating those attitudes and feelings into the issues such as abortion or reproductive freedom, child care, employment, political repression, rape, forced sterilization, crimes against women, and practical actions we need to work on immediately. On the last day of the conference we held a series of workshops around possible actions for women, confronting racism and sexism to move to coalition building, backing a political candidate or being one, community organizing, lobbying, working in minority media or organizing women's businesses. That design should continue to serve us well; working from mutual education to honest dialogue to unified action.

Female Leaders: Who Was Rembrandt's Mother?

Jackie St. Joan

Once women wove blankets
To warm their children
Out of love
And, out of love and the
fierce desire of their own
hearts,
they made them beautiful
Their art did not hang on
museum walls
But covered the bodies of
sleeping children.
(Where is your Rembrandt?)
The men ask us.
She was a Navaho
And the white man killed her.

—Kathleen Thompson

As the poem suggests, many women artistic leaders never have been recognized or allowed to flourish in their work because white male supremacy has circumscribed their existence and limited their roles. Similarly, many women political leaders never have been recognized or allowed to flourish in their work for the same reasons. Today in America, women are not so restricted, yet the women's movement is suffering from a lack of political leadership and a lack of political theory by which to understand the function of feminist leadership. In creating such a theory women must start from what is familiar to them. The Navaho artist based her work in the artistic perceptions she had as a Navaho and as a woman. Likewise, the political theorist

223

can base her work on the political perceptions she has as a mother, as a leader in the family unit.

It would appear that within the family unit, in the role of mother, there is an underlying system by which women operate as leaders. In this article I propose to examine motherhood as a model of feminist leadership, to identify some of the characteristics of the function of mother as they apply to the function of leader, and to compare how society's treatment of mothers is similar to the women's movement's treatment of its leaders. In naming these characteristics, I turn to my own and others' experiences as mothers, and to lesbian feminist literature as sources of information.

Many women carry the common experience as mothers, as leaders in a unit in which others have looked to them for group survival. In addition, lesbian-feminist writers often carry within their work a sense of ethnicity—of women's identification as a people. Literature is a good source because there is at least one thing that good writers and good political leaders have in common—they pay attention to what inspires people (art) or to what moves people to act (politics).

At this point I want to make clear what I am *not* saying. I am not saying that only mothers or only lesbian feminists understand feminist consciousness or are capable of being leaders. All women carry, to a greater or lesser extent, the experiences of motherhood and lesbianism. Most women have, at some point in their lives, taken responsibility for someone else, whether that person was a husband, a child, a boss, or an aging parent. Also, most women have experienced the emotional, if not the physical communion of women, whether as a child among girl friends, in the secretarial pool, or in family relationships. What I *am* saying is that lesbianism and motherhood are *conditions*, either or both of which contain a concentration of experience related to feminist ethics and feminist leadership.

In this article I make broad statements about mothers, statements that need qualification. Although all mothers carry some body of common experience, not all mothers deal with situations in the same way. I am merely exploring a new image of mother-as-leader.

The Motherhood Model

To begin with, I see mothering (or parenting) as a function, and "mother" as a role. How that function and role are performed varies greatly according to the society, race, class, education, and personal style of the woman. In many societies, however, a woman is allowed her identity as a mother only because the survival of the family, as it is structured, depends on a woman's commitment to that role, and the family members' perception of her in that role only. When a woman puts a priority on her personal survival and wants to be seen beyond the mother role, or outside of it completely, she often is seen as a betrayer who is weakening the group. In fact, she is upsetting the power relationships in the family and expecting others to assume some of her responsibility, an expectation against which family members often will rebel, and for which she often is punished (guilt). She then is expected either to return to the mother role, or to become Supermom (Margaret Anderson plus).* Many of the same dynamics that operate to limit the power of women as mothers operate to limit their power as leaders in the women's movement.

Many women I know are looking for a new model of motherhood to replace the Margaret Anderson image we were fed as children by television. Such a model would allow mothers to be real, which includes being angry, not only as women but in that motherhood role itself. A woman who is allowed to be herself, and who also chooses to function as a mother, can function more freely to the betterment of herself both as a person and as a mother. Susan Griffin expresses that image in her poem "I Like to Think of Harriet Tubman":

> And when I think of the President
> and the law, and the problem of
> feeding children, I like to
> think of Harriet Tubman
> and her revolver . . .
> I want men
> to take us seriously.
> I am tired wanting them to think
> about right and wrong.
> I want them to fear
> I want them to feel fear now
> as I have felt suffering in the womb . . .[1]

Mother-as-Leader

When a woman is pregnant, gives birth, and mothers a child, she goes through a process of accepting total, and then less and less, responsibility for someone else's survival. Her letting go of that power and of that responsibility is part of the process required for her own survival as a person and for her children's survival as independent human beings. In the process of letting go, her responsibility is to give accurate information to the child, to inspire her or his spirit,

*Margaret Anderson is the mother in "Father Knows Best."

to teach what survival skills she knows to her young, and to make decisions for the group when they need to be made. Eventually, the mother will have to let go of her mothering role, or she herself will not survive as a whole person. A mother is more than that function which she performs for a time. If she does not let go of that role, her children will rebel and leave her behind. So many women have experienced this painful process from one side or another that it is a clear lesson of women, one that applies equally well to political leadership as to motherhood.

Other characteristics of a mother's power are her children's dependency on her for their survival, and the intimacy of the mother-child relationship. No one wants to be totally dependent on someone else for her survival, and ideally, in a woman-created society, that would not be the case for either mother or child. However, that dependency does exist, although one saving grace to the relationship is that eventually everyone can outgrow it. Part of a mother's job is to foster independence, a by-product of which is to teach children how to be their own mothers and how to function as a mother to others when the situation requires it. In addition, time, over which we have no control, will change the relationship—in fact, time often reverses it.

The source of authority for a mother in the family group is derived from the intimacy of her relationship with her children that holds her accountable to them for their survival as a group. As they become more independent, they become more empowered to call her to an accounting, and ultimately have the power to leave the group or to withdraw their active participation (and love) from the group, thus breaking the intimacy which is the source of a mother's authority.

Another characteristic of motherhood, which some may call spiritual, but which I see more pragmatically as a survival mechanism, is *faith*. Mothers tend to be worriers because they know that their powers are limited, and that they can do only so much to protect and prepare a child. A mother, to survive this worrying and allow the child to be independent, must operate with an assumption that somehow all the lessons got through and that this child will decide what is best for herself. A mother must "act as if" a child will make the proper decision, knowing at the same time that she/he may not.

It may appear to be a contradiction to act as if you believe one thing while knowing that the opposite thing is possible. The ability to live with contradictions, diversity, and tension is another characteristic of motherhood. Judy Grahn's poem, "A Woman Is Talking to Death," beautifully presents a woman's ability to relate to the connections among people, "in an attempt to embrace contradictory elements of experience and responsibility."[2] She describes hating a man who called her a queer and slugged her. She describes how she "fantasized the scene again, this time grabbing the chair and smashing it over the bastard's head, killing him."[3] Then, remembering her first love, an ostracized pregnant teenager, she points to the contradiction in the situation: "now when I remember, I think: maybe he was Josie's baby, all the chickens come home to roost, all of them."[4]

Contradictions, tensions, and diversity within a group require that a mother be flexible, have a sense of humor, and allow herself to react to as well as act on others in the group.

Demystifying Motherhood

A mother empowers her children by feeding their spirits, not by breaking them. A mother can provide some of the conditions by which children can be free to make choices. Part of providing those conditions is to disclose facts, goals, and process within the group. Moreover, a mother can demystify her role and her function by teaching her children how she learned what she's trying to teach them. This process allows her to let go of what appears to be secret knowledge and mystery. Alta describes this process in her poem, "The Ten Commandments of Liberation." She lists nine dos and don'ts, some of which are:

> Thou shalt clean up thine own messes. . . . Thou shalt not use other people. As Tom Hayden used James Rector to advertise people's park, as marxists use workers to overthrow the ruling class, as I just used Tom Hayden for demonstration purposes. . . . Thou shalt revel in what you really are, don't change your looks, don't stop talking, go ahead and be. Thou shalt not endanger other people for an idea. Thou shalt not be ashamed. We are all perverts. We all have pasts we could spend our whole lives denying. . . .[5]

Alta then ends with the tenth Commandment: "Write your own commandments. I am only a person like you. Burn this and memorize yourself."[6]

Similarly, a mother eventually says, like Alta, "Burn this" (what I have taught you—you're on your own) "and memorize yourself." Not only can a mother demystify her role by sharing the process about how she came to understand things, but the very fact of *not* sharing that process can be a means of domination in itself.

One of the subfunctions of mothering is teaching. In general, a mother teaches two things: 1) individual and group survival skills, and 2) how to be a mother. The first is more conscious than the second; the second often is a by-product of teaching the first. In trying to communicate ethics to children, using abstractions such as truth, freedom, justice, and love is a complete dead end. Children simply want to know what makes sense. They have no preconceptions and therefore hold no sanctity to the terms themselves. Being concrete is a good teaching technique.

More often than men, women pay attention to the connections in life and can focus on the relationships between things, events, ideas, people. The two sides of our brains can communicate with each other.[7] At best, women can communicate very concretely, without the splits between mind, body, emotion, and values. Women can combine the rational and the intuitive—hold two contradictory beliefs at the same time, accept that as reality, and still make a decision—still use their power.

And finally, a redefinition of the role of mother must allow her to have faults, to be an ordinary, common woman and not a model of virtue—feminist virtue or otherwise. Mothers are under incredible social pressure to be perfect, and often internalize the pressure to be a perfect mother by setting unreasonably high expectations for themselves. They are also very aware of being in the spotlight among others, especially family, in dealing with their children (since mothering has been defined as *their* function alone). Therefore, a mother feels guilty if she's tired, or if she even wants a private life of her own. The guilt, justifiably, turns to anger, and she may become unable or unwilling to function in her role at all. Society focuses on the unique significance of her role (one false move and the kid's ruined) and blames her for mistakes that may be her child's (or others') responsibility.

The Common Woman

Several lesbian feminist poets have written about the "ordinariness" of women—that it is often the common woman who will rise to an occasion to play an important role, but that it is because it was necessary to do so and she learned how to do so, not because she possessed a certain genius. Judy Grahn has written of the common woman:

> the common woman is as common as
> good bread
> as common as when you couldn't go
> on but did. For all the world we didn't
> know we held in common
> all along
> the common woman is as common as
> the breast of bread
> and will rise

and will become strong—I swear it to
  you
I swear it to you on my own head
I swear it to you on my common
  woman's head.[8]

And Susan Griffin writes about Harriet Tubman, a common slave, who did what was necessary to be done:

and she lived in swamps
and wore the clothes of a man
bringing hundreds of fugitives from
slavery, and was never caught,
and led an army
and won a battle,
and defied the laws
because the laws were wrong.[9]

The motherhood model I have described reveals that women always have functioned as leaders in family and in small groups, and when allowed, or when necessary, in large groups as well. Certain qualities of feminist leadership can be extrapolated from this motherhood model and can be useful to the women's movement in forming a political theory of leadership.

Like motherhood, I consider leadership to be a function that is teachable by some and learnable by others. It is not a given quality with which one is born, although some may perform the function better than others, depending, at least, on the type of task to be accomplished and the group to be affected.

It is also possible that women already have some notions about leadership by which women have operated and which they are in the process of naming and creating. Writer Joanna Russ has pointed out that there is a theme in women's science fiction of the hero with her apprentice, and that hero-apprentice theme is conspicuously absent from male science fiction, which is usually dominated by the Man Among Men. She also notes that in women's science fiction, heroes are often *groups* of women, and that a hero in one group may be on the periphery in another group.[10] Similarly, in the lesbian feminist novels of June Arnold,[11] while one or two women may take leadership in a specific situation, it is the combined efforts and consciousness of the group of women which succeeds.

These concepts suggest a pattern of leadership far different from men's, in which the group focuses on the leader in the center, with him and his constituents fortifying their egos back and forth. The expectation is that he is the leader now, and always and everywhere will be the leader. Male-defined leadership necessarily implies a political inequality between the leader and the constituents. Although it is important that women recognize that we do not have equal abilities (we are not all the same), leadership among women implies, perhaps for the first time in history, a *possibility* of a relationship between political equals. This is especially true when leadership relationships cross/or reverse class and race lines.

Leadership as a Function

The idea of leadership among political equals, if leadership is seen as a *function*, is not the contradiction it appears to be. Just as sexual relationships between women provide the *condition* for equality in that sexual relationship, political relationships between women are not necessarily equal in all respects; those relationships are merely a necessary condition of equality but not sufficient in and of themselves.

Women's organic (i.e., not contaminated by male systems) ways of leading may be a kind of "shifting leadership," which does not expect a leader to always and everywhere perform that function. Marge Piercy expresses the feeling of this leadership pattern:

> I want to be with people who submerge
>   in the task, who go into the fields
>   to harvest
> and work in a row and pass the bags
>   along,
> who stand in line and haul in their
>   places,
> who are not parlor generals and field
>   deserters
> but move in a common rhythm
> when the food must come in, or the
>   fire be put out.[12]

This quality of people "who do what has to be done, again and again," is also a quality of a good leader, who knows how to join in the task with others. If shifting leadership is a valid assumption about female leadership, then it is important that feminists consider that concept and take advantage of that knowledge politically.

In searching for models of leadership, feminists can examine what they know about male leadership and female leadership as they have *been*. To the extent that feminists need to be organized to gain power, we are dependent on our leaders for our survival also. Viewed as a function, leadership involves a pattern of mutual dependency and responsibility. A group empowers a leader with certain responsibilities. The leader, however, requires that the constituents take responsibility for their own tasks within the group and that they perceive the leader not only as the role she plays within the group. For her own survival as a person, the leader must not be seen only in that role. Her letting go of power depends on the ability of others to learn her functions and be willing to perform her role when her leadership time is spent. This not-being-willing-to-let-go-of-power and the not-being-willing-to-accept-responsibility dynamic often destroys feminist organizations. Clearly naming the process that takes place in any transfer of power in an organization is one step in easing that change itself.

What gives a leader authority? Like mothers, many political leaders learn how to function as leaders from other leaders before them, and may pose them as models in their own minds. So, to some extent, a leader's authority may come from the sense of responsibility which the leader has learned from her model. However, the ultimate authority of a political leader, both politically and ethically, comes from the quality of her relationship with her constituents. It is to them that she must give an accounting of her stewardship. No woman is going to pay her dues (to some *one* or some *thing*) and have no say about what those dues go for. If a leader does not account (take responsibility for) her actions, her constituents have the ultimate control to deny the leadership function to her.

In the women's movement, however, this denial of leadership often takes the form of attack on one's personal style and characteristics, and is more often backbiting than an objective evaluation of a woman's capacity in her role as a leader. By not viewing leadership as a function (which includes a large investment of power in one individual), feminists often destroy the political work they have accomplished and the very women who have helped them accomplish it. Expecting a woman to account for her function as a leader is valid politically; expecting her to account for herself personally *because she is a leader* is not.

Leaders and constituents alike need to operate from an assumption of good faith. Like a mother's attitude toward her children, faith is "acting as if" women have courage when we know that many of us are cowards. Faith is the opposite of defensiveness and paranoia. Elitism, on the other hand, is having no faith. Rather, it is developing a prejudice against either the Led or the Leader. From the leader's perspective, it is assuming that women cannot think for themselves, and results in leaving the weak ones behind, powerless and confused. From the constituent's perspective, elitism is assuming that the leader is not looking out for the best interests of the group, and results in the destruction and loss of many valuable women as leaders in the movement. Politically, faith is a survival mechanism that assumes

women are becoming free as individuals and responsible as political
women.

Sharing the Process

Elitism also includes not sharing the process of decision making and
experience with constituents. Leaders can demystify that function (as
mothers demystify their role) by letting go of what appears to be
secret knowledge and mysteries of decision making. Male leaders
often just arrive at a certain point and proceed to give orders. They
often present their position on certain issues as accomplished fact,
without sharing with their constituents how they got to that position
from having no position at all. Much like male journalists, who present only the facts, the news, the headlines of a story, many male
political leaders fail to present the contradictions, the diversity, and
the struggle that comprised the decision.

A feminist leader, like a mother, must empower her constituents by
listening to them and by teaching them what she knows about getting
things done. A leader can do this by sharing the process of her thinking and her experience with her constituents. Good leaders do not
break our spirits or leave us feeling like losers. Leaders, like mothers,
should provide the conditions by which women can be free to make
choices—disclosure of facts, goals, process. Therefore, leaders have
an obligation to tell truly what is happening rather than contrive a
situation so that it will be to their advantage. This is not to say that
leaders cannot plan strategy, goals, or intent. In fact, they must, as
part of their function as leaders. It *is* to say, that those plans must be
part of the disclosure, up front, where everyone can judge for herself.

This process also implies that a leader must be concrete about what
she is saying, and not explain in vague or general terms that are, in
effect, meaningless to others. Not being specific often means not
communicating, which can develop into a means of domination itself.
Constituent responsibility in this regard is to be attentive, and when
practical, to interact with the leader to a point of understanding.

Men have developed the Great Man theory of leadership: a leader
possesses special qualities that account for his achievements, and
which others can aspire to, but somehow will never attain.[13] Women
know better than to believe this myth about male leaders and should
know better than to believe the myth about mothers. Women have
given birth to, have raised, have comforted, have been brutalized by,
and have buried all those Great Men. They have seen him from all
sides.[14] Perhaps this is one explanation of why feminists have been so
distrustful of leaders who pretend to be, or who are presented by the
media as, The Great Woman.

On the other hand, it is often these same feminists who will not allow their leaders to have failings, and who exert the same social pressure on political leaders that is put on the individual mother by society. Someone is looking for a scapegoat and for both mothers and leaders, it's a setup. People want a leader (mother) who has no failings, yet they want to blame her for the group's failings by exposing her faults and destroying her personally. The result of this dynamic is a reluctance on the part of many women to accept leaders who pretend to be faultless; and, more seriously, a reluctance or refusal on the part of many competent women to accept leadership in the movement as long as they are expected by others to be faultless.

Another aspect of this dilemma is that not all women have identical skills, and that many women are denied their own ability to lead by feminists who insist that women are all the same. Some women are better leaders than others, just as some women are better mothers than others. And just as society expects all women to function equally well at mothering, the women's movement expects all women to function equally well at leading. The attitude is that no matter what skills the job requires, the job can be rotated. While it is true that most skills can be learned and that leadership is one of those skills, it is destructive to the task of the group to expect everyone to perform equally well at any task. It is also destructive to the group's task to postpone or limit the scope of the work that needs to be done, until each woman can acquire the skills of everyone else. In this way, our work becomes a personal workshop and our political work ineffective.

It also is true that in a family everyone is not the same. In the heterosexual nuclear family structure, however, leadership functions are usually divided up along sex-role lines. In an efficient family not modeled on the nuclear family model, differences in ability are recognized, and although skills are taught and shared, the survival and efficiency of the group depends on its using the best of its group in certain capacities when specific skills are needed.

Women will not accept leaders or heroes imposed on them, especially ones who are unwilling to share recognition when that sharing is due. Likewise, women will not accept leaders who display no fear, no doubts, no conflicts, and who have all the answers. I believe that women will accept leadership from the common woman who knows what she is doing, and who will tell you woman-to-woman what she knows about getting things done. She will deserve recognition herself, and will share that recognition with others when it is due.

Nevertheless, leaders will not emerge if they receive no recognition for what they have done. No one wants to lead (or to mother, or do anything else for that matter) without receiving some recognition for having performed that function. Male society rewards its achievers in one way or another, thus reinforcing that behavior and encouraging participation in that system. The women's movement seldom does the same, and often is more likely to negatively reinforce women's accomplishments. Until feminists are willing to accept leadership as a valuable and necessary function in a political movement, and are willing to reward its leaders when they deserve credit for their work, the movement will be crippled as a political force and talented women will be continually frustrated. If the romantic rewards attached to motherhood were removed, and women were given a free choice about becoming mothers, how many women would actually choose to do work for which they receive little if any recognition?

Conclusion

We feminists must define our relationships to our leaders, and as leaders, to our constituents. If we don't, our leaders may well define us, or we may find ourselves without women willing to emerge as leaders. This process requires looking at our responsibilities both as leaders and constituents. Taking responsibility for what one does, whether in a leadership function or not, is the first step toward framing a concept of feminist ethics, and of feminist leadership. The motherhood model of leadership is an attempt to uncover what women already know about leadership in a small group, and to create one possibility of a model for women as political leaders, an adaptation of an already existent framework of leadership. This characterizing of the qualities of feminist leadership should not, and need not, be thought of as a creed. It is merely a beginning, with a few clues, a few openers about what we need to define about leadership.

NOTES

1. Susan Griffin, "I Like to Think of Harriet Tubman," Shameless Hussy Press, P.O. Box 424, San Lorenzo, Calif.
2. Inez Martinez, "The Poetry of Judy Grahn," *Margins*, August 1975, 2919 N. Hackett, Milwaukee, Wisc. Beth Hodges, *ed*.
3. Judy Grahn, "A Woman Is Talking To Death," The Woman's Press Collective, 5251 Broadway, Oakland, Calif.
4. Ibid.
5. Alta, "The Ten Commandments Of Liberation," *Burn This And Memorize Yourself*, Times Change Press, Penwell Road, Washington, N.J. 07882.
6. Ibid.
7. Gina Covina, "Rosy Rightbrain's Exorcism/Invocation," *The Lesbian Reader*, Amazon Press, 395 60th St., Oakland, Calif. 94618.
8. Judy Grahn, *The Common Woman*, The Woman's Press Collective, 5251 Broadway, Oakland, Calif. 94618.

9. Susan Griffin, "I Like to Think of Harriet Tubman."
10. From a lecture by Joanna Russ, author of *The Female Man* (Bantam Books), Woman To Woman Bookcenter, Denver, Col., 14 December 1975.
11. June Arnold, *Sister Gin, The Cook and the Carpenter*, Daughters, Inc., 54 7th Ave. South, New York, N.Y. 10014.
12. Marge Piercy, "To Be Of Use," *To Be of Use* (New York: Doubleday n.d).
13. From lectures by Rita Mae Brown, Sagaris, June 1975.
14. This point is dramatically made in the film *The Women's Happy Time Commune*, Women Make Movies, New York, N.Y.

The Beguines: A Medieval Women's Community

Gracia Clark

Editor's Note—The religious revival associated with the twelfth century led thousands of women to found and enter convents. Most of the religious movements of the period, dominated by male clergy, exerted strong pressures to limit women's independence within their nunneries. Against this background appeared a women's religious movement independent of any male impetus or direction—the Beguines.

An understanding of the rise and fall of the Beguines can provide a strength and vision of the viability of present and future groups of women who establish independent communities separate from men. The institutions the Beguines set up to reconcile class differences, to meet the needs of members for food, clothing, housing, and social and spiritual nourishment, as well as the ultimate decline of the movement provide insight into the strengths and weaknesses inherent in various alternative structures. The Beguines are a medieval example of how women can live and work together. Their collapse, and the reasons for it, raise questions for the women's movement today.

Most people believe that during the Middle Ages a deathly stillness descended over Western Europe, freezing its inhabitants into hereditary roles defined by custom and rigidly enforced by feudal orders and the church. Women, in particular, had no rights and no influence except through their men, who exchanged women as political chattels if noble, or as units of labor if peasants.

In fact, during the High Middle Ages (i.e., the twelfth through fourteenth centuries), a large number of women within the mainstream of Christian orthodoxy took it upon themselves to provide spiritual stimulation, recognition, and security for each other.[1] Hundreds of thousands of them built lives of spiritual and economic independence as Beguines in the towns of northern France and Germany and the intervening Low Countries. Contemporaries conferred on these conspicuously pious women a semiclerical respect. Women in every part of society drew strength from personal contact with Beguines and the vigorous alternative they offered to life with men.

Turbulence and instability in medieval society during these centuries gave such women a powerful motivation for self-reliance. Traditional means of delivering daily needs and assuring status could not be depended on. Political groupings shifted constantly. Rapid growth of wholesale trade and concentrated industry, especially in textiles, shifted power to new cities and introduced money and mysterious economic forces into the political process. The booming cloth industry bloated towns with unmarried wage earners. Institutions developed to protect commerce competed openly with rural feudal patterns.

In the twelfth century women who practiced Christian virtue on their own, dressing and living simply and not associating with men, began to stand out as a separate category of person. They followed this pattern of life in many places—in family homes, alone in working-class huts, in townhouses they shared with likeminded relatives, near sympathetic convents, and in remote wild places. In the thirteenth century they began to call themselves Beguines. Their growing numbers, self-awareness, and solidarity enabled them to protect and develop their way of life into the next century.

Not only did Beguinism begin with the independent impulses of thousands of individuals, but it proceeded to take its form from their need to become independent of the established institutions of society. Family life seriously hampered their efforts to act out the ideals of chastity and unworldliness endorsed by the church. It subjected them to living conditions and schedules designed by their husbands and fathers. Just maintaining a family's house and social position meant many hours of irreligious activity. Most young women living at home faced strong pressure to marry and improve the family's financial or political position. Rural women often depended entirely on their place in the family for income. Widows and townspeople controlled their own property but still felt constant psychological pressure to marry. A woman who adopted voluntary chastity proved she could provide herself one of the prerequisites to a spiritual life. Clearly, Beguines had to find alternatives to the family strong enough to protect them from a family-oriented society.

Nunneries were popular, but unsuitable for many women. For one thing, nuns needed considerable family support. Monastic discipline effectively prevented them from earning a living by requiring about six hours of ritual prayer a day and forbidding all contact with the world. The overcrowded convents consequently accepted only wealthy women with enough property to support them for life.

Living Within the Beguines Community

In the towns, Beguines gathered along certain streets much as weavers, butchers, and other tradespeople did. Dayton Phillips'[2] careful compilation of their wills and addresses in Strasbourg uncovers a whole section of town inhabited mainly by women who shared houses, rented to one another, bequeathed houses to their roommates, or provided for the selection of other Beguines as tenants as the present residents left or died. Concentrated in cheap, subdivided houses in the artisan areas of town, they particularly favored land owned by the Franciscan and Dominican monasteries. The friars were willing to experiment with new terms of leasing that did not provide for including women's families. They leased rooms within houses and let tenants leave if they found their own replacements. They wanted to acquire property, so often exchanged a life interest in a house for a woman's farmland in a nearby village. They also would lease at reduced rates to women who agreed to forfeit the right of medieval renters to pass the lease on to their descendents. By such means, a well-defined neighborhood grew up, with Beguines as the nucleus of a larger group of unattached women who were not recognized as Beguines but often left property to other women or Beguines. Phillips estimates that in Strasbourg, this community amounted to 10 to 25 percent of the city, and that other major cities supported communities of similar importance.

Such a large number of houses, each containing up to seven women, provided a wide choice of living conditions. Some houses had reputations for spiritual enthusiasm and austerity, while others catered to women more interested in the independence and respectability available through the Beguine life. Houses varied widely in their rules concerning hours, meals, living expenses, and church attendance. Through the strength of the Beguine community, women could choose these options on their own initiative irrespective of their wealth or past behavior.

The independence of the Beguine movement from clerical leaders or overseers distinguished it from all other Christian groups of the time. Beguines had sought no one's permission to be chaste or thoughtful, and their virtue was not enforced by obedience to their family or religious head. Because they had observed parish duties and adhered to orthodox beliefs, the church hierarchy could, at that time, find no reason to oppose them. Meanwhile, they undermined the church by swaying the spiritual orientation of the time toward virtues that anyone could practice. Humility and compassion did not require the same overhead as esoteric meditation, theology, or dramatic self-abasement. The degree to which Beguines found spiritual stimulation in each other and ignored the church hierarchy obviously unnerved many officials, who kept giving them permission to do the things they already were doing.

Women interested in intellectual and spiritual questions came to the Beguine communities to learn to read and discuss the Scriptures and other popular issues of the day. Most Beguine creative activity took the form of influencing other women, either informally or during house meetings. These meetings were secret to prevent tale-bearing, so most of their content has been lost. Only a few letters survive, between people who met in one place and kept in touch through their wanderings.

Hostile clerics denounced their unnatural thirst for knowledge, interest in theological questions, and respect for each other's opinions. Beguines shocked church observers by arguing with their pastors, debating the Trinity, and weighing the merits of manual labor against those of renouncing all possessions. They directly inspired nuns and laywomen to pursue their own spiritual interests with more energy.

Beguines soon began to provide for themselves the services normally provided through family connections. Very early they contributed to hospitals for their sick and aged. By 1250, in most towns they had formed corporations in imitation of the craft guilds, through which they bargained with city, church, and overlord for various privileges. Sometimes Beguines got tax relief or the right to ply certain trades without joining the appropriate guilds. Whether or not she joined one of the Beguine corporations and enjoyed its privileges, a Beguine arranged her life as she liked. Many women were Beguines for a short time, perhaps after a personal crisis. A Beguine chose the trade that most appealed to her. Beguines commonly nursed the sick; washed wool, cloth, or clothing; baked bread; spun; and ran schools for young girls. Spinning occupied a good part of the female population of Europe. Before widespread use of the spinning wheel, the flourishing cloth industry had an insatiable appetite for wool thread. Carrying only a spindle, a Beguine could settle anywhere and immediately have work. They often traveled to stay with illustrious people or hear famous preachers. They chose their own companions, and any activity they found rewarding could be carried on with honor as part of a chaste and therefore already special life.

Life in the beguinage was informal and quiet. Women lived, worked, and visited in their own homes. Novices and women under thirty lived in a large building, ate together, and met weekly for discussion and correction. The whole beguinage met monthly for mutual criticism and exhortation, at which time infractions of the rules were punished. Beguines controlled their own property and could rent to other Beguines and bequeath part of it as they chose. The remainder, including houses in the beguinage, reverted to the beguinage when the owner died or left. The Grand Mistress, or Martha, administered common property in the name of the infirmary. Sick or destitute residents could get free meals at the infirmary and retire to live there.

Such practical advantages attracted many women to Beguine communities, but they also were the main centers of religious thought for interested women. Nunneries at that time frequently did not even teach their members the meaning of the daily services they recited, though a few were noted for scholarship and mysticism.

Absence of central authority or hierarchy within the Beguine movement let it absorb contributions from women of different social classes without one or another group capturing special influence. By avoiding both economic insecurity and dependence on a central treasury, it could ignore economic leverage. High-born figures often got more publicity, but within the houses themselves leaders emerged from group meetings. Working-class women dominated the movement, since workers numerically dominated the towns and had no other religious option. Many of the houses noted by Phillips had founders or leaders of artisan or peasant origin. Artisan families trained their daughters as independent workers who easily could continue as Beguines, and often gave them experience in skills like money management. Citizens or bourgeoises, a separate, richer class in the towns, enjoyed less independence, but their families often supported the beguinage with its close ties to their beloved city. Therefore, beguinages could absorb numbers of upper-class women without becoming unbalanced.

Sharing skills and support in countless communities built up ties to women in all sections of society. Families sent their daughters to the beguinage to be educated before marriage in reading, religion, and the domestic arts. They returned home with self-confidence from the example of strong women and the knowledge of an independent life always open to them. Many retained sentimental ties to the beguinage and came back in their old age. Beguinism achieved such a strong position in the life of medieval women by uniting the drives for spiritual, social, and economic independence. Women soon found that one goal necessitated the others, and that they had to work together for an environment that promoted their aims. For a half dozen generations, they succeeded very well in creating such environments on a large scale. Women who chiefly desired to leave their former living groups, or to earn their own living in their own way, or to reach out toward a higher spiritual awareness, found that the efforts of other women complemented their own by removing obstacles they had been less aware of.

Beguines at the height of the movement enjoyed more freedom and more power to expand their lives in any direction than any of their contemporaries, male or female. They had conquered class norms almost entirely. While a woman's income or earning capacity still determined her material standard of living, this standard did not govern nonmaterial aspects of her life and was not emphasized as a yardstick of worth. They did, however, show considerable ageism in their choice of leaders. In many sources, the terms "mistresses" and "elder Beguines" clearly represent at least overlapping categories. On the other hand, the authority of the mistresses over their colleagues was extremely limited. They could not force any woman to give up or adopt any practice not covered in the bylaws. Holiness was not expected to coincide with the temporal authority of mistresses, and many young women won distinction for their kindliness, self-denial, or learning.

Beguines Versus the Church

In the early fourteenth century the church managed to check the Beguines' expansion. The commitment to respectability that had helped Beguines reach into parts of society under male control deprived them of a base from which to resist outright orders from the church. Church leaders could not with consistency tell any woman to marry or wear provocative clothing, but they were fundamentally hostile to Beguine independence. After several false starts, they settled on the tactic of requiring women to live in beguinages or organized Beguine houses to enjoy Beguine privileges and avoid ridicule by jealous neighbors and clerics. During the 1320s and '30s, the informal communities of women who had gathered around most concentrations of Beguines dispersed under this pressure. Those who remained became a status group of the church, relatively isolated and known to be concerned with defending their privileges. Soon church authorities made the further demand that they take permanent vows as lay associates of the Franciscans or Dominicans. These vows permitted a more normal life than Beguines already led, but a singular lack of energy followed their adoption. Removing the beguinages' peculiar independence by enforcing obedience to a supervising friar was evidently enough to make them decline sharply into charity homes and sheltered workshops.

Beguines' independence, both from society and each other, appears to have been the lifeblood of their movement. As autonomous women they lived together long enough to have worked out ways of satisfying almost all their needs. We could ask about what weakness did they leave for the church to work on? Perhaps their very lack of central discipline prevented them from resisting forcefully the church's determined efforts to undermine them. On the other hand, their organization into corporations might have created vested interests among members, who later proved willing to abandon their informal sisters to keep their privileges. By all accounts, these privileges alienated their working-class neighbors, who had no such insulation against war and disaster.

Feminists wrestle with similar pressures and questions, and need to consider this past experience from many perspectives. Could the drive for independence be used as a uniting force in our own work or does it have an intrinsic flaw we should respect by avoiding? For Beguines it integrated the transcendent, material, and social spheres of life into a coherent spirit of self-definition, which at its most powerful, made external categories irrelevant.

NOTES

1. Ernest W. McDonnell, *The Beguines and Beghards in Medieval Culture* (New Brunswick, N.J.: Rutgers University Press, 1954).
2. Dayton Phillips, *Beguines in Medieval Strasburg: A Study of the Social Aspect of Beguine Life* (Stanford: Stanford University Press, 1941).

Reflections on Science Fiction

An Interview with Joanna Russ

Q: *How did you begin writing science fiction?*

A: I started writing science fiction in my last year of graduate school after three years of doing nothing but play writing for an M.F.A. from Yale Drama School. I had never written any science fiction before, but had read it since I was twelve and loved it.

Q: *Why did you choose this particular form? Did you see it as having political, social, or moral implications for contemporary life?*

A: First, science fiction is a mode rather than a form (a form would be something like the sonnet, the short story, etc.). It is, basically, anything that is about conditions of life or existence different from either what typically is, or what typically was, or whatever was or is. It is allied to fantasy (which I also write) but is not fantasy—which incorporates as part of its pleasure the impossibility of its material. Science fiction is about the possible-but-not-real. Second, I do not believe that any artist (as opposed to hack) chooses a form; the form chooses the artist, if anything. I did not "choose" s.f. because I saw it as having "political, social, or moral implications for contemporary life." I did not choose s.f. at all. I had always loved it. I read it because horror stories and s.f. seemed to me, from the age of 11–12 on, to be about real life in a way that the classics we were assigned at school were not. Both horror stories and s.f. seem to me in many ways freer and more imaginative than "straight" fiction (although most *avant-garde* fiction has abolished the distinction between realism and fantasy, something nobody taught us in high school). Does s.f. have "moral implications"? Good Lord, is there *anything* that doesn't have moral implications? I don't want to go into the old, idiot song-

and-dance routine about s.f. being prophetic (it isn't) or wonderful for developing the imagination (it rarely succeeds after the first addiction wears off) ... yet I'm still addicted to it. Possibly it's the appeal of the utterly impossible, for a truly first-rate s.f. novel would have to be a great novel, period, and in addition have to surmount the most extraordinary technical difficulties. Forty years ago those who cried out that s.f. was good were voices crying in the wilderness. Now there are ghastly textbooks put out by Prentice-Hall.

Q: *Have your ideas about the role and importance of science fiction changed?*

A: What has changed in my feelings about s.f. is the result of reading it for 25 years. So little of it really reaches the potential of the mode that reading most of it is becoming a chore. Let's say that like a great many critics and readers I remain faithful to the ideal, but deplore most of the practice. Now that s.f. is beginning to be academically respectable, my feelings about its "role" (whatever that is) are mixed. S.f should *ideally* be able to say more about more than other fiction.

Q: *Do you view your science fiction writing as feminist? How do your feminist views affect the science fiction you write?*

A: I am a feminist. Therefore all my writing comes from a *gestalt* or ground-of-being that includes my feminism. I say "feminism" as if it were a set of explicable beliefs, which in part it is, but there is also a kind of basic experience of which I was aware most of my life but which did not find political expression or a vocabulary until about seven years ago. If you want to call both of these "feminist," then yes, of course my writing (all of it, including non-s.f. fiction) is feminist. And it affects what I write, just as everything else I am or have been or have experienced affects what I write. I am currently being beaten over the head in an s.f. magazine by a reviewer of *The Female Man* for this reason. The novel has a great deal of rage in it, which discomforts not only this one reviewer but some women who read and write s.f. The novel is even treated as a blueprint for the future, despite the fact that none of the conditions I describe in the novel exist now or probably ever will. But of course the real target is the taboo against rage, specifically rage against men. Long before I became a feminist in any explicit way (my first reaction upon hearing Kate Millet speak in 1968 was that of course every woman *knew* that, but if you ever dared to formulate it to yourself, let alone say it out loud, God would kill you with a lightning bolt), I had turned from writing love stories about women in which women were losers, and adventure stories about men in which men were winners, to writing adventure stories about a woman in which the woman won. It was one of the hardest things I ever did in my life. These are stories about a sword-and-sorcery heroine called Alyx, and before writing the first I spent about two weeks in front of my typewriter shaking, and thinking of how I'd be stoned in the streets, accused of penis envy, and so on (after that it is obligatory to commit suicide, of course).

It was shifting my center of gravity from Him to Me and I think it's the most difficult thing an artist can do—a woman artist, that is. It's OK to write about artist-female with feet in center of own stage as long as she suffers a lot and is defeated and is wrong (the last is optional). But to win, and to express the anger that's in all of us, is a taboo almost as powerful as the taboo against being indifferent to The Man. Some criticisms I've heard about my latest novel are, for example, that there are no sympathetic male characters in it. Actually the people in it (of both sexes) are not a choice lot, objectively considered, but then I do not think it any artist's business to pretend to a false objectivity. Objectivity is for God and She's not telling. Actually the book is somewhat more complex, inasmuch as the women in it (except for Laur) are really parts of one woman, and the two men (leaving out the spear carriers) are the extremes of sexism *as it impinges on women's lives*. The shift of sympathy is what's being complained about. There are no men portrayed sympathetically because when you are writing about what amounts to a sex war, it is *tempo rubato* to get all misty-eyed about the poor oppressor, as well as uneconomical, aesthetically speaking.

As you can see, I respond to criticism as every writer I know does: by screaming blue murder. But it is hard to convey a distinction that I think very important: that *The Female Man* and "When It Changed" are explicitly feminist because that's what they are about, but that everything else I write must of necessity bear the imprint of the consciousness and sensibility it came from, and that is, of course feminist. I spent three years after *The Female Man* trying to get together some theory of propaganda or persuasion or social analysis in art and haven't managed yet; I only hope I built some of the difficulties and ambiguities *into* the novel itself, as I had tried to do.

Mind you, writing what I call propaganda is no different from writing anything else. But the specific problems (for example, the unconscious picture writers have of the reader) are different.

In the end, *The Female Man* came over as possibly the only kind of propaganda there can be: either a celebration (to those who agree) or a construct which *forces* you through a certain cluster of experiences and states of mind. If you do not agree with the assumptions underlying the "portrait" of this experience, reading the book will be torture and it will make you very angry, but perhaps the only propaganda there can be for a forbidden feeling or belief or existence is simply to present it, as Rita Mae Brown and Jean Genet do. Social analysis or argument (as in Brecht, Ibsen, Shaw) is infinitely more difficult in narrative, and may do much better on stage, where the dialectic of argument is live and much easier to make compelling, or comic, or at least interesting.

To be blunt, I wrote my explicitly feminist work in the same way and out of the same motives and ground I write everything. I did not "decide" to do it. It's an attempt to get my head together—literally, in the novel, where there are at least four women with one head apiece, none of whom is a whole woman until they finally do get together . . . for Thanksgiving dinner. I still think that was a witty bit, you know, Thanksgiving. Hm. Anyway.

q: *How important is it to emphasize female characters as strong and independent?*

a: The crucial question about the feminism of a work is not whether the women in it are strong and independent (though I understand your concern perfectly, having been subjected to generations of Supersimps myself in literature) but whether the assumptions underlying the entire narrative are feminist. A sexist story can exist in which all the characters are crystalline life forms living on a planet of Betelguese—yes, and a racist one, too—because although the characters aren't human, the writer and readers are. What's important is who wins and who loses; a remake of Madam Butterfly, with lots of tears, is not a feminist piece of art, no matter who's written it and no matter what sympathy is extended to the poor victim. Many woman are guilty of this kind of thing as writers. (I like to call it the Joan Didion Syndrome.) Whatever its worth as art (and I think its sentimentality inevitably vitiates it) feminism it ain't. Art is not simple.

q: *Does the women's movement need science fiction and fantasy? Do you think the women's movement has had difficulties in fantasizing, has suffered from an inability to dream?*

a: May the Heavenly Couple bless me, I don't know enough about "the women's movement" per se to know if we should be dreaming more. The inability to dream is just what s.f. is supposed to remedy—and not like pure fantasy. No, I shouldn't say that about fantasy; fantasy is inner space. Most of what publishers call "fantasy" has been written either by men or by women simply imitating the tradition of what already existed. There have always been some women writing s.f., but now that Marge Piercy is doing it, and there is the novel about Ishtar returning as a Bronx house-wife, it does seem to be thriving. Fantasy is extremely difficult in another way, though; there is in it (as Ursula LeGuin points out, at least in the heroic-romance form) *nothing but words*.

Inability to dream—well, everybody needs to dream. It is our spiritual and moral guide. Politics certainly can't be divorced from ultimate goals or ideas about possibilities. The only difficulty I ever encountered with feminists over s.f. was several years ago in the Labyris Bookstore, into which I barged cheerfully (a perfect stranger) and proposed to give the woman there a list of s.f. titles. She seemed rather suspicious and probably with reason—I would imagine they'd had considerable hassling in their existence—yet I learned later they simply could not keep LeGuin's *The Left Hand of Darkness* in stock. It always sold out. I say very angry things about Ursula LeGuin quite often, but it's the anger of disappointed adoration; in some daughterly part of me I feel she's capable of writing something like *War and Peace* about *women*, damn it, and I keep nipping her feet to get her to do so. But *The Left Hand of Darkness* is the nearest thing we have to an androgynous vision. I would like to think that *The Female Man* is a gynandrous vision, so if you put the two into a blender (that is, into your head) and mix well, you may end up with something. To return to your question, some of the distrust some feminists *may* have for s.f. is quite reasonable, since a great deal of s.f. is a kind of misogynist power-tripping of a very absurd and adolescent kind. And since it is s.f. and not realism, this shows far more baldly than in realistic fiction. The mode contains perhaps 100 serious, full-time writers and altogether perhaps 300 from neophyte aspirants to old professionals, so that every range of quality and content is there. A feminist who goes to the novel rack (under "s.f.") and picks at random is likely to be not only bored but genuinely insulted. I can only account for my early addiction by adducing the other, mind-expanding quality of the s.f. works available to me, then, and the fact that, whatever its faults, s.f. does present possibilities per se.

Q: *How do you see the relationship between the visions you have described and possibilities for political change, for example, in the different worlds you see in The Female Man?*

A: Impossible question! Books are not blueprints. They are experiences. The worlds in *The Female Man* are not futures; they are here and now writ large. One man just wrote me a lovely fan letter in which he not only described the structure of the book with a precision that astonished me ("an inward descending spiral") but also mentioned casually that Manland/Womanland was *here-and-now*. A flat statement of it would be that Jeannine's world is the past (but still very much present); that Janet's world is a kind of ideal (into which I put all sorts of quirky things I happen to like,

like public comic statuary); and that Jael's world is here-and-now carried out to its logical extreme. Joanna keeps running from one to the other. Janet's world is the potential one, not Jael's. I've been asked why there are no men in Whileaway, and my only answer is that I tried but the Whileawayans wouldn't let me.

I can't imagine a two-sexed egalitarian society and I don't believe anyone else can, either, though Samuel Delany comes closer in *Trouble on Triton* than anything else I've ever read. Well, here you have the whole thing about s.f. Where else could one even try out such visions? Yet in the end we will have to have models for the real thing and I can find none yet, and that is why Whileaway is single-sexed. So is Gethen in *The Left Hand of Darkness*, really.

Q: *What should women science fiction writers be doing?*

A: Why, writing s.f., of course. Obviously work which deals with sexism and feminism will have an effect on feminism, on antifeminism, and (one would think) on all its readers. The effect could easily be reactionary; there seems to have been a mini-upsurge in antifeminist s.f., some quite naive—for example, John Boyd's "Pollinators of Eden" in which a frigid female biologist is converted to love and orgasm by making it with a giant sentient orchid. She later gives birth to a pod. (I have never been able to figure out quite how serious Boyd's work is, by the way. Yes, I know it's intended to be funny, but *how* funny?) Or even his *Sex and the High Command*, an extremely sexist book in which women win the sex war and exterminate men. That's what I mean about carefully watching a book's assumptions, not just its obvious statements. You don't have to "mean" sexism; all you have to do is remain comfortable and unthinking, if you're male.

By the way, James Blish says he invented the words "hard science" to mean *correct* science, as in "hard copy." Popular usage— "hard" means the masculine range of physics, chemistry, astronomy, engineering, and "soft" means the social sciences—is as neat an example of sexist language as I have ever heard. Phallus worship invades the domain of Sacred Reason. Even "hard" to indicate "correct" or "precise" suggests the same thing. (I prefer "winged" myself.)

To be female or feminine or inaccurate or sloppy is to be "soft." Sexual excitement makes women physically mushy and probably does the same to their minds, if they ever had any. All of Western history (and probably Asiatic, too) is in that pair of words! The horrors of the swamp, the split between mind and body, between power and emotion. Oh dear.

This is the effect of reading sex war books written by men. In one of them God invents a specific form of syphilis (which doesn't show up on a Wasserman test) to give 5,000 insurgent American

businesswomen (who have masculinized themselves via andro-
gens because they can't get raises and promotions any other way,
and who immediately do take over American business, since they
are far more intelligent than their male colleagues) terminal
paresis. Well, *that* one dates back to the "teens." The frequency
with which these books drag in God or "love" (woman falls on
knees, melts—see, "soft"—confesses sins, licks toesies, is converted) suggests to me that men are very uneasy about being able
even to hold their own without divine intervention.

Q: *What has been the role of women and feminism in science fiction
writing?*

A: Women have been in the minority in s.f. from the beginning (if you
characterize the beginning as the 1920s or as the Wells/Verne
period). This is hardly surprising. The only literary genre in which
women have reached anything like a substantial number of
writers working is in the detective story. I don't know why.
Perhaps 1920's s.f., with its emphasis on pulp, he-man adventure,
and (later) on the "hard" sciences, which were assumed to be a
closed book to women, simply did not attract women writers.
There were always some, though to my sloppy historical memory,
they wrote either (generally) adventure stories about he-men or
sexless stories about phenomena in engineering or strange gim-
micks/inventions, just as the men did. There have been a few sentimental ladies' magazine story writers and stories. Pulp fiction
was not a place for any artist; the assumption was that the product was (within limits) standard and that one ought not to be able
to tell a man's work from a woman's . . . as if Dickens ought to
sound like Thackeray and both of them be indistinguishable from
Tolstoy, on the grounds that little things like a writer's era or
nationality ought not to "show"! This commercial attitude still
persists. After all, you can't tell from the Kleenex box whether the
assembly line was staffed by women or men, so why should a
story be different?

Women are still in the minority. In 1973 the membership of the
Science Fiction Writers of America was, roughly, two women to
eleven men. However, the women have been winning a disproportionate number of the prizes given in the field. This suggests to me
that (as in many other fields) women s.f. writers are more rigorously self-selected than the men.

Q: *Can women science fiction writers play a political role in the field of
science fiction and within the women's movement?*

A: Of course they can have a political role within science fiction—if
you mean by this, the internal politics of the field. It is happening
now. One young man has started "The Pig Runner's Digest" to
flout and attack sexism (and its more easily spottable symptom,

misogyny) in s.f. Equal pay is another matter—*everybody* is poor and publishers generally print any novel that holds together (as long as they can underpay you for it). On the other hand, I have heard stories of "Oh, we can't print that; women s.f. writers don't sell," and so on. As in any freelance field where the machines are always hungry for cotton to be woven, nobody cares who picks it. At least I hope so. If things get much more lucrative, they may change. Then again I am in no position to be told to my face that X won't print my novel because I'm female. Or because the novel is feminist. Or it scared the hell out of the senior editor.

Within the women's movement, certainly women s.f. writers can provide spiritual nutriment and visions and (probably) annoyance and everything else to women's movement readers. That is, as writers. As private citizens they can do all sorts of things, obviously. Some women s.f. writers will undoubtedly continue to write about Superduperman (but even there he will be more likely to have a stubborn "girl sidekick") and some won't. The newest generation of s.f. writers of both sexes is largely a generation trained primarily in literature, not science (or science only secondarily), and since the concerns of science fiction are shifting from "hard" science to social structures and psychology/anthropology, it is easier for women (since most women are not trained in science) to enter s.f. What I would like to see, for the health of feminism and the health of s.f., is an influx of new women writers.

The Feminist Workplace

Interview with Nancy MacDonald

This interview of Nancy MacDonald was conducted by Alexa Freeman of the Quest *staff and by Jackie MacMillan, a former member of the Rape Crisis Center, founder and member of the Feminist Alliance Against Rape, and member of the theme development committee for the issue of* Quest *in which this interview appeared.*

Nancy MacDonald recently resigned as administrator of the D.C. Rape Crisis Center. The Center's primary goal is to work toward elimination of rape by attempting to deal with rape in a comprehensive way. It provides direct services to rape victims through counseling and the dissemination of medical information; it provides programs aimed at educating people politically about rape (primarily in the D.C. public schools); and it works to reform institutions connected with rape, including the police department, hospitals and the legal system. The bulk of the funding for the Center comes through a contract with the D.C. government.

This interview was conducted with Nancy to gain some insight into the experience one woman has had working intimately and over a long period of time in a feminist workplace; why she chose to work there and what she perceives as the advantages and disadvantages of such a work choice.

While listening to the tape of this interview, Alexa and Jackie found themselves both disagreeing with and elaborating upon some of Nancy's comments. Many observations about the Center corresponded to their own feminist workplace experiences. At the same time, some of Nancy's comments seemed to apply to a particular type of organizing. In their companion piece, which follows the interview, Alexa and Jackie attempted to draw some generalizations regarding various aspects of feminist workplaces.

ALEXA: What are some of the reasons that women choose to work at the Center?

NANCY: There are many different reasons. Some women are motivated by a sense of outrage caused by an individual attack against them or someone close to them. Others have come to an understanding of the kinds of institutional prejudice and discrimination that exist against women, again perhaps through an individual experience, and they, too, want to do something. Some are bored or unfulfilled in their regular jobs, and are anxious to work with other women to change things. Women have also come to the Center from other crisis centers after moving to D.C. A lot of women express a desire to work directly with victims. New women come especially because they want to counsel victims, and often do not necessarily feel the other work of the Center is as important as counseling and direct contact with victims. Often women who come to the Center haven't thought about rape in political terms, and some don't have very much experience in organizing. So it's a very mixed group.

ALEXA: If that's the case, what process of political education and consciousness raising on the issue of rape goes on at the Center, and what structures have been set up for training women to work at the Center?

NANCY: We've experimented and we've changed our structures continually to deal with this, mainly because there's no guarantee that once you've hung around the Center for a while you're going to have a political consciousness about the act of rape. From the beginning it was felt that no special skills were needed to deal with rape victims other than empathy and the fact that you were a woman. We never felt that you had to have counseling experience or anything like that; we felt that you could learn what you needed to know from the women at the Center.

Training has been very informal in the past, although it has become more structured. Our original orientations were seminars where women who had been around the Center for a while would talk in small groups about areas where they had particular knowledge, such as medical treatment, counseling, speaking, or whatever. The knowledge women gained was primarily from working on the phone and from being in the Center and seeing how things ran. Reading was encouraged—the Center's own literature and books we felt had a good analysis of rape. Now the women who are operating the Center have a formally structured training program, which has ten weekly sessions, and additional political discussions on specific topics. They structure training more traditionally now, because a lot of women who came felt disoriented and needed more structure. Training has always been something we felt we would change based on the needs of the women who were there at the time.

ALEXA: To the extent to which you have different levels of involvement in the Center, what kinds of structures have evolved for decision making?

NANCY: Originally, members had weekly meetings and all decisions were made then. There was a Steering Committee, which was composed of the heads of committees in specific areas such as counseling, self-defense, and so on; the Steering Committee decided overall policy. Regular day-to-day decisions were held over for the weekly meetings. With the advent of a paid staff, it evolved that more and more decisions on a day-to-day basis were made by the paid staff, simply because they were around more. Weekly meetings were no longer necessary; meetings are now held monthly, and we've been trying to develop new structures to keep more women involved in decision making. Of course the staff who are there every day will make more decisions than the people who aren't, but we wanted women who were committed to the Center for a long time, but weren't being paid, to have participation in decision making. One way this has been done is to distinguish between members of the Center and volunteers. A volunteer is a woman who has joined the Center and is being trained but has not yet made a long-term commitment to our work. A member is someone who worked at the Center for six months, has gone through training, and is obviously going to be around for a while; members have the same decision-making capacity as the paid staff.

Another structure for decision making is that on major decisions between meetings, three other people have to be consulted by the woman who is dealing with the matter individually. For example, if *Time* called up and wanted an interview, the woman who took the call would have to discuss it with three other women before making a commitment. We have been very conscious of keeping all the Center members involved in decisions, not just those who are paid.

JACKIE: The Center, from my experience, is an organization women can come into without any background in the women's movement and learn about it there, whereas a lot of groups want only women who have some movement background or experience. Do you consider this one of the functions of the Center?

NANCY: Looking back, it's a place where a lot of women have come who would not consider themselves feminists, but through their work with the Center, they come in contact with the political ideas of the women's movement. They see these ideas in relation to a concrete problem. This experience breaks down barriers that exist between many women and the women's movement. Black women, for instance, who saw the Center as a white woman's place, came and saw women trying to deal with racism and dedicated to meeting the needs of black women in the community. Also, a lot of straight women at the Center had their first conversation with a woman they knew was a lesbian.

It's a place where the political ideas of the movement are personalized—divested of all those trappings that are so alienating to so many women—because just sitting around talking and dealing with whatever you have to do, and learning by doing, breaks down barriers. It doesn't always work, obviously; there have been straight women who have left the Center, freaked out about the fact that someone is a lesbian; some women are alienated by a political analysis of rape, others put off by a chaotic working situation. But at least it's a beginning. I see that now as something really important.

JACKIE: I've heard women talk about the Center as different from the rest of the women's movement, and I think that's largely because many women get their idea of the movement from the media, and they haven't previously been exposed directly to any kind of feminist operation. The Center is not that radically different from a lot of other feminist groups; it's just that the direct contact between women there breaks down some of the myths about what the women's movement is like.

ALEXA: What do you see as important attributes of the Center as a feminist workplace?

NANCY: One is the fact that you can retain a large measure of control over your workplace. As a group we set the hours, divide the work, determine the salaries, and hire and release the staff, based on our judgment of the best way to operate. The decisions we make may ultimately be incorrect, and a lot of times after we've decided something, six months later we kick ourselves; but we have the responsibility, and we learn how to make decisions by making them. That's one area where most women have very little experience, and for newcomers especially, it can be very intimidating. I think that's where support in making decisions is important.

Another positive aspect of the Center is that it provides for support in dealing with personal problems. If you are working in a regular job and your kids get sick or you need to look for a place to live, that's your problem. If you have leave time, fine; otherwise, too bad, and if you can't deal with it—very well, that just means you're incompetent. At the Center, though, we feel that as long as you get your work done and the phone is covered, if you have to take off a couple of days to look for a house or something like that, that's all right. We see problems that women face as set in a political context. That realization, for women who come there, is very important.

Also, there is the possibility for self-education and development in a supportive context at the Center. When you come, you have an opportunity to learn about health, peer counseling, fund raising, speaking, workshops—all kinds of stuff—and you do it in a supportive atmosphere. You're encouraged to try things you never thought about doing before, and this is important, both for your self-concept and for the needs of the Center as well. At the Center, women can break out of traditional "female" behavior patterns without fear of being ridiculed or censured for trampling on male egos. Most important, you understand things that happen to women as political acts in a larger framework, and you see both the need for change and the possibilities for it.

JACKIE: You can make things happen.

NANCY: Also, you can see a lot of contradictions right up front. You cannot escape racism; there's no way you cannot see what happens to black women in the criminal justice system, as opposed to what happens to white women. There is no way you can ignore classism—what happens when an upper-class woman goes to an institution like the police, compared with what happens to a lower-class woman. It's right there. There's just no way you can avoid it.

Something else that was important to me was the chance for personal contact with women who are organizers and leaders, because elsewhere you don't really have access to, or day-to-day contact with, women who are role models in these areas. Seeing that development potential as a possibility for themselves is very important, especially, I think, to young women.

JACKIE: What are some of the negative aspects you've found working at the Center?

NANCY: One of the worst things was the fragmentation. Because the resources are limited, everybody has to do a lot of different things. You begin to feel you can never complete a task, never accomplish anything, only just begin to keep your head above water. You just about get things straight and then, say, a funding crisis comes up, which means everything has to be dropped to deal with City Council. Or you lose your office and you have to look for a new one, and you drop everything to deal with that. This is extremely frustrating.

Next, you see the same problems over and over again. No daytime volunteers; people who come around three or four times and then disappear—these are perennial problems. When you've been at the Center for a long time, it seems as though you never get anywhere in dealing with rape—women just keep on calling. And, too, the lack of financial resources creates really difficult choices; one salary is open: should we hire a Spanish-speaking woman or a black woman? What do you do? Dealing with this kind of dilemma absorbs a lot of energy, and in the end there is really no *right* decision you can make. It can be physically and emotionally exhausting.

I think the negative things work in two ways: number one, they cause people to burn out; women resist and try to cope with them and deal with them until they are too burned out to do anything else. At the same time, while you are in the process of being burned out, you learn very hard lessons about your own personal strengths, about your priorities, about political realities, about your own energy and its limitations. I think sometimes we can do everything and be anything, and then we find out that that isn't true.

ALEXA: I want to discuss the question of volunteerism because that's an issue that comes up all the time in feminist organizations. How do we solve the problems that arise from having paid staff and nonpaid staff, and what do you think are some of the drawbacks volunteerism poses in feminist organizations?

NANCY: I think volunteerism is a drawback. It has a lot of negative effects. It limits the participation of some of the Third World and working-class women because these women need money to survive and they just don't have the luxury of volunteering. It also creates friction between people who are paid and people who are not paid. People who aren't paid for their work sometimes take themselves less seriously. (They are not as dependable—they don't think their work is as important so their self-concept is affected.) Volunteerism also affects the way people look at an organization; people don't think much of volunteers. Outside the organization, the work of volunteers isn't taken seriously. People tend to feel that volunteers aren't capable of handling anything more than shitwork. They don't see volunteers as people who are capable of doing everything anyone else can do.

ALEXA: To me, the question of volunteerism, however, is sometimes even more complicated than that, because I'm not sure that every woman who's a volunteer in a feminist organization would choose to take a full-time, paid job there even if she could. What are some of the reasons women would choose to work full-time in a feminist organization?

NANCY: First, it's not something you just go out and do, like getting a regular job. I don't think it's something you choose; it's something you see a need for doing and you do it. If you get paid for it, that's good—that means you can eat.

ALEXA: Do you seek a job in the movement in the same way you look for other jobs?

NANCY: No, the movement is something you come to for other reasons, like political commitment. It's definitely not the same kind of procedure you go through when you look in the want ads to find a job.

ALEXA: You've mentioned that it's a way of accomplishing political goals, and that's one of the biggest reasons women choose to work in a feminist organization. But what does it mean to that woman in terms of a long-range career? Does she limit her participation in the feminist organization to two years, and then go out and get a job somewhere else? And, if she does, what does that mean for continuity in the women's movement and in feminist organizations?

NANCY: Often negative working conditions preclude long-term commitment to feminist workplaces. When women burn themselves out, they are no longer able to function productively in a group. One way the Crisis Center has dealt with this is to have a Board of Trustees, which is made up of some of the founders of the Center, as well as others with a long-term commitment to antirape organizing. The trustees participate in the hiring of the administrator and oversee long-range policy and goals for the Center. Thus, those women who, for a number of reasons, choose not to participate in the day-to-day workings of the Center can maintain long-term input and continuity.

ALEXA: How does the Center maintain a balance between resolving these internal struggles and accomplishing its external goals?

NANCY: Well, I don't think we have ever really resolved this. We've never let the internal structure become our priority. All along, if something didn't work, we simply changed it; we never made having a perfectly functioning place our main goal. There have been times when problems haven't been dealt with, when things haven't been resolved, when structures haven't been created or changed because the most important thing was to keep the Center functioning. But I think we've struck a pretty good balance. One way to provide internal continuity is through written policy. In 1975 we synthesized a lot of ideas from position papers and other sources into a comprehensive written policy. We went over the minutes from weekly meetings and all the written material at the Center, and we wrote down the political ideas that the old members had been carrying in their heads—about victims, about the criminal justice system, about internal operations, and so on, as well as office procedures. That gave us framework. All this can be referred to; you can hand it to somebody to read, and she can get an idea of what is going on in the Center. It is important for accountability as well, particularly with the diversity of women at the Center. In feminist workplaces, ordinarily, women have a shared level of consciousness about feminism and politics. Because the Center isn't that way, there are inevitable conflicts; the women there don't share the same politics. A conflict arose, for instance, when a woman did something that was contrary to a decision made at a steering committee meeting—because she felt it was the right thing to do. When it was found out, we had a series of meetings that ultimately ended in her resignation. Now we have a clause at the front of the policy statement saying that members of the Center have a responsibility to abide by its policies, to act in accordance with the bylaws, to attempt to change them when necessary, and to resign only when changes acceptable to them do not occur. This seems to be the only solution when women don't all share the same goals.

ALEXA: The fact that you have been able to attract a diverse group of women to the Center is a credit to your ability to reach out to the community. I'd like to hear about that.

NANCY: I have felt that the Center has made a real effort to reach other women, especially through printed matter and speaking. I think it is important to translate politics—which can be so alienating—into something concrete. When you give a speech entitled "The Politics of Rape," for instance, people don't know what you're talking about. So you point out that rape is a political act because it is used as a tool by men to limit the mobility, behavior, and ultimately the power of women. You say that rape functions in the interest of all men, and to the detriment of all women. While not all of us will be criminally raped, we all know the fear of rape, and it alters our lives considerably—the threat of rape affects where we live—and with whom—when we go out and where, and so on. When you relate these concepts to, say, housing security, or being on the street after working late . . . women start thinking about things they have never even thought of as political before, and that they certainly didn't associate with feminism.

It is really important that the politics of the women's movement be translated into concrete experience, and be brought to other women. I think that outreach can best be accomplished through speaking and writing about *very concrete things*.

ALEXA: Let me ask one more question: what do you see as the long-range direction for the Center in terms of your financial survival?

NANCY: Recently the Center has been through a crisis in which the entire contract for the community education program ($29,000, practically the entire operating budget) was cut from next year's

D.C. budget. Dealing with the cutoff of funds often has a very concrete effect on organizing activities—the main objectives of an organization may be sidetracked while organizers fight for salaries and survival. We've had other problems with the city funding agency during the past few years—subtle and not-so-subtle forms of harassment, including city monitoring of our speeches and demands for background information on all Center members. We had to learn how to deal with bureaucrats; when to fight, when to compromise. It takes a lot of time and energy to keep on top of things. We'd like to establish some form of independent enterprise to sustain our work—we've discussed a self-defense school quite seriously, and I joke about starting a restaurant, but we haven't hit on anything viable yet.

One of the positive elements of our recent battle with the city was the impressive amount of community support and pressure we marshaled in defense of our funding. It was very plain to the City Council that we were not going to go away, that our demands had to be met, and that others support our work. Although next year's funding is still not definite there's a sense now that the funding for the Crisis Center just can't be lopped off the budget. I think that the ongoing struggle of the Crisis Center demonstrates the tenacity of most feminist workplaces in dealing with contradictions. We are going to keep on until we reach our goal, the elimination of rape from our lives.

Building Feminist Organizations

Alexa Freeman and Jackie MacMillan

While listening to a tape of the interview with Nancy MacDonald we found ourselves stopping the tape recorder to discuss different points that were raised. We are convinced of the importance of building feminist organizations in the movement, and it is our hope that this interview stimulated discussion for you as it did for us. There are three issues we would particularly like to address: How does a feminist organization operate as an environment for doing feminist work? Why/how does a woman comes to work in one? And finally, how to build long-lasting commitments to our organizations.

What Is the Feminist Organization as Workplace?

A feminist organization provides an environment where work is done that in one way or another builds and strengthens the women's movement—leads toward fundamental change in our society. This feminist work may be paid or nonpaid, full- or part-time. Feminist organizations are important because they provide a visible power base for feminist struggle. Therefore, inherent in our definition of the feminist organization/workplace is that it must be controlled by feminists. No matter how supportive the relationships are that might exist within the women's studies department of a university, or at an abortion clinic, and no matter what the political goals of the individual women working there are, such places cannot be considered feminist organizations unless those women control overall policy.*

Feminist workplaces can vary tremendously with respect to focus, activities, financial base, and so on. The feminist organization can provide a product or service to a particular community as well as jobs and skills development to its workers. It can engage in research or provide educational services. It can transmit education, or ideas, through various media. It can engage in reform activities. A feminist organization can incorporate any or many of these activities for a number of constituencies. Though some feminist organizations are financially self-supporting, others operate on public or private grant money, through income sharing among members or through combinations of these revenue structures. In short, feminist organizations are diverse. And this diversity is positive in many respects; it reflects the grassroots nature of the women's movement. We are beginning to build stronger and more sophisticated organizations based on our own experiences dealing with problems and contradictions. We've learned a lot from our successes and from our failures. Our organizations are essential not only for the concrete goals they set out to perform but as the visible structural forms of the movement, the primary vehicle for attracting new women. Organizations are also models for the future—we build from the bases we have created. We are a young movement and do not have a totally clear theory and direction. But this will grow in part from an examination of the organizations we are building. Work at the feminist organization serves as a base for further developing our political ideas.

This article focuses largely on the relationship between the feminist organization and the individual worker. We have tried to identify some problems and issues that are common to most, if not all feminist organizations. The relative importance and range of solutions will vary according to the nature of the project. A discussion of the feminist organization raises a number of additional questions that are not within the scope of this article: How does a particular

*Many women who identify as feminists feel that they can do feminist work in traditional workplaces. While this is possible, we feel that it is much more difficult than working directly through independent feminist organizations. Feminists working in traditional institutions can do various forms of workplace organizing. In addition, feminists who have credentials can obtain positions of relative power in policy-making levels of private or public agencies. For many years we have been saying that such positions are important for the women's movement. But they are practically useless to us as political tools, unless individual women holding these positions have ties with independent feminist organizations. Feminist organizations acting as support groups can enable feminist professionals to share responsibility for decision making and provide structures for accountability. Such structures can encourage professionals to take risks that they would not and could not take in isolation.

organization relate to the overall movement? How does it relate to the community it operates in, and possibly serves? What kinds of larger networks for support and accountability should the women's movement be developing?

What Brings a Woman to Work in a Feminist Organization?

Nancy MacDonald has focused on some of the reasons women sought out the Rape Crisis Center. The reasons why women are initially attracted to a feminist organization are varied. In many cases, a woman seeks out the feminist workplace because she is dissatisfied with her job, or with her life in general, and looks to the movement for a change and significance. Or a woman may be out of work and looking for paid work, specifically in a movement organization. The work at a particular organization may relate to her professional or academic career interests and thus attract her for that reason; or it might relate to a personal experience (a woman who has been beaten by her husband might become involved in a wife-abuse shelter project, for example). Or a woman might be specifically sought out to work at a feminist project because of her special skills. Some women come to work at a feminist organization because they want to learn about feminism and the women's movement. If a woman comes for any of these reasons, it may be hoped that she will develop a basic feminist political perspective and commitment to feminism through her experiences there. In many cases, women come to work at feminist workplaces for clearly political reasons. They already have a commitment to feminism and the political purpose of the organization.

We certainly need to ascertain the reasons why a woman initially seeks out a feminist organization. Such insights can help us refine and improve our methods of outreach. However, the question we particularly want to address here is why a woman chooses to remain at a feminist organization and continue her work there. This question is critical to the survival, growth, and continuity of our organizations.

What Makes for Long-Lasting Commitment to Feminist Organizations/Workplaces?

The immediate advantages of working in a feminist organization for the individual woman are obvious:* having control over one's work;

---

*These points apply especially to full-time workers in a feminist organization.

learning new skills; developing different self-concepts and the ability to take certain kinds of responsibilities, and thus having a measure of control that is absent from traditional jobs; the opportunity to work in a supportive atmosphere; and generally, the ability to live a largely integrated existence where one's work is an expression of one's life and purpose.

The organization also serves as a base for getting political support and criticism. For example, suppose that, as the result of some special expertise, a feminist is approached by network TV to appear on a major talk show. Assuming that the issue to be discussed is in any way political (abortion, inflation, education, etc.), the situation will be potentially powerful and potentially dangerous. The woman will have to decide whether or not to accept the invitation; and if she does, how best to exploit the opportunity (without in turn being exploited). While ultimately, the individual woman is accountable to no one but herself, she may want to seek support and accountability in making these decisions. If she belongs to a feminist organization where there is a high level of political trust, she might logically turn to that group for advice. Lacking such a base, a woman often makes decisions after consulting individuals—friends, lovers, and the like. By seeking accountability and support from our political organizations we not only strengthen these organizations but also give individuals political and social legitimacy and endorsement for their actions that cannot be gotten elsewhere.

Probably the primary need that the feminist organization fills for individual feminists is to provide a feminist organizational base. Participation in feminist organizations is what makes us part of the women's movement. A feminist organization provides an environment where we not only have shared values and assumptions, but where we are doing work toward shared goals. Without feminist organizations, feminism is limited to an abstract concept. At our workplaces it becomes a living reality. Whether we are full-time or part-time, paid or volunteer workers, this organizational base fills a critical need for individual feminists and for the movement.

The feminist organization as we've described it seems so attractive that one wonders why anybody would choose *not* to work in a feminist organization, or why anyone would choose to leave. Yet, women often turn down the opportunity to work full-time at a feminist organization (and choose part-time feminist work) and women regularly leave paid and nonpaid movement jobs. There are a variety of personal/political reasons why women leave. Economic realities are often the primary concern; most organizations cannot afford to pay salaries, and for those that can, the pay is usually not competitive with other job options a woman may have. A woman may leave, therefore, because she needs some money or more than the organization can provide, greater economic or job security, and the opportunity to make long-range personal plans that require a stable situation. Some women are giving up more and risking more than others when they fully commit themselves to a feminist organization. A woman with children is often laying more on the line by foregoing economic security than a nonmother. A woman from a more secure economic background can better afford to take a lower salary and give up certain benefits that she might have gotten from a straight job. To whatever extent possible, the feminist workplace must provide an atmosphere that enables us to be active and productive as feminist workers without becoming martyrs. If our structures are not sufficiently able to support varying needs among women, then women will leave. Other reasons for leaving might be that a woman's self-concept, social pressures, or career aspirations may lead to a desire for a job that provides greater social legitimacy than movement jobs generally do. Or, a woman may encounter oppressive class or race attitudes or behavior in the organization and decide to leave. Another reason for leaving may be a lack of child-care and other kinds of support for mothers. Finally, personal/political conflicts within the organization may become unresolvable or too emotionally draining for some women. In a feminist organization committed to giving each woman responsibility and control over her own work and to working to develop a political context, there is greater risk of conflict. When conflict is resolved, it is usually because process, accountability, and commitment have been developed within the organization. Nevertheless, conflicts will exist and a woman must be willing to commit the energy necessary to resolve them.

Many of these problems can be eliminated or alleviated; some, such as lack of security and legitimacy, will continue for some time. Even if all of these circumstances disappeared, however, women would still leave feminist organizations. For, in addition to personal decisions, feminists leave feminist organizations for political reasons: A woman may feel that her peer group is too narrow and that this is stifling her political growth; or that she is becoming too focused on one issue or one aspect of the women's movement and that her perspective needs broadening. She may feel that another organization is moving more in a direction that interests her or that she has more to offer another group because of her special skills or insights. If a woman is doing nonpaid part-time work at one organization, and is offered a full-time salaried position with another organization, she may feel attracted by the possibility of working full-time in a movement job. It may be that the organization itself has been unable to grow or evolve along with the individual. It is possible that the woman who continues to develop politically, or who first gains a feminist political perspective in the organization, will realize that this is not where she wants to make her long-range political commitment, and will leave.

At some point an individual may consider working in more than one organization at once. There are benefits to be gained by the organization in having some of its members involved on other projects: they can bring back to the organization creative solutions and new ideas for solving common problems, a strengthening of skills, a greater overall perspective on the movement, an ability to be flexible, etc. The major drawback is that an overextended membership cannot maintain a fruitful commitment to a workplace forever. This pattern is destructive for all involved, because it puts a special burden of covering the work and taking responsibility for the organization on those whose primary emphasis is there.

An organization is strengthened by its members' diversity. But an individual cannot take responsibility for an organization's survival and growth if she is spread too thin.

Our organizations need workers who can take primary responsibility for ensuring that the organization's functions are carried out and that its goals are realized. While some women involved in the feminist organization will place clear limitations on their work, others must take responsibility for coordinating this work and for completing jobs that remain undelegated. Commitment doesn't *necessarily* require that each individual play a central role in the feminist organization. It *does* require that each person take responsibility for ensuring that the organization's work get done. This may mean ensuring that salaries are paid to full-time workers and that those workers are held accountable for the smooth workings of the organization.

Second, commitment to a feminist organization presupposes that the ongoing work done there is important. Organizations must be able to survive over long periods of time in order to be effective and to be taken seriously. Rapid turnover of workers is a handicap to any organization. For the sake of efficiency and continuity it is important for feminists to make long-range commitments to their organizations.

Finally, in making a commitment to a feminist organization, the crucial factor seems to be the recognition that personal interest is intrinsically tied to feminist political struggle and the understanding that the development of strong organizations is essential to that struggle.* A feminist becomes committed to a feminist organization

---

*We do not mean to suggest that all commitment comes from purely altruistic motives (or that feminism is altruistic!). While especially true for full-time workers, some factors that may motivate women include certain personality traits (a need for adventure, an ability to take risk or endure stress); a tendency toward self-righteousness or martyrdom; a desire to force the world to their own personal vision.

or workplace because she recognizes its importance to the overall movement.

Nevertheless, for all the reasons we have discussed (and more) women do leave and will continue to do so. Therefore, it would be useful to establish certain processes through which this can be done with relatively little pain, both for the more permanent members and for the organization itself.

Major decisions that affect the organization should be brought to that body before a realignment of involvement. Clearly, ultimate decisions will rest with the individual, but we should strive for maximizing accountability to and flexibility in our workplaces. This will allow women to make long-term commitments more readily. A woman can restrict her activities rather than totally leaving the organization, if the organization's structure permits. A woman may elect to become a board member rather than an active member, for example. Because of her past work in the organization she has a vested interest in the effective continuance of the group. She may choose to take a leave of absence rather than to leave permanently. Or, if she does choose to make a total break with the organization, a structure can be devised whereby she can phase herself out, by training other women to do her jobs, or finding alternative ways to get the work done so that the organization will suffer only minimally. Even if an organization can continue with the loss of one or more of its members, what cannot be easily replaced is the woman's political judgment and experience. In this case, we must look to and try to respond as part of an overall women's movement. It may be hoped that the woman will be contributing to the feminist movement in another capacity.

We envision and hope that the women's movement will eventually have broader structures for decision making, through which we can determine major areas of work to be emphasized, for example, among feminists on a city-wide basis, or larger. This could take the form of a coordinating council or possibly a political party. A woman could, in a sense, request a change of assignment via this body or possibly have grievance hearings. Such a structure, while it would produce its own set of problems, would nevertheless alleviate others. We are not suggesting it is the only possible form to take; only that it is significant as an idea we've returned to again and again in discussions about problems that organizations have. But, for now, the individual and small peer support groups must make these decisions alone. We think that it is important to be flexible in this process, to recognize that an individual's needs will vary and that at different times an organization's needs will also vary.

Women who remain with an organization see concrete results and experience progress in their work. This kind of personal and political reinforcement produces feelings of hope and a realization of the potential power of feminist organizations. Sustained by such rewards, we will continue to see the need for and share in the work and responsibility of building strong organizations.

Suggestions for Further Reading

PART ONE Power and Practice

Books

Barry, Kathleen. *Female Sexual Slavery*. Englewood Cliffs, N.J.: Prentice-Hall, 1979.

Beauvoir, Simone de. *The Second Sex*. New York: Knopf, 1952.

Daly, Mary. *Gyn/Ecology*. Boston: Beacon, 1979.

Firestone, Shulamith. *The Dialectic of Sex*. New York: Morrow, 1971.

Griffin, Susan. *Woman and Nature*. New York: Harper & Row, 1978.

Huston, Perdita. *Third World Women Speak Out*. New York: Praeger, 1979.

Institute of Cultural Action (IDAC) Document #10. *Towards a Women's World*. Geneva: IDAC, 1976.

Jain, Devaki. *Women's Quest for Power*. Vikas Publishing House of India, 1980.

Latin American Perspectives, ed. *Women in Latin America: An Anthology*. Riverside, Calif.: Latin American Perspectives, 1979.

Marks, Elaine, and Isabelle De Courtivron, eds. *New French Feminisms: An Anthology*. Amherst: University of Massachusetts Press, 1980.

Mernissi, Fatima. *Beyond the Veil: Male-Female Dynamics in a Modern Muslim Society*. New York: Schenkman, 1975.

Millett, Kate. *Sexual Politics*. New York: Doubleday, 1970.

Morgan, Robin, ed. *Sisterhood Is Powerful*. New York: Vintage, 1970.

Redstockings. *Feminist Revolution*. New York: Redstockings, 1975.

Ruth, Steila, ed. *Issues in Feminism: A First Course in Women's Studies*. Boston: Houghton Mifflin, 1980.

Summers, Anne. *Damned Whores and God's Police: The Colonization of Women in Australia*. Victoria, Australia: Penguin, 1975.

Articles

Alpert, Jane. "Motherright: A New Feminist Theory." *Ms. Magazine*, August, 1973.

"The Black Women's Issue." *Conditions Five*, Special Issue, vol. 2, no. 2 (Autumn 1979).

Burris, Barbara. "Fourth World Manifesto." In Anne Koedt, Ellen Levine, and Anita Rapone, eds., *Radical Feminism*. New York: Quadrangle, 1973.

Eisenstein, Zillah, ed. "Theoretical Introduction" and Part 5 in *Capitalist Patriarchy and the Case for Socialist Feminism*. New York: Monthly Review, 1978.

Elshtain, Jean Bethke. "Moral Woman and Immoral Man." *Politics and Society* 4, no. 4 (1974): 453–73.

Freeman, Jo, ed. Part 5 in *Women: A Feminist Perspective*. Palo Alto: Mayfield, 1975.

Gould, Carol, and Marx Wartofsky, eds. Parts 1 and 4 in *Women and Philosophy: Towards a Theory of Liberation*. New York: Putnam, 1976.

Jones, Beverly, and Judith Brown. "Toward a Female Liberation Movement." In Leslie B. Tanner, ed., *Voices From Women's Liberation*. New York: New American Library, 1970.

Lorde, Audre. "The Power of the Erotic." Spinsters Inc. pamphlet, 1979.

Rosaldo, Michelle Zimbalist. "Theoretical Overview." In *Woman, Culture and Society*. Stanford: Stanford University Press, 1974.

Stambler, Sookie, ed. Part 5 in *Women's Liberation: Blueprint for the Future*. New York: Ace Books, 1970.

"Toward a New Feminism for the Eighties." Articles in *Feminist Studies* 5, no. 3 (Fall 1979).

Vetterling-Braggin, Mary; Frederick A. Elliston; and Jane English, eds. Part 1 in *Feminism and Philosophy*. Totowa, N.J.: Littlefield, Adams, 1977.

PART TWO   The Politics of Everyday Life

Books

Abbott, Sidney, and Barbara Love. *Sappho Was a Right-On Woman*. New York: Stein and Day, 1972.

Barry, Kathleen. *Female Sexual Slavery*. Englewood Cliffs, N.J.: Prentice-Hall, 1979.

Boston Women's Health Collective. *Our Bodies, Ourselves*. New York: Simon and Schuster, 1976.

Brownmiller, Susan. *Against Our Will: Men, Women, and Rape*. New York: Simon and Schuster, 1975.

Cade, Toni, ed. *The Black Woman*. New York: New American Library, 1970.

Chesler, Phyllis. *Women and Madness*. New York: Doubleday, 1972.

Chodorow, Nancy. *The Reproduction of Mothering: Psychoanalysis and the Sociology of Gender*. Berkeley: University of California Press, 1978.

Daniels, Kay, and Murnane, Mary. *Uphill All the Way: A Documentary History of Women in Australia*. Queensland, Australia: University of Queensland Press, 1980.

Dinnerstein, Dorothy. *The Mermaid and the Minotaur: Sexual Arrangements and Human Malaise*. New York: Harper & Row, 1976.

Farley, Lin. *Sexual Shakedown*. New York: McGraw-Hill, 1978.

Frankfort, Ellen. *Vaginal Politics*. New York: Quadrangle, 1972.

Gordon, Linda. *Woman's Body, Woman's Right: A Social History of Birth Control*. New York: Viking, 1976.

Hite, Shere. *The Hite Report*. New York: Dell, 1976.

Jones, Ann. *Women Who Kill*. New York: Holt, Rinehart and Winston, 1980.

Klaich, Dolores. *Woman Plus Woman: Attitudes Toward Lesbianism*. New York: Simon and Schuster, 1974.

Martin, Del. *Battered Wives*. San Francisco: Glide Publications, 1976.

Martin, Del, and Phyllis Lyon. *Lesbian/Woman*. San Francisco: Glide Publications, 1972.

Miller, Jean Baker. *Toward a New Psychology of Women*. Boston: Beacon, 1976.

Mitchell, Juliet. *Psychoanalysis and Feminism*. New York: Pantheon, 1974.

Oakley, Ann. *Woman's Work: The Housewife, Past and Present*. New York: Vintage, 1974.

Rich, Adrienne. *On Lies, Secrets, and Silence*. New York: Norton, 1979.

Saadawi, Nawal El. *The Hidden Faces of Eve: Women in the Arab World*. London, England: Zed Press, 1980.

Stack, Carol B. *All our Kin: Strategies for Survival in a Black Community*. New York: Doubleday, 1972.

Vida, Ginny, ed. *Our Right to Love*. Englewood Cliffs, N.J.: Prentice-Hall, 1978.

Women's Press Collective. *Lesbians Speak Out*. Oakland, Calif.: Women's Press Collective, 1974.

Articles

Breines, Wini; Margaret Cerullo; and Judith Stacey. "Social Biology, Family Studies and Antifeminist Backlash." *Feminist Studies* 4, no. 1 (February 1978).

Flax, Jane. "The Conflict Between Nurturance and Autonomy in Mother-Daughter Relationships and Within Feminism." *Feminist Studies* 4, no. 2 (June 1978).

Rapp, Rayna; Ellen Ross; and Renate Bridenthal. "Examining Family History." *Feminist Studies* 5, no. 1 (Spring 1979).

Rubin, Gayle. "The Traffic in Women: Notes on the 'Political Economy' of Sex." In Rayna Reiter, ed., *Towards an Anthropology of Women*. New York: Monthly Review, 1975.

Vetterling-Braggin, Mary; Frederick A. Elliston; and Jane English, eds. Section 6 in *Feminism and Philosophy*. Totowa, N.J.: Littlefield, Adams, 1977.

PART THREE   Feminist Perspectives on Class

Books

Baxandall, Rosalyn; Linda Gordon; and Susan Reverby, eds. *America's Working Women: A Documentary History—1600 to Present*. New York: Vintage, 1976.

Bunch, Charlotte, and Nancy Myron, eds. *Class and Feminism*. Baltimore, Md.: Diana Press, 1974.

Boserup, Esther. *Woman's Role in Economic Development*. New York: St. Martin's, 1970.

Deming, Barbara. *We Cannot Live Without Our Lives*. New York: Viking, 1974.

Evans, Sara. *Personal Politics: The Roots of Women's Liberation in the Civil Rights Movement and the New Left*. New York: Random House, 1979.

Gibbs, Joan, and Sara Bennett, ed. *Top Ranking: A Collection of Articles on Racism and Classism in the Lesbian Community*. Brooklyn, N.Y., 1980.

Kuhn, Annette, and AnnMarie Wolpe, eds. *Feminism and Materialism: Women and Modes of Production.* London and Boston: Routledge and Kegan Paul, 1978.

Lessons from the Damned: Class Struggle in the Black Community. New York: Times Change Press, 1973.

Mitchell, Juliet. *Woman's Estate.* New York: Pantheon, 1971.

Rowbotham, Sheila. *Woman's Consciousness, Man's World.* Baltimore, Md.: Penguin, 1974.

Rubin, Lillian Breslow. *Worlds of Pain: Life in the Working Class Family.* New York: Harper & Row, 1976.

Sargent, Lydia, ed. *Women and Revolution.* Boston: South End Press, 1980.

Scott, Hilda. *Does Socialism Liberate Women?: Experiences from Eastern Europe.* Boston: Beacon, 1974.

Second Class, Working Class: An International Women's Reader. Oakland, Calif.: People's Translation Service, 1979.

Siefer, Nancy. *Nobody Speaks for Me: Self-Portraits of American Working Class Women.* New York: Simon and Schuster, 1976.

Weinbaum, Batya. *The Curious Courtship of Women's Liberation and Socialism.* Boston: South End Press, 1979.

Articles

Benston, Margaret. "The Political Economy of Women's Liberation." In Leslie B. Tanner, ed., *Voices from Women's Liberation.* New York: New American Library, 1971.

Blau, Francine D. "Women: in the Labor Force: An Overview." In Jo Freeman, ed., *Women: A Feminist Perspective.* Palo Alto: Mayfield, 1975.

Bridges, Amy, and Batya Weinbaum. "The Other Side of the Paycheck." *Monthly Review,* Special Issue, vol. 28, no. 3 (July–August 1976).

Brown, Rita Mae. *A Plain Brown Rapper.* Baltimore: Diana Press, 1976.

Caplan, Patricia, and Janet M. Bujra. *Women United, Women Divided: Cross-Cultural Perspectives on Female Solidarity.* London, England: Tavistock, 1978.

Dudley, Barbara, et al. "The National Conference on Socialist Feminism." *Socialist Revolution* 5, no. 4 (October–December 1975).

Eisenstein, Zillah R. "The Capitalist Patriarchy and Female Work." In *Capitalist Patriarchy and the Case for Socialist Feminism.* New York: Monthly Review, 1978.

"Generations: Women in the South." *Southern Exposure* 4, no. 4 (Winter 1977).

Lederer, Laura. *Take Back the Night: Women on Pornography.* New York: Morrow, 1980.

Lewis, Diane K. "A Response to Inequality: Black Women, Racism, and Sexism." *Signs* 3, no. 2 (Winter 1977).

Young, Iris. "Socialist Feminism and the Limits of Dual Systems Theory." *Socialist Review* 10, nos. 2–3 (March–June 1980).

PART FOUR Organizations and Strategies

Books

Atkinson, Ti-Grace. *Amazon Odyssey.* New York: Links Books, 1974.

Covina, Gina, and Laurel Galana, eds. *The Lesbian Reader: Amazon Quarterly Anthology*. Oakland, Calif.: Amazon Press, 1975.

Dalla Costa, Mariarosa. *The Power of Women and the Subversion of the Community*. Bristol, England: Falling Wall Press, 1972.

Koedt, Anne; Ellen Levine; and Anita Rapone, eds. *Radical Feminism*. New York: Quadrangle, 1973.

Hole, Judith, and Ellen Levine, eds. *Rebirth of Feminism*. New York: Quadrangle, 1971.

Jay, Karla, and Alan Young. *Out of the Closets: The Voices of Gay Liberation*. New York: Pyramid, 1972.

Lerner, Gerda. *Black Women in White America: A Documentary History*. New York: Pantheon, 1972.

Morgan, Robin. *Going Too Far*. New York: Vintage, 1978.

Myron, Nancy, and Charlotte Bunch. *Lesbianism and the Women's Movement*. Baltimore, Md.: Diana Press, 1975.

Reed, Evelyn. *Woman's Evolution*. New York: Pathfinder Press, n.d.

Rowbotham, Sheila. *Women, Resistance, and Revolution*. New York: Vintage, 1972.

Russell, Diana, and Nicole Van de Ven, eds. *Crimes Against Women*. Millbrae, Calif.: Les Femmes Publishing, 1977.

Tepperman, Jean. *Not Servants, Not Machines: Office Workers Speak Out*. Boston: Beacon, 1976.

Tripp, C. A. *The Homosexual Matrix*. New York: McGraw-Hill, 1975.

Wallace, Michele. *Black Macho and the Myth of the Superwoman*. New York: Dial, 1978.

Articles

Bunch, Charlotte. "Women Power and the Leadership Crisis in America." *Ms. Magazine*, July 1980.

Ehrensaft, Diane. "When Women and Men Mother." *Socialist Review* 10, no. 1 (January–February 1980).

Freeman, Jo. "The Tyranny of Structurelessness." In Anne Koedt, Ellen Levine, and Anita Rapone, eds., *Radical Feminism*. New York: Quadrangle, 1973.

Hunter, Allen, and Linda Gordon. "Feminism, Leninism, and the U.S.: A Comment." *Radical America* 13, no. 5 (September–October 1979).

Mainardi, Pat. "The Politics of Housework." In Leslie B. Tanner, ed., *Voices of Women's Liberation*. New York: New American Library, 1970.

Morgan, Robin. "Goodbye to All That." In Leslie B. Tanner, ed., *Voices of Women's Liberation*. New York: New American Library, 1970.

Radicalesbians. "Woman Identified Woman." In Anne Koedt, Ellen Levine, and Anita Rapone, eds., *Radical Feminism*. New York: Quadrangle, 1973.

"Reader's Forum on Black Male/Female Relationships." *Black Scholar* 10, nos. 8–9 (May–June 1979).

Rowbotham, Sheila. "The Women's Movement and Organizing for Socialism." *Radical America* 13, no. 5 (September–October 1979).

"Third World Women: The Politics of Being Other." *Heresies: A Feminist Publication on Art and Politics*, Special Issue, vol. 2, no. 4 (1979).

Resources

Aegis: Magazine on Ending Violence Against Women. P.O. Box 21033, Washington, D.C. 20009

Ain't I a Woman (1971–74). Alternative Press Center, 2958 Greenmount Avenue, Baltimore, Md. 21218

Asian Women's Liberation. Poste Restente, Shibuya Post Office, Shibuya, Tokyo, Japan 150

Azalea: A Magazine by and for Third World Lesbians. 306 Lafayette Avenue, Brooklyn, N.Y. 11238

Big Mama Rag. 1724 Gaylord Street, Denver, Colo. 80206

The Black Scholar. P.O. Box 908, Sausalito, Calif. 94965

Broadsheet. Box 5799, Auckland, New Zealand

Brown Sister. Schneider College Center, Wellesley College, Wellesley, Mass. 02181

Canadian Women's Studies/Les Cahiers De La Femme. Centennial College, 651 Warden Avenue, Scarborough, Ontario MIL 3Z6 Canada

Conditions. Box 56, Van Brunt Station, Brooklyn, N.Y. 11215

Fem: Publicacion Feminista Trimestral. Nueva Cultura Feminisista, S.C. Av. Universidad 1855 Desp 401, Mexico 20, D.F., Mexico

Feminist International, Japan. Feminist Inc., Tokyo 4-51570, Japan, or PO Box 2535, Honolulu, Hawaii 96804

Feminist Issues. Transaction Periodicals Consortium, Rutgers—The State University, New Brunswick, N.J. 08903

Feminist Studies. Women's Studies Program, University of Maryland, College Park, Md. 20742

Feminist Review. 65 Manor Road, London N16, England

Frontiers. Women's Studies Program, University of Colorado, Boulder, Colo. 80309

Gay Community News. 22 Bromfield Street, Boston, Mass. 02108

Hecate, A Women's Interdisciplinary Journal. P.O. Box 99, St. Lucia, Brisbane, Queensland 4067, Australia

Heresies. P.O. Box 766 Canal Street Station, New York, N.Y. 10013

ISIS International Bulletin. Case Postale 301, 1227 Carouge, Switzerland

Lesbian Tide. 8706 Cadillac Avenue, Los Angeles, Calif. 90034

Manushi: A Journal About Women and Society. C1/202 Lajpat Nagar, New Delhi 110024, India

Off Our Backs. 1724 20th Street N.W., Washington, D.C. 20009

Quest: a feminist quarterly. P.O. Box 8843, Washington, D.C. 20003

Questions Feministes. c/o Editions Tierce, 1 rue des Fosses Saint-Jacques, F-75005 Paris, France

Refractory Girl. 62 Regent Street, Chippendale, NSW 2008 Australia

Resources for Feminist Research. c/o Sociology, O.I.S.E., 252 Bloor Street W., Toronto, Ontario M5S 1V6 Canada

Signs. University of Chicago Press, 5801 S. Ellis Avenue, Chicago, Ill. 60637

Sinister Wisdom. Box 30541, Lincoln, Neb. 68503

Vindicacion Feminista. Napoles 105-4C, Barcelona 13, Spain

Women: A Journal of Liberation. 3028 Greenmount Avenue, Baltimore, Md. 21218

Women's Studies International Quarterly. Pergamon Press, Headington Hill Hall, Oxford OX3 OBW United Kingdom.

Women's Studies Newsletter. The Feminist Press, Box 334, Old Westbury, N.Y. 11568

Index

Accountability, 132–33
Allison, Dorothy, 212–22
Alpert, Jane, 76
Alpert-Swinton controversy,
    52–53
Alta, 227, 234
Androgyny, 59–66
Apuzzo, Ginny, 212–22
Arendt, Hannah, 18
Arnold, June, 229, 235
Aronowitz, Stanley, 122
Authority: power and, 163–65;
    sources of, 170–71; types of,
    165–67; uses of, 167–70

Bargowski, Dolores, 138
Bay, Christian, 18
Beguines, 236–42
Benston, Margaret, 184
Berson, Ginny, 122
Biases, feminist, 157–59
Black Panthers, 48
Black studies programs, 102–3
Black(s), 12, 20, 40, 48, 131, 133,
    150, 156–57, 255; history
    and, 102–9; -white
    confrontation, 212–22
Blau, Francine, 92
Blish, James, 248
Boyd , John, 248
Braverman, Harry, 122
Brown, Rita, 18, 138, 148, 235
Bryan, James, 86, 93
Bunch, Charlotte, 7, 18, 31, 43,
    148, 160, 219
Burris, Barbara, 184

Caine, T. A., 170, 173
Cantaro, Ellen, 110
Capitalism, 10–13, 33, 35, 73,
    112–18, 161–73, 194

Carroll, Berenice, 5, 9, 117, 122
Casella, Marie, 149, 152, 156, 159
Castro, Fidel, 109
Change, 5–6, 36–37, 50–51,
    116–18
Child care, 3, 22, 74–83, 158–59,
    170, 175–76
Childfree, 78, 82–83
Childraisers, 75–83
China, 30, 116, 118
Civil rights movement, 48, 68
Class, social, 34, 40; attitudes,
    139–48; consciousness, 72,
    125–26; feminists on,
    123–85; lesbianism and,
    71–73, 219–22; privilege,
    95–97, 196–97, 203; race
    and, 149–60. *See also* Lower
    class, Middle class, Working
    class
Cleaver, Eldridge, 48
Cobb, Jonathan, 19, 148
Collectives, feminist, 28, 79,
    119–21; Beguines, 236–42
Commitment, 265–66
Common woman, 228–30
Communist party, 48, 53
Community, children and, 82–83
Consciousness raising, 6–7, 24,
    131, 133, 158, 197, 219
Cooptation, androgyny as, 62–63
Covina, Gina, 234
Cultural feminism, 25–26, 45n,
    50–51, 192
Culture, 150–51
Custody, child, 80–81

Daniels-Eichelberger, B., 160
Daly, Mary, 59
Davis, Angela, 48
Davis, Rene, 97n

deBeauvior, Simone, 92
DeCrow, Karen, 160
Dependence, economic, 11–12, 170
DuBois, W.E.B., 15, 19

Economy, changing, 76–79
Edelson, Carol, 31
Ehrhardt, Anke, 60, 66
Elitism, 33, 40, 94, 231–32
Engels, Frederick, 19, 42, 43, 121, 175–79, 182, 184, 185
Equal Rights Amendment (ERA), 3, 17, 192, 197
Establishment jobs, 94–100
Evans, Sara, 161, 173

Family relationships, 11–12, 21, 77–83, 86, 126–29, 159, 179–80, 224–25
Fava, Maria, 149, 155
Female Man, The, 116, 244–45, 247
Feminism, passim. See also Cultural feminism, Lesbian feminism, Nonaligned feminism, Radical feminism, Socialist feminism
Feminist Credit Unions, 209–10
Financial resources, sharing, 136, 206–11
Firestone, Shulamith, 76, 184
Fisher, Beverly, 56, 135, 138
Freud, Sigmund, 183–84
Friedan, Betty, 12, 18
Furies, The, 31, 67, 68

Garcia, Inez, 107
Gearhart, Sally, 199, 201
Gilman, Charlotte, P., 92
Goldman, Emma, 92
Grahn, Judy, 226, 228, 234
Gramsci, Antonio, 39, 42
Greene, T. H., 19
Greer, Germaine, 76
Griffin, Susan, 225, 229, 234–35
Group identity, 131–32
Guttman, Herb, 105
Gynergy, 64–66

Harris, Bertha, 56
Hartsock, Nancy, 52
Haynes, Elizabeth, R., 110
Heilbrun, Carolyn, 61–62, 66
Hermaphroditism, 59–60
Heterosexuality, 11n, 27–29, 68–71; class and, 219–22; privilege and, 70–71, 73, 197
Hill, Judah, 147
Hill, Monica, 92
Hobbes, Thomas, 5, 14
Holiday, Billie, 104, 110
Hurston, Zora Neale, 107

Industrialization, 21, 80–81, 168
Inheritance Laws, 176–78
"Integrity," androgyny as, 63–65
Interaction of processes, 37–38
Issues, women's 137–38, 153–59

Jackson, Bessie, 105
Jackson, Diane, 149, 153, 154, 157, 160
Job performance, sexual harassment and, 87–89
Johnston, Jill, 76
Jouvenal, Bertrand de, 5

Kaplan, Abraham, 6, 17, 122
Kardiner, A., 9
Kennedy, Ethel, 75
Kollias, Karen, 56, 138, 160
Kornegger, Peggy, 56

Labor force, women in, 11–13, 40, 112–21; sexual harassment of, 84–93
Lane, Robert, 173
Language of Social Research, 5
Lasswell, Harold, 6, 17, 122
Lazarsfeld, Paul, 18
Leadership, feminist, 8–10, 132–33, 223–35
Left, political, 32–34, 41, 44, 47–49, 34, 145–46
Left Hand of Darkness, The, 247–48
Legitimation of authority, 167–70

LeGuin, Ursala, 247
Lesbian feminism, 228–29; class and, 71–73, 219–22; female separatism and, 22–29; politics of, 67–73, 192; subculture, 152–54
Levison, Andrew, 148
Lévi-Strauss, C., 177, 184
Lewis, J. G., 213
Liberalism, 145–47
Little, Joanna, 107
Lower class, 15–16, 113n, 128–29
Loyalty, institutional, 98–99
Lukacs, Georg, 8, 18, 35, 180–81
Luxemburg, Rosa, 40, 43, 194

McCourt, Kathleen, 127, 138
MacDonald, Nancy, 251–59
McDonnell, E. W., 242
MacPherson, C. B., 18, 19
Male supremacy, 27–29, 164–71, 192
Marcuse, Herbert, 121
Martinez, Inez, 234
Marx, Marxism, 4–5, 14, 18, 19, 34, 42, 43, 47, 113–14, 117, 121, 122, 161–63, 174–85
Matriarchy, 40, 176
Maynard, Joyce, 93
Middle class, 8, 16, 21, 71, 87, 90, 113n; attitudes, 133–35, 140–48; mothers, 75–77; privilege, 95–97, 136, 196–97; reformist groups, 156–57, 192
Millett, Kate, 18, 184
Minorities, 13, 153–54, 218–22
Mitchell, Juliet, 17, 19, 173, 184
Money, John, 60, 66
Money: attitudes about, 202–3; in feminist organizations, 263–64; need for, 204–6; redistribution of, 206–11
Motherhood, 74–83, 171; demystifying, 227–28; expendability of, 79–80; model, 224–27
Mother-right, 176–78
Myron, Nancy, 31, 148

National Black Feminist Organization, 133, 157, 212–22
National Congress of Neighborhood Women, 149
National Organization for Women (NOW), 48, 135, 191, 201, 208
Nehru, Jawahlarlal, 56
Nin, Anais, 15, 19
Nolan, James, 62, 65, 66
Nonaligned feminism, 44–56; concept, 46–47; history and, 47–50; manifesto for, 54–56; race and, 151–52
Nuclear family, 77–78, 86, 159

Olah, Suzie, 185
Olivia Records, 119
Organizations, feminist, 8–10, 16, 41–42; accountability in, 132; blacks in, 215–16; building, 260–67; work in, 115–21, 251–67
Origins of the Family, The, 175
Ortner, Sherry B., 185

Parsons, Talcott, 4, 17, 122
Patriarchy, 10–13, 73; capitalism and, 161–73, 180–82; ideology of, 180–83; socialist feminism and, 32–35, 161–63, 174, 178–80; work under, 112–18
Phillips, Dayton, 242
Piercy, M., 6, 111, 116, 122, 230
Pohl, Frederick, 122
Political action groups, 207–10
Poverty, 85, 95–96, 139, 142
Powell, Betty, 212–22
Power, 3–19, 116–18, 163–65
Power and Society, 6
Privilege: class, 95; heterosexual, 70–71, 73; patriarchal, 178–80; sharing, 210–11; work and, 94–100
Professional women, 136, 139–48
Property, women as, 177–78
Prostitution, as male/female paradigm, 85–86, 88

Public/private spheres, 14–15, 162–63, 168

Racism, 12–13, 21, 34, 40, 142, 149–60, 212–22, 255
Radical feminism, 161, 191–93
Rape, 93, 158, 251–59
Rape Crisis Center, 251–59
Rational-legal authority, 165–70
Raymond, Janice, 66
Reform: conditions for, 199–201; evaluating, 195–98; groups, 155–57; long-term goals of, 193–95; radicals and, 191–93; and reformism, 189–90
Reid, Coletta, 148
Revolution, 23–26, 38–39, 135–38
Rickman, Geraldine, 133, 138
Room of One's Own, A, 61
Rosaldo, Michelle, 185
Roszak, Betty, 185
Rubin, Lillian B., 148
Russ, Joanna, 116, 122, 229, 243–50
Russell, Bertrand, 3, 17, 122
Russell, Michele, 110

Sachs, Karen, 185
Sagaris Collective, 212–13
Sanday, Peggy, 173
San Diego Women's Studies Program, 131, 138
Schmitz, Marlene, 31
Science fiction, 229, 243–50
Secor, Cynthia, 64, 66
Self-concept, 7–8, 16, 130
Sennett, Richard, 19, 148
Separatism, female, 20–31, 49–50, 56, 65–73
Sex roles, 21, 133
Sexual harassment, 84–93
Shafer, Carolyn, 96n
Sheridan, Mary, 122
Shields, Emma, 105, 110
Shortridge, Kathleen, 92
Simone, Nina, 101, 105
Sloan, Margaret, 133, 138
Small, Margaret, 31

Small groups, 6–7, 229
Smith, Bessie, 105
Snobbery, class, 143–47
Socialist feminism, 51, 134; as mode of analysis, 35–36; patriarchy and, 32–35, 161–63; politics of, 39, 67–73, 174–75, 192; race and class and, 154–55
Socialist Feminist Conference (1975), 32–43, 52, 55, 67
Status systems, 169–70
Stein, Robert, 92

Tabb, William K., 18
Tax, woman's income, 208–10
Terkel, Studs, 86, 93, 112, 121
Third World, 34, 40, 142, 153, 156, 158, 212–22
Till, Emmett, 107
Tillich, Paul, 64
Tillmon, Johnnie, 128, 138
Tokenism, 34, 96–98
Toomer, Jean, 105, 110
Traditionalism, 167–70

University women, 107–10

van den Berghe, P. L., 27, 31
Volunteerism, 256–57

Weather Underground, 53, 56
Weber, Max, 173
White supremacy, 10–13, 194
Willis, Ellen, 134, 138
Woman on the Edge of Time, 116
Woolf, Virginia, 61, 66
Working class, 15, 21, 113n, 203; educated, 140–41; family, 126–27; mothers, 77, 87, 90; women's movement and, 125–38, 155–57, 196, 220
Working poor, 127–28
Working Women United, 84, 86, 91
Workplace, feminist, 115–21, 251–67

Young, Marilyn, 122

Zaretsky, Eli, 19, 162, 173, 184

About the Authors

Ginny Apuzzo, a lesbian feminist activist, was a delegate to the National Women's Conference in Houston in 1977 and is at present a member of the platform committee of the Democratic National Convention. She is executive director of the Office of Administrative Trials and Hearings, New York City, and is on leave from Brooklyn College.

Charlotte Bunch, a theorist, activist, and teacher who has been organizing feminist activities since 1968, was a founder of The Furies—a lesbian feminist collective in Washington, D.C.—and of *Quest*. She has edited five anthologies on feminism, has written for a variety of publications, and is at present working on issues of international feminism.

Gracia Clark trained as a historian, a plumber, and an anthropologist. She recently lived with matrilineal market women in West Africa and is now writing articles and a thesis from her group home in Washington, D.C.

Beverly Fisher-Manick is a feminist, community organizer, mother, housing director, contradictory perfectionist, working-class, multiethnic Detroiter, procrastinator, woman-lover, anticapitalist seeking basic change and survival for herself and her daughter.

Jane Flax teaches political theory at Howard University and is a psychotherapist in private practice in Washington, D.C. She has written articles on feminist theory, psychoanalysis, mother-daughter relationships, and critical theory that have appeared in a variety of journals.

Alexa Freeman, a founding member of *Quest*, has worked for ten years as a political organizer in feminist, gay, leftist, and city politics in Washington, D.C. A founder of the D.C. Area Feminist Alliance, she currently serves on the D.C. Commission for Women.

Marilyn Frye is, in patriarchal terms, an associate professor of philosophy at Michigan State University. According to her own naming, she is a gynosophiliac lesbian writer and teacher.

Nancy Hartsock has been an active feminist since 1969, and was a member of the original *Quest* staff. She is currently an assistant professor of political science at The Johns Hopkins University and works with the Women's Union of Baltimore.

Karen Kollias has done work related to poor and working-class people for more than twelve years, much of it in the feminist movement. Since 1977 she has continued her work through the Office of Neighborhood Self-Help Development in the Department of Housing and Urban Development.

Nancy MacDonald is a former member of the Washington, D.C., Rape Crisis Center, affiliated with the Feminist Alliance Against Rape, and a co-founder of *Aegis: A Magazine Against Violence Against Women*. She will receive a B.S. in nursing from the University of the District of Columbia in 1982.

Jackie MacMillan is a current member of the *Quest* editorial staff. She was co-founder of the *Feminist Alliance Against Rape Newsletter*, which at present is part of *Aegis: A Magazine Against Violence Against Women*. She has worked with the Washington, D.C., Rape Crisis Center since 1972 and is a member of the Center's board of directors.

Mary McKenney is a science editor in San Francisco. She would like to thank Peggy DuPont for her invaluable contributions to the article reprinted in this volume.

Linda Phelps was one of the founders of the Kansas City Women's Liberation Union and has also been a participant in the civil rights, antiwar, and socialist movements.

Betty Powell, a black lesbian feminist activist who used to teach French in high school, is now professor of language theory and methodology at Brooklyn College, CUNY. She has spoken at numerous colleges and community group meetings and on radio and television as an advocate for feminists and lesbian feminist issues, and is a founding member of the Astrea Foundation for social change.

Janice Raymond is assistant professor of women's studies and medical ethics at Hampshire College and the University of Massachusetts-Amherst. She is the author of *The Transsexual Empire: The Making of the She-Male* in which a fuller treatment of the androgynous issue appears.

Joanna Russ teaches creative writing at the University of Washington and has just completed a nonfiction manuscript, "How to Supress Women's Writing Without Really Trying."

Michelle Russell has lived and worked in Detroit since 1970 and has been an activist in numerous political organizations, in schools, and as a free-lance writer and graphic artist. She is at present living and working politically in Grenada in the West Indies.

Deirdre Silverman operates toy stores in upstate New York. She previously taught sociology and women's studies at Ithaca College.

Jackie St. Joan is a lesbian feminist who lives in Denver, Colorado. She works as a lawyer and as the mother of two children. Her writings have appeared in *Quest: A Feminist Quarterly*, *Our Right to Love*, *Big Mama Rag*, and Maureen Brady's *Give Me Your Good Ear*.

Lucia Valeska, a feminist activist in Albuquerque from 1967 to 1979 and a founder of women's studies at the University of New Mexico, is co-executive director of the National Gay Task Force and one of *Ms.* magazine's "Women to Watch in the '80s."